One Pitch from Glory

A Decade of Running the Red Sox

Lou Gorman

www.SportsPublishingLLC.com

ISBN: 1-59670-067-X

Publishers: Peter L. Bannon and Joseph J. Bannon Sr.
Senior managing editor: Susan M. Moyer
Acquisitions editor: Noah Adams Amstadter
Developmental editors: Elisa Bock Laird and Dean Miller
Art director: K. Jeffrey Higgerson
Dust jacket design: Heidi Norsen
Project manager: Kathryn R. Holleman
Imaging: Heidi Norsen
Photo editor: Erin Linden-Levy
Vice president of sales and marketing: Kevin King
Media and promotions managers: Courtney Hainline (regional),
    Randy Fouts (national), Maurey Williamson (print)

Printed in the United States of America

Sports Publishing L.L.C.
804 North Neil Street
Champaign, IL 61820

Phone: 1-877-424-2665
Fax: 217-363-2073
Web site: www.SportsPublishingLLC.com

To my wife, Mary Louise.
Her love, devotion, and support have been the wind
beneath my wings
from the very first day we both said, "I do!"
She makes all things possible in my life.

"Lou Gorman is baseball through and through. His book, *One Pitch from Glory*, is a special insight into the innerworkings of Major League Baseball with candor and knowledge seldom available to the average baseball fan. Gorman has enjoyed a tremendous baseball career, a true gentleman, who for the past 40 years has meant so much to Major League Baseball. It's a must read."

—Spencer "Herk" Robinson
Former executive vice president and
general manager of the Kansas City Royals

"In more than 30 years in baseball, I have never yet met anyone who does not like or respect Lou Gorman. Lou is considered one of baseball's pillars of integrity, decency, and knowledge. He has touched countless lives among baseball fans, our nation's military, and numerous collegiate institutions.

"His work in this book gives the reader a great look at the innerworkings of a major league team and chronicles some of the interesting things about our national pastime that the reader would only get from reading *One Pitch from Glory*."

—Mike Port
Assistant general manager of the Boston Red Sox and
former general manager of the California Angels

"Lou Gorman has had a prominent, successful, and storied history in baseball. He recounts these experiences in an interesting and enlightening manner, which all fans of the game will find informative and entertaining."

—Talbot M. Smith
President of baseball operations for the Houston Astros

"Lou Gorman is a baseball legend, and few people had the breadth of experience in baseball as he does. He has given so much to the game and now gives so much to the readers of this book with his rich, inside account of all that takes place in professional baseball. This book is a must read for anyone who loves the game."

—Ron Shapiro
President of Shapiro-Robinson & Associates

"Every fall during our organizational meetings, one of the first agenda items was, 'What is Lou Gorman doing? What are the Red Sox doing?'

"He is a fierce competitor, but also one of my most trusted peers. Lou's word and his handshake were his bond."

—Pat Gillick
Former general manager of the Toronto Blue Jays and the Seattle Mariners

Contents

Foreword

Lou Gorman is a born storyteller, and in *One Pitch from Glory* he has a terrific tale to tell.

It begins at Shea Stadium in 1986 when the Red Sox stand one out away from winning their first World Series since 1918. While that painful loss will be etched in the memory of Sox fans forever, the familiar sequence of events comes to life in an entirely new way through Gorman's unique vantage point as general manager. We follow him into the Sox clubhouse after the crushing defeat. We see the emotions of the owner, the players, and the staff. We share Gorman's discomfort when he has to tell the players that Boston's mayor has inexplicably scheduled a parade in their honor the following day. We hear the players' "chorus of groans, moans, and unrepeatable epithets," and we share Gorman's anxiety the next morning as he wonders if any of them will actually show up.

When, one by one, the players and their families arrive, until nearly the entire squad is assembled, we absorb Gorman's relief and even more, his immense pride in his team. Still, the question remains: "Would the fans be there to greet them?" The answer is a resounding yes as fans come by the hundreds of thousands, standing five deep, cheering passionately for their beloved players, going wild when Bill Buckner's name is called. It is a remarkable moment that will touch the hearts of every reader.

With that stirring opening, Gorman takes us through the ups and downs of his tenure as general manager. We travel with him to the winter meetings. We see the thinking behind the controversial trade that sends minor leaguers Brady Anderson and Curt Schilling to the Baltimore Orioles for veteran pitcher Mike Boddicker. We grimace when Jeff Bagwell is traded for pitcher Larry Andersen, based on scouting reports that mistakenly predict that the young infielder would never have more than average major league power. We get an inside view of the negotiations to keep superstar Roger Clemens while letting Dennis Eckersley go to the Oakland A's. We remember the antics of "Oil Can" Boyd and the front-page stories sparked by

Margo Adams when she revealed her long affair with Wade Boggs. We smile at the memory of Mo Vaughn rounding the bases.

We find ourselves commiserating with manager John McNamara when he is fired, rooting for the hometown kid, Joe Morgan, when he is hired, and then feeling stunned only a few years later when Morgan, too, is abruptly fired. We listen in as Gorman tells Sox stalwarts Jim Rice and Dwight Evans that the team is letting them go. Both men had been with the Sox their whole careers. Neither took it well. We are emotionally involved because in every instance Gorman shares his own feelings with the reader. As a youngster of 17, his dream of being a major league player is shattered when the Phillies release him from their farm system after only a few months in camp. That memory returns every time he has to release a player, making the hateful task almost impossible to carry out.

We watch the Sox win division titles in 1988 and 1990 only to lose four straight games both years to the Oakland A's in the playoffs, with Dennis Eckersely providing hauntingly brilliant relief for his new team. Three years later, Gorman hears his own unwelcome news—the owners have decided to replace him as general manager. Dan Duquette would now take over control of the club.

"After some 36 years of living and breathing baseball operations on a daily basis," he writes, "often 12 to 13 hours a day for 365 days of the year, my days of dealing with players and player personnel had finally come to an end. I would miss it greatly."

But the story does not end there because the Sox keep him on as executive vice president. Which means, as he tells us in the epilogue, that he, like the current Sox brass, enjoyed that magical October night in 2004 when the long beleaguered Sox finally win the World Series championship that had eluded them for nearly a century. As he takes us through the joyous parade route, his mind inevitably harkens back to the more poignant parade that followed the devastating loss in 1986. It is the perfect ending to a rousing story filled with telling details, wonderful anecdotes, witty asides, and heartfelt emotion.

—Doris Kearns Goodwin

Acknowledgments

I am forever grateful to so many people that encouraged me, helped me, and inspired me to undertake the challenge of writing a book about my years with the Boston Red Sox. I originally approached Bill Reynolds, the very talented author and sports columnist of the *Providence Journal*, to work with me on this endeavor. I had been contemplating writing this book for some time but shied away from the challenge until I met with Reynolds and he agreed to work with me on this project and got me started.

As we began the work, we had a difference of opinion as to how we would write it and ended up terminating our relationship on very cordial terms. I then proceeded to write the rest of the book on my own. But it was his confidence in my ability and in my material plus his encouragement that prompted me to go forward with the challenge. I am, however, forever indebted to him.

The final manuscript, chapter by chapter and page by page, was typed by Mrs. Terry Young in Portland, Maine, and Wendy Duffy in Cambridge, Massachusetts, They did so while editing mistakes and grammar and more miraculously deciphering my handwriting. Their contributions were invaluable. I also had some limited typing done on a chapter by Brenda Cook, a dedicated Red Sox fan, and I am grateful to her as well.

I am indebted to Page van Astwerp for her assistance in the early going when she made to me some recommendations that were invaluable.

So many members of the Red Sox staff were extremely helpful in providing me with priceless assistance with research, recommendations, and whatever else I requested.

Thanks to Dick Bresciani, the current vice president for publications and archives for the Red Sox and formerly the talented and longtime director of public relations. He provided me with a great deal of assistance and suggestion while I proceeded to write the book. I am grateful for his professional input.

To Pam Ganley, she has been a constant help to me in so many ways, and I am continually indebted to her. To Debbie Matson, to Rod Oreste, to Cathy Fahy, and to Julie Cordeiro, they have also been helpful in so many ways and I am most appreciative.

To attorney Daniel Kahn, who while at Harvard Law School spent three weeks at Fenway Park doing statistical research for the book for me. I thank him for his contributions.

My grateful appreciation goes to Dr. John Goodson, doctor of internal medicine at Massachusetts General Hospital, professor of internal medicine at Harvard Medical School, and my personal doctor. He has been enthusiastically involved in the writing and progress of the book since the beginning. He has literally served as a mentor to me. His generous insights, expertise, and sincere interest have been an inspiration to me and I am most grateful.

Special thanks to William Martin, the author of *Annapolis, Cape Cod, Back Bay, Harvard Yard, Citizen Washington*, and others, for his interest, constructive criticism, and professional guidelines. As a neighbor and friend, he has offered critical insights and recommendations that were invaluable. His kindness in doing so is much appreciated.

I am also indebted to Professor Steven Greyser of Harvard Business School. Professor Greyser had served as a marketing consultant for the Red Sox in the past and teaches a course in sports marketing—a class he personally developed for graduate students in the MBA program. He was kind to review some of my writings and to offer a number of constructive comments and recommendations that were helpful.

Some of the most helpful and constructive counsel, however, came from my very best critic, my wife, Mary Louise. She became my final proofreader, correcting my spelling and on occasion my grammatical structure, page by page and chapter by chapter. Her contributions and suggestions were invaluable, but most of all her understanding, patience, and encouragement were my inspiration to undertake the challenge of writing this book in the first place.

I would be remiss if in writing this book about the Red Sox, I did not at least recall the memories of two of the greatest Red Sox legends ever, namely Helen Robinson, who for 60 years was the Red Sox receptionist at Fenway, and the incomparable Sherman Feller, the Fenway voice of the Red Sox for decades. They were greater than life and their imprint on Red Sox history and all of us who worked at Fenway is everlasting. It is impossible to write or talk about Red Sox baseball without recalling their impact on all of us and they were very much with me as I wrote this book.

I am also gratefully indebted to Elisa Bock Laird and Dean Miller of Sports Publishing L.L.C. for their professional assistance and counsel and for their recommendations in the editing of my book. Without their guidance the final product could not have been possible.

Thanks to Noah Amstadter, also of Sports Publishing, because it was his initial interest to consider publishing the book, which helped bring it into print. I thank him for his interest and help.

Thanks to the marketing skills and enthusiasm of Courtney Hainline, also of Sports Publishing, for her help in promoting the book.

I owe a debt of gratitude to agent Jay Acton, who encouraged me to write the book and assisted me in finding a publisher. I extend my sincere thanks.

Finally I am most grateful for the assistance and support that I received from so many. It would have been an even greater challenge without their contributions or encouragement. My thanks are heartfelt.

Introduction

As 1984 began my total concentration was on the upcoming season and the New York Mets organization. I had been with the Mets for four years after a four-year stint with the Seattle Mariners, and we were really starting to make some headway. I was very happy with the Mets.

A couple of weeks later, everything changed. Frank Cashen, the executive vice president and general manager of the Mets, called me into his office. I was very close to Cashen; it wasn't a boss-employee relationship.

"The Red Sox have called, and they want permission to talk to you about a position. I think it is running the baseball operations, but I am not sure about the title," Cashen said. "I am going to give them the right to talk to you, but I am going to have the right of first refusal. We really don't want you to leave."

I was taken aback by the news.

"Frank, I really don't want to leave. I am happy here at the Mets and with what we are doing here," I said. "I enjoy working with you and I think the ball club is on the verge of winning a pennant or even a world championship."

"Well, I want you to know that we want you to stay here," he said.

"Frank, you know the Red Sox is the only organization I would ever consider talking to. I grew up in New England a longtime Red Sox fan. To run my own show once again and back in New England close to home is tempting." I paused. "Frank, I'll talk to the Red Sox ownership, but in all sincerity Frank, I'm not sure I want to leave the Mets organization. I do thank you for the opportunity to talk to them."

As I left his office, I was torn. I knew that we had a wealth of talent in our farm system and were on the verge of turning the Mets into a highly competitive ball club, quite possibly a championship ball club. If I left the Mets organization now, I would once again not share in the spoils (as had also happened to me when I left the Royals) I felt confident the Mets would attain. On the other hand, the Red Sox were one of the premier franchises in all of Major League Baseball, and the job would bring me back to my roots, my family, and my educational foundation. It would also take me home to my beloved Red Sox.

I had never considered that somehow someday I could find myself fulfilling my childhood dream to become part of the Boston Red Sox, let alone be their general manager. As a youngster growing up in South Providence, Rhode Island, I was a diehard Red Sox fan, albeit a card-carrying member of the Red Sox Nation. I would fall asleep in my room listening to the marvelous Curt Gowdy, then talented Jim Woods and Ned Martin, and finally the wonderful deep-toned Ken Coleman as they covered Red Sox games. Their descriptions and analyses of the action mesmerized me, and I dreamed of the day I might be able to become a major league ballplayer for the Red Sox in Fenway Park, just like my hero, Ted Williams.

Filled with that passionate desire, I spent hours after school on the playing field of Richardson Park imitating everything Williams did—his stance, his swing, his ambling gait—but the results were not even close. I never became discouraged, and I continued to work at it.

When I was about 10 years old, my dad told me he was taking me to a game at Fenway Park. I was beside myself at the thought of getting to go, for the first time in my life, to Fenway and seeing Williams perform in person. I hardly slept the night before because it was a dream fulfilled. When I arrived at the ballpark, my dad took me to the ticket counter where he purchased our tickets. The excitement, the clamor, the sound of the vendors hawking their wares, and the colorful crowds pushing and shoving their way into the turnstiles thrilled me. When we finally walked into the park itself, the playing field came into view. It was immaculately manicured—the green grass so rich in color was brilliant and appeared almost iridescent in the bright sunshine. Then suddenly my gaze caught sight of the Green Monster that towered some 37 feet above left field. I almost felt I could reach out and touch it. It stood magically there, intriguing, challenging, and inviting every batter.

I made my dad, who was not a fan of baseball, stay for the entire game, as I stood transfixed at the battle between the two teams that unfolded before my eyes. I wanted to watch every single at bat by Williams, and although the Red Sox lost the game, Williams hit a two-run homer in his second at bat. I was ecstatic.

After the game, I asked my dad, who was a fire captain at the time but would later go on to become a battalion chief for the Providence Fire Department, if we could go to where the players parked their cars and wait. After enough pestering, he agreed. I wanted to get a look at Williams or the experience that day, despite how glorious it had been, would not be complete. As I stood outside the players' parking lot, miniscule in size compared to the crowded throng of devoted fans, I worked my way to a great viewing spot. Suddenly the players started to appear. Two players came out looking for their wives, who were in the waiting in the parking lot.

"Johnny! Bobby! Please sign our autographs!"

The two men turned to the crowd and began to sign.

I turned to an older gentleman, who stood next to me, and asked, "Is that Johnny Pesky, the shortstop?"

"Yeah, and the other player is the second baseman, Bobby Doerr," he answered.

Another player now emerged from the park and the crowd began to holler, "Dominic, please sign an autograph for us!"

Before I could ask the gentleman, he said, "That's the 'Little Professor,' center fielder Dominic DiMaggio."

The fans began to push us toward him. I was caught up in the excitement as I watched this scene unfold. I kept the lookout for Williams, but he had yet to appear. Then a huge cry went up from the crowd.

"There he is! There's 'The Kid'!"

The fans began to chant, "Ted! Ted! Ted!"

They crushed in and I had yet to get a good look at him. I pushed myself to the front of the rabble, and there was Williams, tall, angular, and movie-star handsome, signing a few autographs. I stood in awe.

But just as suddenly as he appeared, a taxicab pulled up, Williams jumped into the backseat, and he was gone.

I left to find my dad and head for home. It had been reward enough to see him. It had been a very special day.

As the seasons passed, my love for the Red Sox grew. I savored their victories and anguished in their defeats. I recalled their entire lineup position by position season after season. I began to understand that once you are a Red Sox fan, you are a Red Sox fan for life.

I continued to make some moderate success as a ballplayer at the amateur level, the American Legion level, CYO level, and the high school level.

I drew some attention from professional baseball scouts and I began to harbor some hope that maybe a Red Sox scout would have some interest in me.

At the end of my senior year, the Hearst newspapers sponsored a major event in New York City at Polo Grounds, where the company held tryout camps across the nation to bring together 30 of the top amateur ballplayers to compete against a team comprised of New York's finest amateur talent in a much-publicized game called Brooklyn Against the World. It showcased the top amateur talent before a sellout crowd and 40 or 50 major league scouts. In New England, the regional Hearst game was to be played in Fenway Park with the New England All-Stars playing against the Boston All-Stars before an afternoon Red Sox game. I started at first base for New England; the legendary Harry Agganis started at first for Boston. We played the game and waited to hear the results of who would go to New York.

I had been thrilled to play at Fenway, and I was just enjoying the moment. As I walked off the field, the Red Sox players were headed onto the playing field to begin their pregame workouts. I found myself directly in the path of Williams. I could hardly look at him I was so excited.

Then I heard him say, "Hey, kid, let me see your bat. I watched you swing the bat in your last two at bats. I think your bat speed is a bit slow."

With shaking hands I handed him my bat. He took it in his hands and held it a moment.

"This bat is too heavy for you. You should swing a lighter bat."

I was speechless and in a trance.

"Thanks," I managed to mumble.

As Williams headed for the batting cage, he turned back to look at me and said, "Good luck, kid."

My parents found me after the game. My dad immediately wanted to know if I had made the cut to go to the big game. I just smiled at him.

"Dad, I don't care about the big game. I just met and talked to Ted Williams!" I replied.

At that moment I didn't care if I went to New York because I was somewhere close to heaven because I had jut met in person and spoken with Ted Williams. That was paradise enough for me.

I would eventually sign a professional baseball contract with the Philadelphia Phillies but after struggling at the plate I was released outright. Thus ended my dreams to be a part of the Red Sox.

But I now had another chance—at least to serve the team in the front office and I had to at least consider the offer. I had continued to follow my team from Boston—game by game, season by season—throughout my college, Navy, and professional front office baseball jobs. My love never wavered.

A couple of weeks after they contacted the Mets, I flew into Boston and met with John Harrington, a managing partner of the Red Sox; Haywood Sullivan, the current executive vice president and general manager; and Jean Yawkey, the principal owner, for lunch at Jimmy's Harborside Restaurant. It was a very cordial business luncheon. They wanted me come to Boston to initially serve as the vice president and director of baseball operations, but within the next year, Haywood would step down as the club's general manager, because he would become a general partner, and I would then be given the title of vice president and general manager. They offered me a four-year contract with incentives where my previous years in professional baseball would be grandfathered into the Red Sox pension plan. They told me I was the primary candidate to take over the baseball operations. It was a very persuasive presentation, and so I asked them for a week to make up my mind, which they agreed to. But they did mention that they had other viable candidates in mind and I had better make up my mind—soon. I told them I'd be back in touch with them shortly, and I flew back to New York.

A couple of days after I arrived back in New York, Cashen and I met with Nelson for lunch at 21. Nelson wanted me to remain with the Mets and offered to match whatever the Red Sox had offered to me. He told me that as long as he was involved with the Mets ownership, I had a job.

"Whatever they offer you, I will match it. I want you to stay with us. Whenever Frank Cashen decides to step down as the executive vice president and general manager, the job is yours," Doubleday promised. "Now let's have lunch."

I went back to the office with everything that had happened and been said in the back of my mind. I went home early that day. My wife, Mary Louise, and I spent the better part of the evening mulling over my decision to stay with the Mets or go home to the Red Sox. We talked about it at home and then went out to dinner to talk about it some more. I had been totally happy with the Mets, Cashen, the ownership, Joe McIlvaine, Al Harazin, Steve Schryver, and the entire Mets baseball operations staff. We were like a happy family despite how cliché that might sound. To leave would be difficult, very difficult. Deep within my gut however, I knew my deep-seated love of the Red Sox and the opportunity to go home to my roots was too much to overcome. After wavering back and forth, I made the decision. I was going to accept the Red Sox offer.

That next morning I went to Shea Stadium for what I felt was the last time to meet with Cashen and tell him of my resolution. It was one of the more difficult executive decisions I would ever have to make, and I struggled to tell Cashen of my decision to leave.

After a number of extremely difficult goodbyes, I was on my way to Boston to join the Red Sox organization and a whole new adventure and challenge. Little did I ever realize that just two years later I would be back in Shea Stadium, yet this time as the enemy battling the New York Mets for the world championship.

My immediate challenge, however, was to begin to assimilate the talent and staff of an entirely new organization—and not just any baseball organization. This was the Red Sox. They had always been one of the more successful and illustrious organizations in all of professional baseball. Their history was the stuff from which legends are created, and I would now be privileged to become a part of that great history.

My first two years with the Red Sox were spent learning the organization and the staff in place. I familiarized with the system that was in place and how the people within the Red Sox approached baseball operations. I really wanted to learn how to read the scouts in place and to know how to analyze their judgments. I needed to get to know the minor league system and the talent within the system. After my first year manager Ralph Houk decided to retire and so I was faced with finding a new manager and putting together a coaching staff. Haywood recommended a close friend John McNamara, who he had managed together in the Oakland minor league system. We met with McNamara and decided he was the man for the job. In 1986, Haywood became a limited partner, and I became the general manager.

When I came to work for the Red Sox, I wanted to be the one who would take them to the promised land and win a world championship. Two years after I joined the Red Sox, I found myself on the threshold of that dream as we faced the New York Mets—the team I had assembled into National League champions—in the 1986 World Series.

CHAPTER 1

Games 6 and 7
The Dream Dies

I found it almost impossible to contain myself.

My mouth was dry and my heart was beating rapidly. Could I even dare to consider what was about to occur? Was it only a dream or was this really happening? Sixty-eight years of frustration and anguish was about to come to an end. The Red Sox were about to win the World Series for the first time since 1918, and I was their general manager. Me, a kid who had grown up in New England with the Red Sox as my first love.

The silence in Shea Stadium was eerie. More than 45,000 fans were sitting in stunned disbelief as they prepared to accept the inevitable. Millions more watched on national television. Back in New England, fans by the thousands were on the verge of a celebration they had awaited for nearly a century. It was the sixth game of the World Series, the top of the 10th inning.

I turned to my wife, Mary Lou, and whispered, "Remember this moment. We're about to make history."

One of the ironies of this game was that it almost didn't happen. As Richard Brenner wrote in his book *The World Series, the Great Contests:* "A funny thing happened to the Boston Red Sox and the New York Mets on their way to the World Series—they almost watched the California Angels play the Houston Astros."

Two weeks before, our club had been down three games to one against the Angels in the American League Championship Series. In the ninth inning of the fifth game in Anaheim, 54,000 screaming Angels fans were putting on a remarkable display of jubilation. Their team held a 5-2 lead, and the Angels were about to go to the World Series for the first time in their history. The crowd was literally dancing in the aisles.

Things quieted down a bit, however, when a Don Baylor home run cut the Angels' lead to one. We were soon down to our last out, and the fans' excitement began to creep back up, louder, louder, until it became a nearly unbearable din. Their moment of destiny was at hand, and the fans seemed willing to scream it into being.

And I was beginning to be concerned. Not so much about the loss of the game, but about the fans who were beginning to crowd the aisle that led to the exit. I was accompanying Jean Yawkey, the widow of Tom Yawkey, who had bought the Red Sox in 1933. It seemed impossible to get her out of that stadium without being pushed or even crushed by revelers caught up in the celebration.

In all the commotion, I didn't realize that Rich Gedman had been hit by a pitch, which had sent the Angels to their bullpen for one of their top relievers, Donnie Moore. Dave Henderson was coming to the plate.

Meanwhile, I was desperately trying to spot a security guard in the crowd, which by now had completely filled the aisle that led to the nearest exit. My back was to the playing field when I heard the crack of the bat. I turned in an attempt to follow the arc of the ball's flight, but everyone in the stadium was on their feet and my view was blocked.

I never saw the ball leave the park. It was the resulting silence that made me realize that Henderson had just hit one of the most dramatic home runs in Red Sox history, a shot that kept our wildest dreams alive.

Even though the game went into extra innings before we won it, the playoffs had been turned around. Our manager, John McNamara, called it "the best baseball game, the most competitive game, I've ever seen."

The Angels wouldn't recover from this heartbreaking loss. Not when the teams returned to Boston and—for at least one member of this fine team— maybe not ever. Moore, the man who delivered that series-changing pitch, would take his own life a few years later. There were many who speculated that his depression was partially caused by the haunting memory of giving up that homer, of making the pitch that spelled the beginning of the end of the Angels' shot at their first pennant.

Once we got back to Fenway, we won the sixth game 10-4 behind starter Dennis "Oil Can" Boyd and relief pitching by Bob Stanley. We went on to win the seventh game 8-1 with Roger Clemens on the mound. It was the first American League championship for the Red Sox since 1975.

Meanwhile, the Mets had been involved in a dramatic series of their own against the Astros. The Mets had been considered a favorite in the National League series but had approached the playoffs with an air of over confidence that bordered on arrogance, an attitude that would often antagonize their opponents. Darryl Strawberry seemed to epitomize this cockiness. No other player on the club was more disliked.

However, I honestly believed that the Astros might have been the tougher club for us to face. I felt we were a better team than the Mets, that position by position, we had the edge. But I also knew that for the most part, pitching would determine the outcome. Although I had confidence in our staff, the Mets pitchers were outstanding. They had led the National League with an earned run average of 2.63 and had four excellent starters in Dwight Gooden, Ron Darling, Bobby Ojeda, and Sid Fernandez.

But we matched their ace staff with talent of our own. Roger Clemens was dominant. He had won 24 and lost four in his breakout season, striking out nearly 250. (In fact, when I was with the Mets, I had drafted Clemens out of junior college and we had made every attempt but failed to sign him. Had the Mets been able to sign him, however, it might well have changed baseball history.) Left-hander Bruce Hurst had gone 13-8, but he had struck out 170 batters in 167 innings pitched and had maintained an ERA of only 2.99. I also felt the Mets were vulnerable to left-handed pitching. "Oil Can" Boyd had also finished the season 16-10 with a 3.79 ERA. "The Can" was a tough competitor and he relished pitching in big games. I felt the overall depth and balance of our ball club gave us an edge over the Mets.

Going in to the World Series, we knew it wasn't going to be easy. It never was. Yet, here we were in Game 6, and we were about to win the world championship—for the first time in 68 years.

Making it even more emotional for me was the fact that just two years earlier, I was working for the Mets as their vice president and director of baseball operations. I had joined them in 1980 when my old friend Frank Cashen set out to rebuild the organization. I had previously worked for Cashen in the Orioles organization, as their director of player development, and we had helped steer them to their first world championship in 1966.

When Cashen landed the job with the Mets, the organization was struggling to compete. But in addition to a law degree, Cashen had a deep hands-on understanding of the needs and problems of developing a competitive organization. He was an excellent administrator and chief executive, one with vision. He also brought a confidence to the job that was felt by the people around him. He never shied away from delegating authority and responsibility. It was a trait I deeply admired, and our working relationship was one of mutual admiration and respect. Our friendship continues to this day.

I was proud to be part of the very effective and talented staff Frank had assembled to help him pull off the job at hand, which was nothing short of bringing an organization in shambles back to its glory days, to let the New York fans relive the days when they could root for those "Amazin' Mets."

And the two principal owners—Nelson Doubleday and Fred Wilpon—were a superb duo, totally committed to doing what was necessary to the development of a successful winning club.

Just two seasons had passed, and now I sat in Shea Stadium rooting with every ounce of emotion in my body to defeat the club I had helped put together. I had learned long ago that baseball was a game of irony as well as one of hits, runs, and errors.

I had never seen Mrs. Yawkey so intense or nervous as she was at that moment, anticipating what was about to unfold in front of her. What could she possibly be thinking? What emotions must she be experiencing? How many memories? Tom Yawkey had poured both his heart and his pocket-book into the team until his death. The Yawkey family had been synonymous with the Red Sox for generations. Yet, in all those years, they had never won a world championship. It was the one thing that always eluded them, their one great regret, even though they had come so close in 1946, 1967, and 1975—so close, they could taste it. I knew more than any other owners in baseball, the Yawkeys deserved to win a World Series. I desperately wanted to be the one to win it for them. It would be a symbolic "thank you" for all they had done for baseball and New England. It would be the one great shining prize that could come close to repaying them for all the emotion—and the money—they had so willingly invested in the Red Sox.

The team had taken an early 2-0 lead behind Clemens, who had proved himself to be the best pitcher in baseball that season. He also was one of the most intense competitors I had ever been around, someone who cared more about winning than about his personal stats. And although there would be some critics who would claim that Clemens never won the "big game," I considered him a true winner in every sense of the word. He had a great arm, and he gave 100 percent of his guts and ability every time he took the mound. Without question he was one of the greatest pitchers in Red Sox history and on his way to baseball's Hall of Fame.

Clemens surrendered two runs in the bottom of the fifth, but we came back to go ahead 3-2 in the top of the seventh. By then, he was working on a four-hitter with eight strikeouts and only two walks. He'd come within six outs of capturing a World Series victory—a dream he would chase for another 13 seasons before getting the ring in 1999 with the New York Yankees.

In fact, he had led the Red Sox into the World Series with a 24-4 record, and he would go on to become not only the Cy Young winner but also the Most Valuable Player in the American League. This was a rare feat but well deserved in light of his spectacular season.

But going into the eighth inning, he had developed a blister on the middle finger of his pitching hand; it had begun to bleed. This was hindering the delivery of his slider and his breaking ball. His potent fastball was the only pitch left in his arsenal.

So when the Red Sox came out of the dugout in the bottom of the eighth, Clemens was out of the game, even though he had been outstanding. When he stayed on the bench, the national media was stunned, as were Red Sox fans everywhere. This was one of the biggest games in Red Sox history. Why was Clemens being lifted?

This was to become one of the major controversies of the Series. The question at hand was whether Clemens had "asked out" of the ball game or McNamara had made the decision for him.

McNamara insists that Clemens asked to be removed and indicated that the pitcher had told him he couldn't continue.

Clemens adamantly disputes this, saying, "The decision was entirely McNamara's. He was the one who made the decision. My finger was bleeding, but it was up to him whether I stayed in or not. I had nothing to say about it. There was no way I was asking out. I told McNamara I could get it done with my fastball."

Bill Fischer, the pitching coach, corroborated the fact that Clemens's finger was bleeding when they looked at his pitching hand in the bottom of the seventh inning.

Later, when I talked to both Clemens and McNamara about the incident, both held fast to their original statements. Knowing Clemens as well as I did, I found it difficult to accept that he would ever have himself taken out of a ball game—particularly a World Series game in which he had only six outs left to make. He is just too tremendous a competitor. On the other hand, I had a great deal of respect for McNamara, both as a baseball man and as a person. He had been straightforward, honest, and upfront with me at all times.

I've spent a lot of time trying to put this conflict into perspective. The best I can surmise is that when Clemens's hand was examined between innings by McNamara, Fischer, and trainer Charlie Moss, they asked Clemens if it was bothering him. When he indicated that he was having some difficulty throwing his breaking ball, McNamara may have misunderstood Clemens's response as an indication that he wanted out of the game. In the intensity of that critical moment—a pivotal point in a World Series game that was the key to fulfilling the most heartfelt baseball dream of every member of the team as well as millions of long-frustrated Red Sox fans—it is certainly possible that some confusion could have developed.

One thing I know for certain is that Clemens is a tremendous competitor. I doubt that he would ever have taken himself out of a game that could have been the culmination of his lifelong dreams. Yet I also know it doesn't make any sense for McNamara to have removed Clemens if he was physically sound, in command, and only six outs away from winning the World Series.

Calvin Schiraldi, whom we had obtained the previous winter in a trade with the Mets, was the new pitcher. While I was with the Mets, we had drafted him out of the University of Texas, where he had been Clemens's teammate on a squad that had won the national championship. At the time, many scouts considered Schiraldi the best collegiate pitcher in the country and an even better prospect than Clemens. Schiraldi had been honored as the college pitcher of the year. In the late part of the season, Schiraldi had been a savior for us. Combined with Bob Stanley, he had given us an outstanding bullpen.

As Schiraldi warmed up, I remembered how he hadn't been too happy about our decision to make him a relief pitcher. He had always been a starter in college. But once he accepted the change, he began to relish it. I was confident that he could save the ball game for Clemens. In so doing, he might become one of the biggest heroes in Red Sox history. Never again would Schiraldi pitch a game where there would be more riding on every single pitch.

Over in the Mets dugout, I spotted manager Davey Johnson. I had known him since he was a young player in the Baltimore organization when I was the director of minor league operations and player development for the Orioles. I vividly remembered the spring of 1966 when Johnson, after about a year and a half at Triple-A Rochester, had a great spring training and manager Hank Bauer penciled him into the lineup over veteran Jerry Adair. He went on to play in the big leagues until 1978, played in four World Series, and was an All-Star three times. He then managed one year in the minors before leaving baseball. In 1981, I contacted him at his Florida home and offered him an opportunity to manage in the Mets organization. It took a great deal of persuasion, but he finally agreed. I started him in Double-A. The following season, I convinced him to serve as a roving instructor and talent evaluator. I was offering him the opportunity to look over all the talent in our organization before giving him the Triple-A manager's job at Tidewater (Norfolk, Virginia), the next season. A year later, on my recommendation, Cashen made him skipper of the Mets.

Now he was leading the opposition.

And I thought of all of the players in the Mets dugout whom I was involved in acquiring or had signed myself. Strawberry and Gooden had been first-round draft choices. I could recall many conversations I had had with Strawberry about the pressures of playing in New York and the temptations of being a celebrity in the Big Apple.

Strawberry had such great talent and the potential to become a Hall of Fame inductee. He generated tremendous power from a graceful classic swing. For a big man he had excellent range in the outfield, good speed, and a strong throwing arm. His future and promise were limitless.

Dwight Gooden was also a very special talent with a great arm and a great young man, whom we had drafted and signed out of a Tampa, Florida, high school. He also had the potential to become one of the very best pitchers in the major leagues and was capable of pitching his way into baseball's Hall of Fame.

So much irony and so many memories. My wife later said she had never seen me so nervous or uptight during a game. In a sense, I suppose I saw this as the culmination of my career. Two teams that I was intimately familiar with, battling each other for the world championship. I wondered if anyone else in the history of the game had ever found themselves in such a situation.

The Mets came back to tie the game at three runs apiece with a single run off Schiraldi in the bottom of the eighth. Both clubs failed to score in the ninth, and the game went into extra innings.

In the top of the 10th, Henderson led off the inning with a towering home run into the upper deck façade off a low inside fastball. As he gleefully danced around the bases, I began to fantasize that he was Moses reincarnated, leading us once again to the promised land of postseason glory—as he had so dramatically done against the Angels back in the ALCS. When he reached home plate, our entire ball club stormed out of the dugout to greet him en masse.

The Sox now led 5-3 and were only three outs away from immortality.

It was difficult for me to sit still. I was tempted to go find some place to walk off the tension, yet I was unable to move, as if my every emotion was strained to the breaking point, pinning me to my seat.

Wally Backman led off the Mets 10th with a fly out to left fielder Jim Rice.

Two outs away.

Then Keith Hernandez flied out to center.

One out away.

The tension and excitement were overwhelming me. For some unknown reason, I began to recall the many minor league parks I had been in, all those games in all those ballparks, so many nights spent building my career. Lakeland, Florida; Kinston, North Carolina; Dubuque, Iowa; Elmira, New York; Aberdeen, South Dakota; Bluefield, West Virginia; Billings, Montana; Thomasville, Georgia; Stockton; San Jose; Rochester; Syracuse; Tacoma. All those innumerable places. All the years and all the games.

One more out and all those nights in my long baseball lifetime would be redeemed.

For one brief moment, the Shea message board flashed, "Congratulations to the Boston Red Sox, World Champions." But as quickly as it appeared, the message was gone.

It seemed like a joyful harbinger of a foregone conclusion, of inevitable victory.

Our players were on the front steps of the dugout, ready to charge onto the field in a massive celebration—the biggest any Red Sox team had experienced in 68 years. I thought of the incredible revelry this was going to set off in Boston. It might never end. The city had waited for this victory for so very, very long; it seemed to be almost for an eternity.

Time seemed suspended. I was transfixed, mesmerized, and spellbound. It was surreal.

With two outs, Gary Carter singled to give the Mets a glimmer of hope. Kevin Mitchell was coming to the plate to hit for pitcher Rick Aguilera. Mitchell singled to center.

Schiraldi then proceeded to get two strikes against Ray Knight. We were only one strike away from euphoria for thousands and thousands of Sox fans.

Two outs. Two strikes on Knight. And a two-run lead. There was no way we could lose now, I said to myself, "No God could ever be so cruel to allow this victory to slip away."

But Knight singled up the middle, and Carter scored the Mets' fourth run.

McNamara walked to the mound and signaled to the bullpen for Stanley. He had been with the Red Sox for 10 years, had saved 123 games, and won 100. And he'd had a good year, appearing in 66 games as a tough competitor, someone who had never made excuses for a bad performance. He had been a frequent target of some fan abuse over the years, but he always handled it well. I had a great deal of respect for him.

In his normal fashion, Stanley ran in from the bullpen. McNamara patted Schiraldi on the back and handed the fate of the team over to Stanley. As the closer warmed up, his pitches appeared alive. The tail on this fastball was exceptional.

"I've never seen his fastball have so much movement," I said to Haywood Sullivan, a general partner of the team who was sitting beside me. Haywood, an ex-major leaguer, agreed.

I was convinced that Stanley would blow the Mets away.

The Mets' next batter was Mookie Wilson, their diminutive left fielder who for most of the season had played center field. He and Stanley began the battle that was the truest essence of baseball.

It was a classic confrontation, the baseball version of the gunfight at the OK Corral: the pitcher with everything on the line and no room for doubt or error.

Lee MacPhail, the American League president, suggested to our party— Mrs. Yawkey, John Harrington, and Haywood—that we should start toward our clubhouse to ready for the presentation of the world championship trophy. We were seated next to our dugout and the ramp that led to the clubhouse. I wondered who would want to make the acceptance speech. I also began thinking about what I would say to the fans of New England and how to apologize for nearly 70 years of frustration and agony. We had the greatest fans in America, fans who had supported the team through so many long fruitless years. I wanted to be able to say something to somehow salve all the past's painful wounds, if that were ever possible.

At that moment, two of our front office staff—Larry Cancro, director of marketing, and director of broadcasting Jim Healey—were frantically rushing between our clubhouse and the Mets clubhouse to borrow the Mets' champagne supply. I couldn't remember why we had not brought enough champagne into our clubhouse in anticipation of a celebration with one more victory that would give us the world championship. I couldn't recall whether it was an oversight or superstition, but right now it was the furthest thought in my mind. I was totally absorbed in the action on the field and on our desperate need for one final out to end it all. Nothing else mattered at this point. Looking over at Mrs. Yawkey, I could see for the first time the faint traces of a smile of long, long awaited satisfaction.

We had already left our seats when the ball got past catcher Rich Gedman allowing Mitchell to score the tying run of the ball game.

Wilson had kept fouling off pitches, barely getting a piece of Stanley's snakelike movement. With the count even at 2-2, Gedman had called for a fastball down and in at the knees. He'd set up just to the right of the middle of the plate. As Stanley started to go into his windup, he had wondered why Gedman had not moved to the inside of the plate, but he had assumed that the catcher would shift as the pitch made its way to the hitter. Inexplicably, Gedman moved too late, and Stanley's pitch, with its outstanding movement, darted down and in, glancing off Gedman's glove as it made its long trip all the way to the backstop. Mitchell raced home with the tying run.

Had it been a wild pitch or a passed ball?

Dale Ford was the plate umpire and reportedly stated that the pitch might have been a marginal strike and should have been caught. Wilson later said that he thought Stanley was attempting to pitch him away or his pitches were tailing away to the outside of the plate, so Wilson was crowding the plate inside. Wilson was crowding the plate so much, Gedman would claim that his view of the inside pitch was blocked as Wilson dived to avoid being hit.

The official scorer ruled it a wild pitch, but there were many who thought it was a passed ball that the catcher should have blocked. The issue over whether it was a wild pitch or a passed ball would strain the relationship between Stanley and Gedman for months after the Series concluded.

But that would come later. Now the game was tied, and the entire scenario had changed dramatically.

Unbelievably, the Mets were back from the dead. Adding insult to injury, Mitchell had been in the clubhouse taking off his uniform and phoning for a plane reservation home only minutes before he was called to bat.

Our group froze in it tracks, almost in disbelief, too stunned to accept what had just happened. It could not be possible for us to lose this game. It just couldn't. The anguish and agony would be too much to take.

We trudged back to our seats. On the pitch that got by Gedman, Knight had moved into scoring position at second base. We had gone from one pitch away with a two-run lead to a tie ball game. And now the Mets had the winning run on second base. My heart was still pounding hard against my chest, only now with a sense of impending disaster. My wife reached over to grab my hand.

"We're going to win this ball game," she said.

I desperately wanted to share her confidence, but everyone else in our group was deeply concerned and as apprehensive as I was.

The count was three and two. Wilson and Stanley battled on, and two more pitches were fouled off. The already excruciating tension just kept increasing.

What happened next will live forever in Red Sox infamy. It would be one of the most tragic defining moments in World Series history. Our dream of winning the first world championship since 1918 ended with Mookie Wilson's next swing.

Wilson topped the ball off the end of his bat, sending a slowly bouncing ball to Bill Buckner at first base. It was a routine play, one that should have ended the inning and kept us in the ball game.

Wilson, who had good speed, charged down the baseline as Buckner got into position to field the ball. Buckner had made innumerable plays just like this in his career. As the ball approached him, it was twisting and turning like a cue shot on a pool table. He was in perfect position to make the play. But as he bent down to field the ball, it inexplicably, incomprehensibly scooted through his legs into short right field. Knight scored to give the Mets the 6-5 win.

The unthinkable had happened. Pandemonium broke out throughout Shea Stadium. Fans exploded into thunderous shouts of disbelief and overwhelming joy at this stunning turn of events. Our party was in absolute silence. It was almost impossible to accept what had just happened. Every emotion, save a dull sickening anguish, drained from our bodies.

It was a defeat so crushing as to be almost impossible to accept or live with. They say that grown men don't cry, but I came awfully close as I watched the delirious Mets players celebrating around home plate. They knew they had come back from the dead, and that both the emotion and momentum of the Series were now in their favor.

Mrs. Yawkey simply stared out onto the field in stunned silence, a thousand lost hopes playing across her face.

I had wondered at the start of the inning if McNamara had given any thought to removing Buckner for defensive reasons and replacing him with sure-fielding Dave Stapleton, a move he had made throughout the playoffs. It seemed like an obvious switch to make.

Later I asked McNamara, why not Stapleton? Had he given it any thought?

"I thought about it," he told me, "but I felt Buckner deserved to be on the field when we won."

McNamara was a very sentimental and caring man. But this time, I felt he had allowed his emotions to overshadow his baseball logic, which should have dictated that he remove Buckner at the top of the 10th. I'm equally certain that Stapleton expected to be on the field that inning.

On the other hand, Buckner had been superb defensively throughout his long career and had just set an assist record for first basemen the season before, however, a succession of injuries *had* severely limited his mobility. However, this play had nothing to do with those problems, and I'm convinced that if the same play were to occur again, Buckner would have made it 10 out of 10 times.

Buckner had played the entire ALCS against the Angels and the World Series in intense pain. He had re-injured his right ankle, a recurrence of an old and serious injury that he had suffered seasons ago while playing for the Dodgers. He had torn away much of the muscle and tendons attached from his ankle to his foot. In the last few weeks of the regular season sliding into second base he re-aggravated the same ankle and foot, bone scraping against bone, ever so painfully.

Prior to every playoff game and the World Series we had to freeze his ankle in ice, tape it, and then place him in hightop shoes. His mobility and range were severely restricted.

"I hate to say I missed that ground ball," he said later. "I was playing deeper than usual, and I knew that Wilson was extremely fast. The ball seemed to be spinning off the end of the bat, and I was seeing the ball well. The ball had so much spin on it, I kept looking for it to bounce. But it never did. It just kept skipping and spinning, and it got under my glove. It's hard to believe I missed the ball. I thought later, I might have taken my eyes off the ball to see where Wilson was coming down the line, but I honestly felt I saw the ball well. I don't recall ever missing a ball like that in my past career."

But in the 10th inning of Game 6 of the 1986 World Series at Shea Stadium in the borough of Queens, just one pitch from glory, the ball dribbled away and so did the hopes and dreams of millions of Red Sox fans everywhere.

Finally, we got up and started to move out of the stadium. Protocol has it that the home team hosts a postgame party, but Mrs. Yawkey was in no mood to attend a Mets celebration. The concessions at Shea were handled by Harry S. Stevens, the same company that ran the concessions at Fenway Park. One of their executives offered us a room to sit in while we waited for crowd to leave Shea and provided us with some drinks and hors d'oeuvres. The room was sparsely furnished with a few packing cases scattered here and there. It was a drab and depressing place—perfectly suited for our state of mind.

As we began consoling one another and trying to raise some glimmer of hope for Game 7, scheduled for the next night, Mrs. Yawkey motioned for me to sit next to her. She looked me straight in the eye and said, "You know, your manager just cost us the world championship." I began to respond, but she continued, "Do you understand what I'm telling you? Your manager cost us the world championship."

I just kept nodding while she kept staring into my eyes to make sure I was getting the message. I knew what Mrs. Yawkey was implying, not stating, that McNamara should have replaced Buckner with Stapleton for defensive purposes in the bottom of the 10th inning. She obviously recognized Buckner's limited mobility, and with the ultimate victory all but in our grasp, we needed to have our best defensive ball club on the field. From that moment on, I knew that it was only a matter of time before McNamara would be gone.

It was like a wake in there. We all knew what we had lost, and each of us felt the enormity of that defeat. We had come so close to grasping the Holy

Grail of professional baseball and, in a dramatic and painful fashion, watched it cruelly snatched from our reach.

We also knew that it was going to be extremely difficult, if not impossible, to regain the momentum that had swept us to the brink of becoming world champions. Just one pitch. The slimmest of margins had kept us from the most glorious of victories. What could ever define heartbreak more starkly than that?

Eventually, we left the room and the others headed for the limousines that were to take them back to Manhattan. I decided to ride the bus back with the players, and when I got to the clubhouse, the scene was chilling. It was like sitting in the middle of a morgue. Despite the fact that there was another game to go, the players seemed to know they had just let the Series get away from them. Their spirits couldn't have been any lower. As we rode back to our hotel, all I remember hearing was the hum of the bus tires. Everything else was a deadly, sickening silence.

Former columnist Mike Barnicle of *The Boston Globe* once wrote, "Baseball is not a life and death matter, but the Red Sox are."

As I sat on the darkened bus, consumed, disillusioned, and surrounded by disappointment, I knew all too well what those words meant. I didn't have a very good feeling about Game 7, either.

I tossed and turned all night long, unable to nod off into a peaceful slumber as I pondered over and over again whether our ball club could ever come back from such a devastating defeat. I had visions of an embarrassing rout, because the morale of our ball club had to be at an all-time low. It would take a miracle to revitalize the spirit and soul of our team. Maybe I should have been praying to the patron saint of hopeless causes to intercede on our behalf.

The seventh and final game of the 1986 World Series was scheduled for Sunday, October 27, at Shea Stadium. Twenty-four hours previously, I had been convinced that instead we'd all be on our way back to Boston for probably the most tumultuous celebration the city had seen since the end of World War II. The disastrous and agonizing defeat of the previous night had snuffed out that glorious dream.

When Sunday finally arrived, it was bleak, overcast, and beginning to rain. As the morning progressed, it just came down harder and harder. It was becoming evident that a serious question was arising as to whether the game would even be played this afternoon.

I tried to read the New York morning papers, but the accounts of the Mets' miraculous victory and pictures of the 10th-inning celebration turned me off, so I tossed them away.

By 9 a.m., our traveling secretary Jack Rogers, who was unquestionably one of the best in the business, called my suite to inform me that our bus to Shea would be delayed because of the weather. He told me that the commissioner and league officials planned to go to the stadium around 10 or 10:30 to inspect the playing field and determine if the game could be played. I looked out the windows of the Grand Hyatt Hotel, our New York headquarters during the season, and the rain was coming down in torrents. If this continued, the game would be postponed until Monday. That might be a big break for us. It would give our ball club one more day to put the loss behind them. I knew it wouldn't be easy to forget Game 6, but at least I could hope that a day's delay would help.

At 10 a.m., McNamara called and asked me to come to his suite. McNamara said that he had an idea he'd like to get my opinion on. When I arrived, he was sitting at a table drinking coffee and going over the Mets' player statistics he had written out on a yellow pad. He offered me a cup of coffee. I could tell from his demeanor he couldn't stand discussing the painful events of the night before, and this echoed my sentiments exactly. The damage had been done; we couldn't reverse the events of the previous day no matter how much we might want to. The only challenge facing us now was to find some way to come back and win. It would be a monumental task at best. I tried to impress upon McNamara how important it would be for him to find a way to inspire the ball club with the opportunity that Game 7 offered them, despite their despondency after Saturday's loss. We still could come back and win a World Series championship; the door was still open if we could just pick ourselves up by our bootstraps.

McNamara had an idea that he felt might give us an edge. It was "Oil Can" Boyd's turn to pitch. "The Can" may have been a character off field, but on the mound, he was all business. He was a great competitor, and he gave a solid effort every time out. But he'd had some rocky outings during the postseason.

Boyd had won 16 ball games that year and had pitched 214 innings. He had won a ball game in the ALCS 10-4, but he had lost one 5-3. Then he had pitched the third game of the World Series at Fenway and lost 7-1, allowing six earned runs.

McNamara proposed that we bypass Boyd for Game 7 and send left-hander Bruce Hurst instead. McNamara felt that the Mets could be beaten by a lefty, and Hurst had already triumphed twice in this World Series: He threw a four-hitter with eight strikeouts in Game 1 and pitched a complete Game 5 with six strikeouts. If the game were rained out, as it was looking like it would be, he would be pitching on three days' rest instead of his usual four. But McNamara was convinced that Hurst could handle it. After all, when Game 7 was finished, Hurst would have the long winter to recover before he threw another baseball.

McNamara hoped that Hurst could give him seven innings; Schiraldi could pitch the eighth, and Clemens could come in to close. I thought it just might work. But the biggest challenge would be telling Boyd. It was the opportunity of a lifetime for him, and I knew he was desperate to prove himself in such a significant game. It would be no easy thing to talk him out of the starting assignment, and I knew he was bound to be emotional about it.

I assured McNamara that I would back him up, and I would be glad to stay while he talked to Boyd. But McNamara felt like delivering the news was his responsibility, so I left it up to him. Before leaving the suite, though, I gave McNamara as many words of encouragement as I could muster. I felt like he needed a pep talk before he met with the players. He had to be as upbeat as humanly possible to face his ball club after Saturday's disaster.

When I got back to my room, my wife told me I had a message to call the commissioner's office as soon as possible. I'd also received a call from John Harrington, which I figured he'd placed on behalf of Mrs. Yawkey, inquiring about the status of the game.

I immediately got on the phone with the commissioner and talked to Bill Murray, a longtime executive there. He said there was a strong possibility the game would be canceled until Monday night. He said the walk-through showed that field conditions were nearly unplayable. He promised to get back to me within the hour with an update. I passed on the news to John Harrington and McNamara, as well as Jack Rogers. He had already notified the players of the potential postponement.

Then I sat down to a late breakfast with my wife, who was making every effort to avoid discussing our loss. She tried all sorts of light and mundane topics to take my mind off the night before. I couldn't shake it, though, and I began playing the game over and over in my mind. I figured the players were doing the same thing, and I wondered how much they would carry these thoughts back onto the field. We had mentally dug ourselves into a chasm of excruciating and painful memories, and it would be almost impossible for this team to climb out. If they didn't, Game 7 would be over before it even started.

That's when the visions of a one-sided catastrophe started to really loom before me. I knew I was rubbing salt into a wound that would be all but impossible to heal. Somehow, our ball club had to be convinced that they could come back to win the final game. I knew how difficult that really would be, but if we had any chance to win at all, we had "to believe" we could do it.

The phone rang, and McNamara was on the line. He had talked to Boyd who, though very unhappy with the manager's decision, had reluctantly agreed but was extremely upset and left the suite in anger. I fully understood his reaction. He was such an intense competitor. Right after McNamara called me, Bill Murray from the commissioner's office called me to tell me the game had been canceled and would be played Monday night.

After I informed everybody in our organization, I briefly considered having McNamara call a team meeting. But I quickly re-thought that notion, figuring that a night away from the game might be just what the players needed. McNamara could get them together in the clubhouse tomorrow night before the game. That seemed to make more sense.

Monday evening finally arrived. It was a clear, cloudless night with a slight touch of fall in the air. The rain clouds had long since dissipated, and some 55,000 fans were jamming their way into Shea Stadium. They had come to witness the kill. I could detect their frenzy and excitement as they came storming through the turnstiles into Shea Stadium, which I had once called my second home. Somehow it made me recall the citizens of ancient Rome flooding into the Coliseum, hungry for the blood of Christians being fed to the lions. It was a terrifying and sobering image, and I quickly tried to erase it from my mind.

I dropped my wife off with the rest of the Red Sox party in the box seats behind our dugout and headed for the clubhouse. It was unusually silent there, but I tried to imagine it was a feeling of quiet confidence. I was encouraged, even hopeful. I walked by Dwight Evans and Bill Buckner and wished them both luck. They acknowledged me with a nod and went back to dressing for the game. McNamara had spent a good part of the past few hours with his coaching staff and then with his pitcher and catcher once again reviewing our advance scouting reports on the Mets' hitters and their overall strengths and weaknesses.

Like all ball clubs that make it into postseason playoffs, they assign their top professional scouts to cover in depth their upcoming opponent at least a week or two before they meet them in competition. The advance scouting reports are in exacting detail, player by player, pitcher by pitcher, game situation by game situation.

I had never been aware of the importance or tremendous value that advance scouting reports could be until I read the advance scouting report that Jim Russo, one of the Orioles' special assignment scouts, had turned in on the Los Angeles Dodgers. I was with the Orioles as their director of player development, and we had defeated the Dodgers in the 1966 World Series. It was a remarkable detailed analysis of every single player on the Dodgers' roster. It spelled out every move, action, and reaction of each player in every game situation both offensively and defensively. What pitch gives the hitter the most trouble? Which pitch does he look for in which situation? What pitch does a particular pitcher throw for an out pitch on which count on the hitter? The defensive alignment of the infield and outfield in each situation. Who has the strongest throwing arm in the infield and the outfield? Who runs on the ball club and on what count? etc. etc. I read the report in awe and became forever a true believer in the vital contribution that an advance scouting report can make.

I had assigned Eddie Kasko, our scouting director and an outstanding baseball man; Rac Slider; Joe Stephenson; and Wayne Britton to provide our advance scouting on both the California Angels and the New York Mets. They had done an outstanding job, and the detailed reports on the Mets ball club were superb. I had added my input on the Mets players, but the advance scouting reports were in much greater detail and scope. We had actually constructed a book on the Mets, player by player, for McNamara and the coaches to use to brief our players and to refer to throughout each ball game. It was a standard procedure to create a book through advance scouting on every club in your league, which is maintained in the dugout, and it is referred to throughout the ball game by the manager or coaches. The playoff reports are even more detailed.

I went into McNamara's office, where Haywood was already engaging in some banal small talk with our manager. McNamara was still reviewing his lineup card. As I took a seat, one of the American League officials poked his head in and asked for the lineup to pass on to the media. It was looking like an all-time television audience was going to be tuning in to the final game of an already dramatic Series. And I knew that despite the painful and tragic loss on Saturday, a huge audience of New Englanders would still be watching.

Before we knew it, it was time for them to head out onto the field. Our ball club was introduced to a constant crescendo of boos. Nevertheless, the team seemed upbeat, and I hoped that it wasn't just superficial. Maybe a day off had helped put Saturday night out of their minds.

As the Mets were introduced to a thundering ovation, each took a place in the home plate area in front of their dugout. My eyes scanned each player, bringing back a host of memories. So many of these players I had been involved in acquiring while I was with the Mets as their vice president of baseball operations.

It was a ball club I knew all too well. It was almost incomprehensible that they were now the enemy. Gooden, Strawberry, Fernandez, Backman, Aguilera, Dykstra, Mitchell, Wilson, Mazzilli, Ojeda, Orosco, McDowell, Sisk. I had worked so hard to help assemble much of this team; a team that now stood between our Red Sox and our chance to become immortals in the annals of Boston's baseball history.

And even the coaches. As starter Ron Darling headed to the bullpen with Mel Stottlemyre, their pitching coach, I remembered convincing Cashen to hire him, having become so enamored with his abilities when he worked for me in Seattle.

When the pregame ceremonies concluded, the noise level subsided just slightly and 55,000 fans readied themselves for a Mets victory. That din would rise and fall throughout the game, but rarely did it subside below a deafening roar. That roar just added to the overwhelming tension and anxiety of our group as we sat back to witness the drama unfolding. We felt the burden of the ages—the years of discouragement and pain felt by the Red Sox Nation. And though I'd had more of a hand probably than anybody in orchestrating the circumstances that led to this particularly poignant moment in baseball history, I was now just a bystander.

The first inning was scoreless, as both Darling and Hurst got out of it unscathed. It was in the second inning that our jubilation began as back-to-back homers by Evans and Gedman lifted us all out of our seats and gave us a lead.

We had a 2-0 lead right out of the gate, but I remember greedily wishing we'd had more men on base to take advantage of those hits. We needed a bigger cushion for Hurst. But at least we had a lead, and I quickly reminded myself to be grateful for small favors.

But we had been so humbled on Saturday night. Hopefully we'd learned our lesson about letting over confidence creep into our thoughts. This ball game had a long way to go, and we were painfully aware of what cruel bounces the baseball could take.

A little extra insurance came before the end of the inning when Wade Boggs hit a line drive to center to bring in Henderson, who had walked. Sid Fernandez would replace Darling on the mound in the third inning. From that point on Fernandez would take charge and all but shut us down. Going into the sixth, however, we were still clinging to a 3-0 lead.

Hurst had been in complete control to that point. He was pitching masterfully, and it really seemed that McNamara's gamble had paid off. Could I dare even dream for a moment that we were finally going to win it all? We only had 12 more outs to go; yet it seemed an eternity. Hurst had only allowed one hit and no runs. I felt like closing my eyes and praying away the four remaining innings. After nearly 70 years of Red Sox frustration, it seemed the baseball gods should at least lend me an ear.

But I have always felt very strongly that we aren't owed anything, not in life and certainly not in baseball. Whatever you're given in this world, you have to earn on your own merits. And a lot of luck. Baseball was no different.

I knew we had to knock Fernandez out of the ball game to make any headway. He had been extremely tough since the third. And I felt a terrible gnawing in the pit of my stomach because I recalled that I had been the one who was responsible for acquiring him from the Dodgers. He had been a major force during this World Series.

In the top of the sixth, Hurst got the first Mets batter out. He then gave up back-to-back singles. Fischer went out to talk to him. I began to squirm in my seat. Maybe Hurst was running out of gas because he'd only had three days' rest. I looked over to the bullpen and saw that McNamara had Schiraldi warming up. I was beginning to have a bad feeling about this. Hurst was looking uncomfortable and uneasy, pawing at the rubber, and that was making me uneasy also. Hurst had always epitomized poise and class during his entire career; he was the embodiment of professionalism. But right now, however, he seemed to be tiring, uneasy, and disturbed.

The bases were loaded with one out. Keith Hernandez was coming to the plate. Hurst had worked the count in his favor, but he couldn't close the deal. Hernandez lined a single to center field. The hit made it a 3-2 ball game, and the momentum was changing. That one pitch might well have been the defining moment of the ball game.

Hurst had been so exceptional to this point—not only in this game but in the entire Series. He had pitched 23 innings and had an outstanding 1.96 ERA. When you factored in his performance in the ALCS, he had pitched 36 innings and struck out 29 batters for an overall ERA of 2.40.

Oftentimes in the thousands of games I have seen in my career, a game comes down to one pitch, one play—a single instant that stands out in the innings of otherwise routine baseball. Even when a ball game is lost by a wide margin, the beginning of the end can often be traced to one misplay, one fundamental mistake that opened the floodgates and turned things around. Hurst's fastball, left up high and over the plate, was that moment in Game 7.

Later, long after the World Series was done, Hurst would tell me, "If there was one pitch in my entire career that I would give anything to take back, it would be that pitch Hernandez hit," he said. "I knew if I could get him out, we would win the World Series."

This might sound a bit like braggadocio, but I firmly believe he was right. Hurst was a quietly confident and humble man. When he made that statement, I never doubted his sincerity or the validity of his statement. It well might be an accurate assessment, because if he had gotten Hernandez out, we might just have won that ball game and the World Series.

The crowning blow came next. Gary Carter came up and looped another single into right field where, despite a valiant effort, Evans barely missed making the play. We were tied at three apiece.

McNamara made the decision to remove Hurst from the game at the end of the inning. He sent Tony Armas up to bat for him in the top of the seventh, and Armas struck out. After the game, the media questioned this move, saying McNamara should have stuck with Hurst for the seventh. Despite the Mets' three runs in the sixth, Hurst had only allowed four hits. Hurst said later that he had felt strong enough to continue, but the decision was made to replace him. Schiraldi was brought in. It was a very difficult call, but McNamara was understandably worried about Hurst working with only three days' rest. His last outing had been a complete game, and McNamara had planned to go with Schiraldi in the eighth, anyway. Hurst did appear to be tiring. It would be easy to second-guess the decision to remove Hurst, but McNamara never doubted that it was the right move.

McNamara was also aware that we couldn't afford to fall any further behind. The Mets had a great bullpen, and he knew our scoring chances were dwindling. Removing Hurst had been a gutsy call, but I understood his reasoning.

As Schiraldi took the mound, I glanced over at the team owners. Everyone had the same tense, anxious look, a look I knew was on my face also.

Haywood leaned over to me and said, "I thought Hurst might do it again. He had great stuff tonight. But let's hope Schiraldi has it."

I nodded as confidently as I could. If Schiraldi couldn't keep us in the game right now, we were finished.

The first batter that Schiraldi faced was first baseman Ray Knight. It was like Game 6 had come back to haunt us. These two had faced off in the 10th inning Saturday, and despite Schiraldi jumping ahead of Knight in the count, no balls and two strikes—one pitch away from ending the Mets inning—Schiraldi had given up a single into center field. He had been pulled after that, and the rest was history.

Things were not to turn out any better this time around. Knight was ahead in the count from the start. Then, in the blink of an eye, he lined a fastball over Shea's left-field fence. The Mets had taken the lead.

Schiraldi was unnerved; that was clear. The Mets sent up Lenny Dykstra to pinch-hit for Kevin Mitchell. Dykstra promptly singled to right field, past a diving Marty Barrett. Then Schiraldi uncorked a wild pitch, sending Dykstra to second.

I whispered to myself, "Mac, get Bill Fischer out there now and settle down Schiraldi. We can't let this game get out of hand."

The next batter singled past Buckner at first, just barely out of his reach, and Dykstra raced home to score the Mets' fifth run. The fans were dancing in the aisles, and the cheers were becoming torturously loud.

Finally, McNamara came out to get the struggling Schiraldi. He had retired only one batter on a sacrifice bunt, giving up three hits and two runs and leaving a runner in scoring position. It was lefty Joe Sambito's turn. Schiraldi's performance had been disastrous, and we were now once again in a deep hole.

Sambito intentionally walked Mookie Wilson but then gave up another walk and a sacrifice fly. When the inning was finally over, the Mets were three runs ahead. Stanley was brought in to finish out the inning, but the damage had been done.

We were on the brink of total collapse. Haywood looked so frustrated. "Our bullpen has really been awful," he sighed.

I knew he was right. As I looked over his shoulder at Mrs. Yawkey, I could see the anguished look on her face deepening. I didn't want to even imagine what she must have been thinking. All I could do, though, was pray for divine intervention.

Dykstra stayed in for the Mets and took over center field as the game headed into the eighth. Wilson was moved to left. It was a good managerial move, one that gave the Mets great speed and exceptional coverage in the outfield.

Buckner led off for us and sent a looping fly into center field for a hit. Jim Rice followed with a line drive single over to center, advancing Buckner to second. It was painfully clear Buckner was still suffering with his injured ankle, and he was barely able to run at all. It greatly hampered his speed around the bases. Evans then lined a rope to right-center field for a double. Buckner and Rice both scored, and hope sprung eternal once again. The score was 6-5. We were back within a run. Hopefully this rally would rejuvenate the dugout. We still had a shot to win this ball game, and that moment of truth was now.

But then the Mets went back to their deep bullpen and brought in Jessie Orosco. As he stood on the rubber taking his warmup pitches, I recalled his early days in the major leagues when we had brought him up from Triple-A Tidewater to join the major league ball club. George Bamberger was the manager. In his early appearance in relief he would struggle badly, and Bamberger was about to re-assign him back to Tidewater. When Bamberger, Cashen, and I discussed Orosco, Bamberger indicated that Orosco had no confidence in himself. I suggested to Bamberger that he bring Orosco into game situations when the game was not on the line. It allowed Orosco to have some success and build up his confidence and his belief in himself. After Orosco continued to get hitters out more and more often, Bamberger eased him into more critical game situations and Orosco began to respond with great success. An outstanding career was born as Orosco went on to become a top-flight relief pitcher in a career that would span more than 20 years.

Over the course of the season, Orosco had won eight ball games and saved 21. Only Roger McDowell had saved more for the Mets, with 22. Orosco had only worked one inning on Saturday, so I knew he probably was rested enough to stay out there a while and go long if he had to. There were no tomorrows. Spring training was five months away.

The first batter he faced was Gedman. He hit a ball hard, but unfortunately right to second baseman Wally Backman. A foot to either side, and Gedman would have been on base. Henderson was up next. He had run out of miracles, though, and struck out. McNamara knew that all it would take was one great swing of the bat, and we were back in it. So he sent up Don Baylor to pinch-hit for Spike Owen. But Baylor grounded out. We were still hanging in there precariously, but time was running out.

In the bottom of the eighth, Eddie Romero took over for Owen at shortstop, and Al Nipper was sent out for Stanley. Stanley had faced only one batter but had done his job by ending the inning. The first batter who Nipper faced was Strawberry. I felt uneasy about his confrontation. Nipper had won 10 games during the regular season. I knew he was a hard worker and a tough competitor, but his stuff wasn't overpowering. Strawberry was the kind of batter who wouldn't allow you to make a mistake. Especially with a fastball. In his last start, Game 4, Nipper had allowed seven hits and three earned runs and struck out only two. He took the loss in that game.

Nevertheless, Nipper quickly got ahead in the count. I tried to read his mind, to know what he planned to throw next. Before I could read him, though, he released his next pitch, Strawberry swung, and the ball was long gone. Over the right-center-field fence. The Mets fans were delirious, screaming, "Straw, Straw, Straw." Nipper looked furious, both at himself and at Strawberry who was reveling in his home run trot. Nipper never forgave Strawberry for that, and later bitterly recalled it as "hot dogging." The Mets were up 7-5.

I was dumfounded. I've never been able to understand why a pitcher would throw a pitch in the strike zone when he's in control of the count. Nipper had delivered the pitch with two strikes and no balls—why would he then throw something in the strike zone the batter could handle? Nipper should have pitched to the black of the strike zone, tempting Strawberry to swing at something that could have ended up as a harmless ground ball or pop fly. I would see this happen time and time again in my career in baseball—a pitcher in a controlling position, only to lose command of the game with a poor pitch when he could have made the hitter chase a pitch or two. It never made any sense to me, and it was infuriating to lose a ball game on a dumb pitch when the pitcher had the count in his favor and the hitter in a hole.

And I also knew that most left-handed batters, such as Strawberry, are generally low-ball hitters. Nipper could have gone up and in on Strawberry. It seemed so easy from where I was sitting, but then again, I wasn't the guy out there on the mound. Besides, all my theories didn't matter because the ball was now in the stands and we were down two runs.

Knight was up next. Again Nipper went up in the count, no balls and two strikes. But again, he gave up a hit on his next pitch—a single up the middle.

Fortunately, Dykstra grounded out, but Knight was able to move to second. Hoping to set up a double play, McNamara decided to intentionally walk Rafael Santana. Orosco then came to bat. The conventional thinking would have had him try for a sacrifice bunt, but he was a poor bunter. Instead he swung away and launched a bouncing ball over the mound and into center field for a hit. Knight scored.

McNamara had to reach into his bullpen again—he went to Steve Crawford, a righty. Crawford hit Wilson with a pitch, loading the bases. Backman then hit a bouncer to Boggs at third, who was able to cut down Santana at home. Crawford got Hernandez to ground out and finish the disastrous inning. With only three outs to go, the dire straits we were in reminded me of an old Navy saying: We were "in-extremis," indicating that two ships were about to collide. It defined our grim situation at the moment.

Orosco took the mound for the Mets in the top of the ninth. Romero led off the inning and fouled a high fly ball just to the left of first base where Hernandez hauled it in. One out.

Boggs came up next. He hit a grounder to Backman at second, who handled the ball with ease and cut down Boggs at first. Two outs.

The fans were reaching a fevered crescendo. You could tell that Orosco was feeling it. The Mets were about to pull off another dramatic comeback win. Another amazing victory—one that would make them world champions. Fifty-five thousand voices were chanting as one, "Jessie, Jessie. Jessie." The very stadium was rocking and shaking.

Orosco backed off the rubber and tugged at the visor of his cap. Nervously he bent down and fidgeted with the rosin bag. The roar was now incredible as he got back into position and eyed the batter, Marty Barrett. Orosco squinted for the sign, while Barrett—our last hope—stepped out of the batter's box, obviously feeling the enormous pressure of the moment and nearly deafened beyond concentration by the shouts of the fans.

It only took four more pitches. Barrett went down on strikes. The quickness and the finality of it were numbing. All it took were four final swings to signal the end, to finally and irreversibly kill the dreams of thousands.

This game can torture you in so many ways. It could have been us; it should have been us. We came so close to being the ones savoring this remarkable exaltation and joy. Instead, we had let our chances of everlasting fame slip from our grasp.

I looked into our dugout—already mostly empty as our players quickly tried to turn their backs on the celebration going on just a few feet from where they had just lost it all. I was sharing their frustration. Boggs was one of the few left, just sitting there with his head in his hands in a position of absolute anguish. Clemens was there, too. But he was staring out at the scene before him. He stayed an interminable minute or two before he quickly turned and headed into the clubhouse. He hadn't even gotten his chance to come in to finish the game.

Haywood took me out of my trance.

"Mrs. Yawkey wants to leave. Why don't we get going?" he said.

I was afraid to even look at her, knowing the pain she must have been feeling.

What was so ironic about this Series was that Rice, who had driven in 100 runs during the regular season, didn't bring in one. Clemens, who had a brilliant season and who would go on to win the Cy Young and AL Most Valuable Player awards, didn't win a single game. Hurst won two and had a 1.96 ERA for the Series but was undone by that one bad pitch to Hernandez. And Buckner, who'd been a great contributor all season long as well, bringing in 102 RBIs, hit only .198 and will be forever and unfairly remembered for his infamous misplay. Forgotten in all of the hand wringing over the Series' outcome was Barrett, who tied a major league Series record with 13 hits and had a .433 average, and Evans, who hit .308 and drove in nine runs.

The Mets had put together two dramatic victories. There was no one thing or one play that had inspired their victory. No witchcraft or curse. We had been given the opportunity—many opportunities—for victory, and we just hadn't gotten it done. It was that simple. We had lost the Series between the white lines. It was partly the vicissitudes of luck, but primarily our failure to grasp victory, a victory we once held in the palm of our hands. There were moments to question and decisions to ponder over in the months and years ahead.

I knew that some of McNamara's decisions would be dissected, analyzed, and questioned by the media and fans all winter long. Regretfully, it's forgotten that it was McNamara who took this team farther than anyone dreamed possible at the beginning of the season. We came to the brink of a world championship, so much farther than anyone ever gave him credit for or that anyone ever dreamed was possible.

Our trek to the waiting buses was made in silence. The procession reminded me of mourners slowly departing a funeral. Sox ownership had graciously brought all the team's fulltime employees and their spouses down to New York for the final games. It was a large group who made this sad walk to the parking lot behind the right-field fence. Everyone was lost in thought, reliving the depressing memories of the past two games. It took a while for the players to shower and dress, and while we waited for them, the silence of our group was nearly as deafening as the jubilant Mets crowds, who were still lingering in the stadium and the parking lots.

Eventually, out the window, I saw the players begin to trickle into their waiting bus. I suddenly recalled the mayor of Boston's request for our participation in a parade in downtown Boston the next day at noon. Nothing could seem more incongruous. As I watched the players filing by, I couldn't conceive of how I could ever ask them to return to Fenway tomorrow morning to participate in a parade. It almost seemed like an insult for me to ask them.

I thought about discussing it with Haywood and Mrs. Yawkey, but one glance across the aisle at their downcast faces let me know that this was no time to even mention the word *celebration*. Instead, I whispered to my wife that I needed to go make some inquiries. I knew I had to talk to someone about this, so I sought out our public relations director Dick Bresciani. Though I'd only been with the team a couple of years, Bresciani had been with the Red Sox for a number of years. He was a hard working and extremely capable and talented baseball executive. His reputation throughout all of baseball was outstanding and well deserved. I wanted his counsel.

When I got over to his seat, he was just the sympathetic ear I was looking for. He, too, recognized that convincing anyone to celebrate the events of the past few days was all but impossible. He suggested I call Mayor Flynn's aide, even though it was after midnight by then, and see if we could convince them to excuse the team from this obligation. He agreed that the whole idea of suggesting a parade to our team seemed like a disaster waiting to happen.

As I headed to the pay phone, I passed by the last of our players on the way to the bus. I knew they would be followed, as always, by traveling secretary Jack Rogers. Suddenly I heard a loud cry of anguish. Players started yelling for trainer Charlie Moss. I ran over to where the commotion was. I could see someone lying on the ground. Before I got there, I saw some of our players come running off the bus, heading back into the stadium.

The man on the ground was Rogers. At first, I thought he'd had a heart attack, but then I saw the blood on his forehead and scalp. Moss was already there attempting to minister to him. Rogers was unconscious, and it looked like he had a pretty serious head injury. Moss was hollering out for someone to get team doctor Arthur Pappas.

It seemed that one or two young Mets fans had been throwing bottles at our team as they left the stadium and evidently, one of those bottles had hit Rogers. I scanned the stands, trying to spot the culprits, but the only people in sight were the stadium clean-up crew. Then I remembered the players who had run back inside. I knew they were in there looking for revenge, and that serious trouble could be brewing. Because I couldn't do anything to help Rogers, I had to get a handle on that situation before anyone else got hurt. I started looking around for McNamara. We had to get our players back on the bus. He immediately summoned his coaches to assist in retrieving the players and getting them on the bus.

A small crowd had arrived on the scene. Haywood and John were there, as were a couple of Mets officials, who offered their assistance. Rogers was conscious by now, but Dr. Pappas wanted him to be taken to the hospital immediately to be examined for a possible concussion. Someone went to get Rogers's wife, Ellie, off our bus so she could be with him for the trip to the hospital.

The whole ugly incident just seemed to top off the misery and agony we had just been through for the past few days. It made the whole idea of a parade in Boston even more pointless.

And I still had to make that phone call. I hurried into the stadium and got though to the mayor's aide. But I got nowhere. He quite simply stated that the parade was set, and it would be extremely embarrassing for the Red Sox to back out at this 11th hour. Convincing him to the contrary, I now knew, was hopeless.

There was nothing left for me to do but hurry back to the bus so we could get out of there. As I ran back, a Yogi Berra quote kept echoing in my head. "If you can't catch the ball, you catch the bus. If you can't catch the ball, you catch the bus… "

I couldn't remember where I heard it, and I don't know why it popped into my head at that moment. It just seemed apropos. We'd dropped the ball on this World Series, and all I really wanted to do now was get on the bus and put Shea Stadium far, far behind us.

The parade continued to weigh heavily on my mind. When I finally got up the nerve to mention it to John Harrington as the busses made their way to the airport, he wasn't very encouraging.

"It doesn't make make sense to me, and I can't imagine the players going for it," he said. "Handle it the best way you can."

We finally climbed aboard our charter flight home, I started doing the math. We weren't going to arrive back at Fenway until after 4 a.m. The players would be tired and frustrated, thinking about nothing but packing up and going home for the winter. The thought of standing in the middle of the clubhouse and trying to convince them to return at 11 a.m. was going to be an unpleasant end to an already horrible evening. I had little choice in the matter, but I knew I wasn't going to be popular. I spent the entire plane ride dreading this speech, while simultaneously trying to come up with the right words to convince the team to participate.

When the plane touched down at Logan, it was an emotionally and physically exhausted ball club that made its way to the busses to take us back to Fenway. There wasn't much conversation, and I was completely lost in thought. My wife leaned over toward me.

"I know how disappointed you are," she whispered. "But I'm still proud of what you accomplished. The Mets were very lucky."

I loved her deeply for all the support she had given me through the years. Her words helped give me some encouragement for the task at hand.

A few minutes later, we made the final turn of our journey, onto Yawkey Way. And I couldn't believe what I saw. A huge crowd, 3,000 or 4,000 fans, were waiting at the entrance of the ballpark. Thousands of people were clapping and cheering as we pulled in a couple of hours before dawn. The fans cheered each and every player as they headed into the clubhouse. The sight of all those magnificent people was an extremely emotional moment for all of us. The crowd started chanting in unison, "Go Red Sox, go Red Sox." People were shouting out, "We're proud of you." It was one of the most touching displays I've seen in all my years in baseball. It made me more

determined than ever to convince the team that we had to show our gratitude by doing this parade. We owed it to these incredible fans.

When I got to the clubhouse, the players were packing up. I hustled into
McNamara's office.

"Mac, the parade is still on," I blurted out.

He dropped the gear he was packing up and looked at me in sheer disbelief.

"You're not serious, Lou," he said.

I assured him that I was and told him about my conversation with
mayor's aide.

"John, I did everything I could to stop this," I told him, "but I need you
to go out there and tell the players not to leave till I talk to them."

It was pretty obvious that McNamara was stunned and growing angry
with me.

"Damn it," he said. "These guys don't want to be in a parade. We didn't
win. They want to go home."

I knew he was right, but I also knew I had absolutely no choice.

McNamara finally agreed to let me have a chance with them but said he
had to talk to the team first.

"I can't blame them if they don't go along with you," he told me. "Good
luck."

I knew I was going to need it and started preparing for one of the toughest selling jobs of my life. There would be some resistance, maybe a lot of
it. The best I could hope for, I figured, was something less than total rejection.

McNamara and I walked into the clubhouse, and he called for attention.
The players, most of them half asleep already, struggled to focus on
McNamara.

"I want to thank every single person in this clubhouse for the great effort
you've given me all season. I know it was painful not to win the big one, but
you guys had an outstanding run. I'm proud to be associated with each of
you. Have a great winter. And let's report to spring training next year determined to win it all.

"Now, Lou Gorman has some comments to make."

I moved to the center of the room and cleared my throat.

"Gentleman, I want to echo Mac's comments. All of New England is
proud of the great season you gave us all. It is a season that will be remembered through the ages.

"Now I have a very special request to make of you all, from the ownership of the Red Sox, the mayor of Boston, and the great fans who have supported us so faithfully. Despite the fact that we didn't win it all, those fans want to honor you and thank you for the excitement you brought them this season. They want to hold a parade and celebration later this morning… "

There was a chorus of groans, moans, and unrepeatable epithets. I had to stem this tide of dissent immediately, or the cause was lost.

"Gentlemen, gentlemen," I shouted over the din. "Listen, guys. I understand your opposition to this, and I did everything I could to cancel. But the mayor insisted that the fans needed this opportunity to thank you. It'll only last an hour or two, and you'll be creating some memories for these people that will last a lifetime. The parade's on whether or not any of you show up. I'm just here to ask you, on behalf of the entire organization and your thousands of fans, that you be there. To ask you not to let them down."

I looked around, really looked into at all of those exhausted, dispirited faces, and I had no idea whether I'd gotten through to a single one of them. There was nothing left for me to do, so I left the clubhouse. I couldn't tell whether the mumbling and groans that I heard on the way out was a good sign or just a final rejection.

The crowd was still outside as my wife and I drove away from the park. My mind was churning, thinking about how embarrassing it would be if no one showed up for the parade, how badly these great fans would be disappointed. I truly had no idea what would happen. But it was out of my hands, and I was slowly slipping into exhaustion. Now I just had to focus on trying to get a few hours of precious sleep after one of the longest, most trying and challenging nights of my life.

When I arrived back at Fenway around 10:45 a.m., there were already three or four flatbed trucks waiting, as well as a dozen or so Boston motorcycle cops waiting to escort them along the parade route. My stomach was churning as I thought about what would happen if there was no one to stand on those trucks, no one to escort.

As soon as I stepped into the clubhouse, I was a little encouraged, though. Three or four players had already shown up. I walked into McNamara's office.

"Looks like a great day for a parade, Mac," I greeted him, hoping to sound upbeat, trying to convince myself of my own optimism.

"Yeah, let's hope there are some players around to be in it," he said without looking up from his desk.

Knowing I wasn't going to get anywhere with him, I went back out to the clubhouse to get myself a cup of coffee. Already, some more players had arrived. Mike Greenwell was there and I gave him the same greeting.

"Looks like a great day, Gator."

"If some fans show up," he replied, doubt in his usually cheerful voice, "then maybe it'll be worth the trip."

"Mike," I told him. "These are the greatest fans in the world. They've been with us all season long. I think we'll be surprised."

Jim Rice had just walked in and heard our conversation.

"Hope you're right, Lou," he chimed in.

And the players just kept coming. I could hear their wives and kids in the family lounge next door. My spirits were lifting by the minute. I just couldn't get over the character and class of this bunch of ballplayers. I was overwhelmed with pride.

I went back to McNamara's office until Joe McDermott and his assistant Steve Corcoran came in to tell us that we should be leaving shortly. McDermott was a longtime Red Sox employee and did an excellent job as the director of stadium operations. He and Corcoran handled game-day security and operations superbly, and McDermott would always insist he hadn't missed a Red Sox home game at Fenway in more than 20 seasons. As we were conversing, in came Captain Charles Celucci, of Boston's Finest, to inform us the police escort was ready to roll and the players and their families should begin to climb aboard the trucks to start the parade.

As the players and their families began to leave the clubhouse, I couldn't believe my eyes. Nearly every player was there. Their families were milling around, and the clubhouse was a beehive of activity. It was an unbelievable and heartwarming sight. I looked over at McNamara, and I could tell he was just as surprised as I was. Already, it was a remarkable morning.

Before we left, McNamara addressed the players.

"I want to thank you all for showing up. I know it was a helluva request to have you guys come down here this morning. Thanks."

Then I stepped forward.

"Every single member of this organization also thanks you. I know there's a huge crowd out there waiting to say thank you. Let's go enjoy the moment."

The players hadn't let me down—now came the moment of truth. Would the fans be there to greet them? I had little doubt, but for a team that had experienced such heartbreak, I didn't want this to be another one.

It was a picture-perfect fall day as we started rolling down Boylston Street, where the crowds were waiting, four and five deep. They were cheering wildly, calling out the players' names. Hundreds more well-wishers were hanging out of windows as we passed. Confetti was raining down all around. It was a spectacular sight, a monumental outpouring of sentiment. Banners and signs lined the parade route. "Hey Red Sox, thanks for a great season," read one. Another said, "The Mets may have won, but the Red Sox are #1!"

I thought back to 1966, when I was with the Orioles and that team had won the World Series, the first in the organization's history. That celebration paled in comparison to this expression by the Boston fans. The players were clearly overwhelmed. It was impossible not to be.

The outpouring of love and affection for the players was extraordinary. There had to be close to a million fans paying tribute to the ball club and their families. I could feel the goose bumps.

The closer we got to City Hall, the louder the cheers became, as the throngs grew thicker. I was astounded—I couldn't have ever imagined anything this touching, any gesture this remarkable. I was grateful in so many ways—mostly that we hadn't called this off and that so many players had gotten past their own personal pain to be able to enjoy this moment.

When we got to City Hall, the plaza was jammed with thousands. There were bands playing. The players climbed off the trucks and walked up the steps of the building where they could overlook the jammed plaza. One of the bands struck up "Take Me Out to the Ball Game," and the whole place began singing along.

Mayor Flynn and Governor Dukakis were waiting there for the players, and when they had all taken their places, the mayor silenced the bands. It took him a little while to quiet down the crowd before he could begin thanking the Red Sox for their courageous effort all season long, including the World Series. A thunderous ovation followed. He began to offer his congratulations when the crowd exploded again in a chant of "Red Sox, Red Sox, Red Sox."

Then it was my turn to speak. The ovation that greeted me is something I'll never forget. Once the crowd quieted, I started in.

"I regret that we didn't bring home a world championship trophy to share with you today. All of us in the Red Sox organization are forever grateful for your support and devotion. You are the greatest baseball fans in America. We have been overcome with your tremendous support and your affection. I promise you we will not rest until we finally win a world championship for you. Today, you have given us a day we will long remember. We love you. We thank you."

The mayor then asked Red Sox radio broadcaster Joe Castiglione to introduce the team. Castiglione made some great comments about the season and the excitement of the World Series as well as his pride in being part of it. As he introduced each of the players to deafening applause, I couldn't help but notice that several of them looked misty eyed. It was all but impossible not to be swept up in the emotion of the day.

Once again the crowd went wild and started chanting the players' names. As I returned to my seat, Castiglione asked me if there was a chance of getting a few of the guys to speak. Before we had left Fenway, I had asked Clemens, Buckner, and Rice if they would say a few words at the rally. At that point, the response had been unanimously unenthusiastic. But now, I thought they might be willing to address this amazing crowd.

Castiglione called up Clemens first. The thunderous ovation after his introduction must have lasted four or five minutes. Clemens stepped forward with his family and raised his arms to quiet the crowd. After he thanked them all for their incredible support, he finished with the sentiment we all so keenly felt, "You're the greatest fans in the world."

Rice followed. The response the crowd gave him seemed to reflect their gratitude not only for his performance that season, but for the many great years he had given them. I could tell that Rice was overwhelmingly touched. Like Clemens, he didn't say much, but it came from the heart.

Castiglione then called up Buckner. As Buckner hobbled up to the front to speak, the crowd went wild. It was almost impossible to quiet them. I could tell that this response had moved him, a man of few words under the best of circumstances, almost beyond the ability to speak. Buckner's way of expressing himself had always been to put on his uniform and do his job on the field. Nevertheless, Buckner probably summed it up best when he concluded his brief remarks with, "Thanks. We needed this."

Finally Castiglione called upon Hurst to speak and the huge throng of fans gave him a huge ovation, one that seemed to last three or four minutes. Hurst tried to quiet the crowd and then began to speak.

"We thank you for this day and this tribute. You're the best fans in the world. We'll never forget this day. Thanks."

After some words from McNamara, the bands struck up again and the celebration was over. We got back on the trucks for the ride back to Fenway.

Before we left, though, I made sure to find Mayor Flynn. I had to let him know how glad I was that he hadn't let us back out and miss this incredible, incredible day.

As we were riding back to Fenway Park with a police escort from what had been an astounding celebration and as I looked at the faces of some of our players within my view, it was clearly obvious that almost every man had been very emotionally touched by the outpouring of love from the fans. It had been an overwhelming experience for them, something that they had never anticipated after having lost the World Series. I now felt thankful that the mayor and his staff had held firm to their desire to hold the parade and that I had convinced the players and their families to participate—even under duress. I had done so with great reservations and trepidation, concerned that the whole idea might have been a disaster.

Today was a glorious moment, one that our players and all of us would remember forever. I went into the clubhouse to talk to some of the players and wish them well over the winter months. I then thanked all of the coaches for a great effort and proceeded into the manager's office to wish McNamara well and thank him for a great season also. We shook hands, and I told him I'd be in touch in a week and we'd begin to talk about next season.

I left the clubhouse and went into the empty ballpark. As I stood gazing at the Green Monster, I began to think about what we'd have to do to get back to the World Series again next year. One thing for certain, no matter what happened, the dream to win it all would never end.

I went to find my wife and head for home. Tomorrow would be the beginning of the next season, because the end of one season is in reality only the beginning of the next.

CHAPTER 2

1987

A Season of Disappointment

When the major awards were announced at the conclusion of the 1986 season, Roger Clemens was named the Cy Young award winner following his 24-4 won-lost record, his league-leading 2.48 ERA, and 238 strikeouts in 254 innings pitched, and he was also selected as the Most Valuable Player in the American League; legendary Hall of Fame pitcher Sandy Koufax and the Tigers' Denny McLain were the only starting pitchers in baseball history to win both awards in the same season. Added to his brilliant season he had been selected as the MVP in the major league All-Star Game. The *Sporting News* selected him as the major league Player of the Year. Clemens had been spectacular.

In addition to Clemens winning the two major awards in the American League, John McNamara was selected as the major league Manager of the Year. McNamara was also selected by the *Sporting News* as Co-Manager of the Year for Major League Baseball with Hal Lanier, the Houston Astros' manager. I had extended McNamara's contract in 1986 during our pennant-winning season based on the job he had done in turning the ball club around from the past season when the Red Sox finished 18½ games out of first place.

Over the winter months I worked hard to attempt to put together some sort of trade to improve our ball club for the 1987 season. Each day of the winter meetings I met with our staff of scouts, and McNamara, Eddie Kasko, Eddie Kenney, and Haywood Sullivan. We brainstormed for an hour or more to find some basis for a trade that would enhance our ball club; but despite all of our efforts, we left the winter meetings unfulfilled. That winter I was chastised to a greater or lesser degree by the local media, in particular the daily talk shows, for failing to "pull the trigger."

Not only was I not able to make a beneficial trade, I faced a number of tough contract negotiations over the course of the winter, and by the end of the offseason, they were beginning to wear on me more than any other season in my baseball career. In the early years of the game and prior to the creation of the basic agreement and the advent of agents dominating the marketplace, contract negotiations were much more amicable and much less controversial for me. I met with each player man to man and attempted to arrive at a mutually agreeable settlement that was fair and equitable in both the player's mind and in management's mind. Certainly there would be differences of what was fair and equitable based on the marketplace and the player's personal opinions of his worth and contribution to the ball club's success; however, in just about every case I was able to arrive at a settlement that was acceptable to the player, and we would part with a sense of fairness, trust, and friendship. I never tried to deal with a player by holding the upper hand with power and control in light of the reserve clause but always with a sincere attempt to find a middle ground that was fair for both parties. It is one thing to win a particular battle but in the end lose the war, because when the player leaves your office, he still wears your team's uniform, and the attitude he takes with him will carry into the clubhouse and onto the playing field. I always felt that the players' trust of management was vital to building a relationship that was absolutely essential to creating the kind of morale that developed a winning attitude.

In the earlier years of professional baseball, long before my time, I am certain that some organizations or management and/or ownership officials were not reasonable or fair in dealing with some players and that there was an abuse of power and control, but the creation of the players association (a.k.a. union), the legacy of Marvin Miller, and the enormous infusion of agents onto the scene have changed dramatically the ownerships' and the players' positions of strength in this game forever. The players association has become an enormous administrative and economic force in the game that allows them to influence or control a major part of the future direction of Major League Baseball. Marvin Miller changed the economics of baseball forever.

Oftentimes, in fact more often than not, in today's game contract nego-tiations for a single player may result in seven, eight, or 10 meetings with an agent to finally reach an agreement. The agents, by the nature of their profession, ingratiate themselves to their clients to gain their confidence and commitment, and because they are generally working for commissions, they pound away to obtain the maximum dollars for their client, and manage-ment represents the enemy indirectly. The bond of friendship and trust between the player and the general manager is oftentimes strained to the breaking point, because many times the negotiating sessions can become frustrating, time consuming, and confrontational.

In addition to the negotiating process, I ran all contract proposals that would be made to our players by John Harrington and Haywood Sullivan, my two bosses.

These two men formed with Jean Yawkey a triumvirate that made all of the executive decisions for the Red Sox organization. Haywood was a long-time career baseball man who had held a position at every level of the major league hierarchy, starting as a backup catcher and eventually becoming a minor league manager, a coach, a major league manager, a scout, a scouting director, a general manager, and finally an owner. Haywood was basically from the old school, and the revolutionary changes in the game did not sit well with him. The prospect of agents, the enormous escalation of player salaries, and the concepts of salary arbitration, free agents, and grievance procedures were repugnant and difficult for him to accept. He was also immune to media criticism and ignored their comments or requests. He had many fine qualities, and if you were a friend, he would stand by you through thick and thin. He had a friendly personality, a great sense of humor, and a great love of the game. I enjoyed working with and for him. However, dealing with him on financial matters—such as contract salaries, budgets, and general financial needs and matters—was a daily challenge. In these matters he was a bit parsimonious to say the least. Yet I admired him a great deal and had a great relationship with him.

John had a solid business background and had served in numerous exec-utive financial positions in both the league office and with the Red Sox. He would eventually become the president of the Yawkey Foundation and a limited partner in the ownership of the Red Sox ball club. John, as the pres-ident of the Yawkey Foundation, became Mrs. Yawkey's alter ego and a de facto acting general partner of the ball club, speaking and acting for her in all club matters. (Upon the death of Mrs. Yawkey in 1992, John, as the foundation's president, assumed the role as the Red Sox's chief executive officer. Eventually in 1994 Haywood decided to accept a sizeable cash buy-out, and John assumed the position as the chief operating officer and chief executive officer of the Red Sox with total control and responsibility for the operating of the entire organization.) John was more receptive to the fiscal resolutions in the game. He had an analytical approach to financial matters and was more open to accepting salary increases, to a point. However, John was much more sensitive to their comments or criticism. At times John would tend to delve too much into minutia, but he was always willing to listen to your position or your proposal. His door was always open to me, and I enjoyed working with and for him. We had both served as naval officers, and we developed a bond of friendship and mutual respect that permeates our working and social relationship to this day.

After having failed to negotiate a successful contract with catcher Rich Gedman, a local nondrafted high school player, and his high-profile agent Bob Wolff in 1985 when Gedman had hit .295 with 18 home runs with 80 RBIs, we had gone into salary arbitration and the Red Sox had won the decision. After losing the decision, Gedman had released Wolff and signed on with Jack Sands, a local Boston agent whom I had negotiated with in the past. In 1986 Gedman was coming off probably his poorest season in the past two and a half seasons, hitting only .258 with 16 home runs and 65 runs driven in. Sands came to the negotiating table asking for a three-year contract worth $3 million plus incentives. They argued that Gedman had been added to the American League All-Star team, and because of that he should be paid $1 million a season on a three-year guaranteed contract. I countered with an offer of $2.6 million, a sizeable increase over his current contract, with incentives that could increase the offer. It was summarily rejected by Sands. We continued to negotiate through the winter months, but we made little or no progress. As the weeks dragged on and Gedman was not signed, I became concerned that if we did not reach an agreement before January 8 under the terms of the basic agreement, we could not re-sign Gedman until May 1 and he would miss all of spring training. I continued to negotiate with Sands, hoping to find a way to reach an agreement that would satisfy both sides.

As spring training approached, Gedman was missing and I had a major hurdle to overcome to get Roger Clemens under contract. I did not want to drag out the negotiations because Clemens was a vital part of our ball club and his presence in our starting rotation was essential for our ball club to have any success whatever. Clemens's contract, however, would have an impact on our entire payroll because one player's salary impacted every other player's salary on your ball club to a greater or lesser degree. Comparative salaries in today's baseball market are benchmarks for agents and for salary arbitration.

His agency was the Hendricks Sports Management group out of Houston, Texas. The president of the group was Randy Hendricks, a graduate of the University of Texas Law School. Randy was very intelligent but a tough negotiator who could, on occasion, be caustic and combative, but he got results for his clients. He could be intransigent, tenacious, and formidable, particularly if he held the leverage in the negotiations. He was, however, always a man of his word and upfront when you dealt with him. There was never any question of his ability as a negotiator. He came in well prepared and well armed and pounded away with his demands relentlessly. When you were negotiating with him, you knew you were in for a battle. He would appear almost to be imperious at times, but all he was concerned with was getting the best results for his clients, and in the final analysis that really is the bottom line. Over a period of years, the HSM had built up a sizeable stable of clients, including some of the more high-profile players in Major League Baseball. Randy also was a force in the players association, and his opinions were sought after and respected in labor negotiations by the union.

His brother, Alan, an officer in the agency, was more outgoing, open, and engaging. He projected a warm friendliness that I found amenable to deal with.

I take nothing away from Alan's intelligence or his ability to negotiate a deal, but the final decision that concluded any negotiation with the HSM had to be made by Randy. There were some general managers in the game who felt this was merely a good guy–bad guy scenario, which was orchestrated intentionally by the Hendricks brothers, but that was an opinion I never shared.

In the end, you would always recognize that Randy and Alan were dealmakers. It would always be a battle, they would push you to the limit, and yet somehow we would always get the differences resolved and the deal done.

Clemens was coming off a spectacular season, and I knew that I would be facing a major battle with Randy and Alan to work out a final contract. Right from our very first meeting with HSM, I came to the conclusion that it would take a two-year contract to get Clemens signed. I let John and Haywood know that and kept the two-year deal in the back of my mind as the negotiations progressed. In his book *Within the Strike Zone*, Randy indicates that it was his idea to go to a two-year contract to reach a settlement, and at a point in the negotiations, when we were at a total stalemate, he did, in fact, propose a two-year contract offer to us.

Clemens had a base salary of $340,000 in 1986, and he also had incentives that would allow him to earn another $115,000. He earned all of his incentives in 1986, and so his gross earnings were $455,000. I talked it over with John, Haywood, and John Donovan, our executive vice president and general counsel, and suggested that I put an offer on the table of $500,000 plus incentives that would allow him to very easily earn an additional $200,000 or $300,000 in incentives, which would enable him to earn $700,000 or $800,000 for the 1987 season. In my mind I was hoping to sign him for something less than $1 million in his base salary but provide some incentives to let him earn $1.1 or $1.2 million if he attained all of the incentives.

The Hendricks brothers suggested that the very first week of spring training we get together to work out a contract settlement for Clemens. They had a number of clients on the Houston Astros ball club, and they would generally rent a condo for two or three weeks in the Kissimmee, Florida, area where the Astros trained. I asked John Donovan to accompany me on the trip to Kissimmee.

Donovan was extremely supportive and someone I could always call on to support me on contract proposals or budgetary needs to ownership. We became fast friends. I was always deeply appreciative of his legal counsel and advice. I missed him a great deal after his untimely death.

Our visit to Kissimmee was delayed for various reasons, but finally on March 5, Donovan and I drove over to meet Randy and Alan. As we drove over, I told Donovan that when I put my initial offer of $500,000 on the table, Randy would hit the ceiling and we might face a tirade that could get unpleasant. I suggested that we stop at Olive Garden to grab a quick bite and some libation to at least have some enjoyment, because the rest of the evening might not be too pleasant.

We arrived at the condo where the Hendricks brothers were staying and after the usual introductory comments and conversation, Randy got straight to the point.

"Well, Lou, what is your contract proposal for Roger?"

"$500,000 plus incentives."

"Come on Gorman, cut out the jokes. What is your real offer?" Randy asked.

I again replied, "$500,000, plus incentives."

"You're serious, aren't you?" Randy retorted as if stunned.

I indicated that I was.

"If you think that Roger will accept that offer," he roared, "you're sadly mistaken. I'll tell you one thing, Gorman, I'll be in your camp tomorrow morning to hold a press conference and expose your ridiculous offer, and Clemens is walking out, period."

At that point, I knew there was no point in continuing the conversation. I never even got to spell out the incentives. After Randy continued his tirade, I suggested to Donovan that we head back to Winter Haven.

As we drove back to camp, I turned to Donovan, who appeared a bit taken aback by the entire proceedings.

"Well, John, what did you think?"

"Do you go through this sort of thing in all of your contract negotiations?" he asked.

"Not every negotiation, but some can be unpleasant. You never do get used to the unpleasantness, the acrimony, or the challenges of striving to work out a contract negotiation."

As we continued our drive back to Winter Haven, I mentioned to him that we could anticipate a media circus the next morning when Randy showed up in our camp to address the media. I told him all hell would break loose, and I would be at the center of the storm.

"Do you think Roger will walk out of camp?" Donovan asked.

"John, if Randy Hendricks tells him to walk out, Roger will, and it'll be Randy's way of putting enormous pressure on us to force a settlement. I regret that it will happen, but I'm afraid it will. I just hope the negotiations don't drag on too long; we need to get Roger signed and ready to open the season. He's a key to our success."

Little did I realize at that time how prolonged the negotiations would become. As it turned out, the absence of Gedman and the specter of Clemens walking out of camp and missing spring training were the harbingers of a season of disappointment to come.

The next morning Randy and Alan held a press conference, jamming a huge entourage of print and electronic media into our pressroom for their announcement. Randy told the press we had insulted Clemens with our offer and that Clemens was walking out of camp that morning to protest the Red Sox contract tender. He said Clemens would not return until a satisfactory agreement could be reached. He detailed our offer, spelled out what Clemens had earned last season, and indicated that for Clemens's brilliant season we were prepared to offer him only a nearly $45,000 raise.

I knew that I would be the next target because I could see the horde of media racing across the ballpark in my direction. It was almost as if they realized their story would become a major story, not only in the New England area, but throughout the entire sports world. For our media it always seemed a negative story would have greater impact. And the more controversial it was, the better.

When they finally came storming into my office, requesting an interview to explain the basis of our proposal, there was a panic in their demeanors and questions. I was well aware that my position was tenuous, and with Clemens now gone from spring training, the media found me fair game. I calmly tried to explain that the overall potential of our contract offer to Clemens included very earnable incentives that would provide him with the opportunity to earn as much as $800,000, but I had not been able to adequately spell out those incentives in my initial meeting with the HSM.

The media began to fire questions one after the other almost in staccato fashion.

"How could you let Roger Clemens walk out of camp?"

"What was I going to do about it?"

"Why did you offer him such a low base salary?"

Their general attitude seemed to be as if all was lost and the franchise was about to collapse. Naturally, I was not elated that our number-one starter was walking out of camp and we might open the season without him, but somehow I was confident we'd get him signed and hopefully soon.

"Gentlemen, I'm certain that the sun will set tonight, and I'm also certain it will rise tomorrow morning and I'll have lunch tomorrow afternoon and we will get Roger Clemens signed," I blurted out in an attempt to break the desperate attitude that pervaded the interview. I wanted to dispel the doomsayers and bring a lighter and more positive spin to the proceedings.

Columnist Dan Shaughnessy of *The Boston Globe* would have a field day with my response, and it would be quoted time and time again. Shaughnessy, who is a talented writer, in time became one of my toughest critics and would oftentimes damn me with faint praise. There were times I felt that his criticism was totally unjustified, but I began to recognize that he tended to be negative by nature. To him the glass was always half empty and never half full.

When the press conference was concluded, I went to meet John, Haywood, and Donovan to decide how we would now address the problem of Clemens walking out of camp and the overall contract offer. I was confident that the rest of our ball club and the media were waiting to see what action, if any, we'd take in dealing with the situation. We decided that we would have to fine Clemens for each day he was not in camp. It was not a desirable situation, but it had to be done. We proceeded to put out a press announcement that Clemens would be fined $1,000 a day for every day he was not in camp. HSM made light of our announcement, but it remained in effect.

There was one humorous incident that occurred during this time that lightened the mood of camp while I was trying to get Clemens, Gedman, and other players signed. One day, Winter Haven's police chief came to see me to tell me that a local county sheriff was going to serve a warrant for one of our players, pitcher Dennis "Oil Can" Boyd, because he had failed to return two or three rented videos a year ago and the proprietor of the video store had filed a complaint indicating that they were stolen. After the chief left, I placed a call to the video store and spoke to the owner. I apologized profusely for Boyd's oversight in not returning the videos, and I told him I would pay what was owed him for the loss of the videos plus interest. After some ardent negotiations, he agreed to a settlement in return for dropping the charges against Boyd. I asked Jack Rogers, our highly respected and very capable traveling secretary, to write out a check for the amount and deliver the check to the owner that morning. When I spoke with the owner, I had no idea what the video titles were. All I wanted was to avoid any inkling of this problem getting into the hands of the media, because we didn't need any more negative press.

After handling the situation, I informed Boyd of the situation and let him know it had been taken care of. He thanked me and I assumed that would be the end of it. The next couple of days would prove me wrong.

Even though the charges were dropped, somehow the original charges and the warrant appeared on a daily police blotter where the court reporter for the local paper noticed the warrant and mentioned it to the local sports reporter, who was covering us in spring training. The word spread quickly throughout the electronic and print media who were covering our camp about the incident. To make matters worse, the media got hold of the names of the videos, all of which proved to be X-rated. The media were poised to have a field day with the story.

When that day's workout was finished, I attempted to get to the clubhouse to forewarn "Oil Can" that the media had found out about the videos, but I was detained by a phone call from another general manager, and the media got to him first. When I got to the clubhouse, he was ranting and raving at them in a highly emotional state. I attempted to intervene and hustle him out of their presence into our trainer's room, but it was no easy task. Finally, I slowly eased him into the trainer's room and calmed him down. I explained to him how the media found out and told him the press would probably make it the butt of their humor but to ignore them and consider the source. I'm not certain it pacified his anger, but at least I had him (or the press) out of harm's way.

Naturally the story ran on the front page, no less, of the local *Winter Haven News Press* the next day, and it became the source of much humor and buffoonery in the media back in New England. It did however, provide a bit of levity but unfortunately at "Oil Can" Boyd's expense.

After Clemens walked out and we announced the fine, we continued to try to get Clemens signed. I made a new offer with the same base salary of $500,000 but with earnable incentives now totaling $450,000, which would give Roger a legitimate opportunity to earn $950,000. My offer was summarily rejected, and Randy countered with an offer of $2.5 million for two years. It was obvious we were now very far apart in getting a settlement. It was March 20, and Clemens had now been out of camp for 14 days; I also had not successfully signed Gedman to a contract, and he was absent from spring training as well.

Five days later, HSM scheduled a press conference to be held in their office in Houston. Clemens addressed the local Houston media and a number of Boston media who had flown in for the press conference. He stated that he was remaining out of camp until an equitable resolution of the contract negotiations had been reached, however long that would take. Randy announced during the press conference that they would entertain a one-year deal of $950,000, the total of our base cash offer plus the total of our incentives, or a two-year offer of $2.4 million. A few days later they reduced their offer to two years for $2 million.

In an unusual turn of events in our negotiations with HSM, the commissioner of baseball, Peter Ueberroth, contacted Haywood and suggested that they both fly to Phoenix to meet with Randy Hendricks to discuss

Clemens's contract. (Randy had suggested to the commissioner not to involve me in this meeting because I always had to go to Haywood or John to get approval for contracts.) Haywood discussed the proposal with John, Donovan, and me because he was concerned that they were bypassing me, and that as ownership, he would be put on the spot to say yes or no to a proposal while he was there without the benefit of discussing the offer with the rest of us. I wasn't concerned in the slightest in not being invited, just as long as we could get Clemens signed to a one- or two-year agreement that kept him within his base salary—under $1 million on the average for two years—as we had previously discussed, and John agreed it was worth a trip to see if we couldn't get this resolved and get Clemens back in camp.

Ueberroth and Haywood left for Phoenix, and we kept any mention of his trip away from the media so that they did not muddy the waters at this critical juncture. Ueberroth got the parties together for a meeting and left Haywood with Randy and Clemens at the Sunburst Hotel in Scottsdale, Arizona, to iron out a tentative agreement with Haywood. They had agreed that Clemens's contract would not exceed $2 million including incentives, and because the basic terms were acceptable to both parties, Clemens should report back to spring training immediately. Haywood and Randy had shaken hands on the agreement. All that was needed now was for Clemens to sign the contract.

When Haywood returned to Winter Haven, he told John, Donovan, and me that Randy would fly in to meet with me, and I would draw up the contract for Clemens to sign. It would be a two-year contract for approximately $1.7 million plus incentives. I should also work up an incentive package and run it by Randy, but the overall package, including incentives, was not to exceed $2 million.

By the time Clemens came back to Winter Haven, spring training was just about over so we had Clemens stay behind to work out with some of our organizational staff and get him to pitch some simulated innings against some live hitters from our minor league system.

At the opening of the season Randy met with me back in Boston, and we finalized the total terms of the contract, but the one fly in the ointment was the daily $1,000 fine we had assessed Clemens for walking out of camp. He had been out of camp for 21 days, totaling $21,000 in penalties. Randy wanted us to forget it completely, but to do so would set a bad precedent. I told Randy the fine had to stand. After a great deal of discussion we agreed to apply the $21,000 fine to Clemens's Rocket Booster Club to purchase

Red Sox tickets for inner-city youngsters. It was a creative approach to resolve the problem.

The final draft of the contract was as follows:

1987—$600,000
1988—$1.2 million

      Incentives*:

Cy Young award	First Place:	$150,000
	Second Place:	$100,000
	Third Place:	$50,000
MVP award	First Place:	$150,000
	Second Place:	$100,000
	Third Place:	$50,000
All-Star team selection:		$50,000

* Any incentive earned in 1987 would automatically be applied to the base of his 1988 contract but could not exceed $200,000.

In my mind, we had actually signed Clemens to a contract that averaged $900,000 per year in the basic contract minus incentives. Everything considered, if Clemens had been paid up to $1 million for 1987 and he had a decent season in 1988, in all probability he could have exceeded $1.5 to $2 million in his 1988 contract. I felt it was a good signing for the Red Sox, and one of Boston's top sports columnists, Will McDonough, wrote a column in which he applauded the Red Sox for it, claiming it was an exceptional contract negotiation by the team.

I was delighted that we had finally settled the Clemens contract dispute and he was back. I had him back working out, but it would be some days, or weeks, before we would have him back in our rotation. I had to hope and pray that this late start would not dramatically impact his performance once we had him back in the rotation.

While I was negotiating with Clemens, I also was trying to retain Tom Seaver, who I had acquired in a trade with the Chicago White Sox for Steven Lyons on June 29, 1986. Seaver would finish 5-7 with a 3.80 ERA and pitch in 104 innings for us. Five of Seaver's losses were by three runs or less, and he had had knee surgery, which had put him on the disabled list during the American League Championship Series and the World Series. But even at age 42, he could still pitch, and I was hopeful that a physically sound Seaver could complement a pitching staff of Roger Clemens, Bruce

Hurst, and Dennis "Oil Can" Boyd for the 1987 season. But Seaver's contract called for a base salary of $950,000 plus $300,000 in incentives. I wanted to offer him a base salary of slightly more than $1 million with realistic incentives that would give him the opportunity to earn $1.4 million total. Our major league team payroll was around $18 or $20 million, and I was attempting to control it at that level if at all possible.

As Seaver, his agent, and I continued to negotiate salary terms for the 1987 season, we could not agree upon an acceptable package. I was surprised when Seaver made the decision to retire and end a great career that would take him straight to Cooperstown and baseball's Hall of Fame.

The loss of Seaver would become even more significant as the events that led up to the opening of the 1987 season unfolded. We would open the season without Clemens ready to pitch and with our starting catcher, Rich Gedman, still not signed.

The entire offseason of 1987 proved more difficult because a league-wide controversy was developing as teams, the players association, and agents were trying to finalize player contracts for the upcoming season. After having difficulty getting free agents signed by ball clubs, Randy Hendricks and a number of other agents were convinced that there was a concerted effort by the major league ball clubs to attempt to control the escalation of players' salaries—a activity called *collusion*—and some began to make public statements that players' contract negotiations were being orchestrated out of the commissioner of baseball's office in New York. Eventually the media began listening to the agents' outcries, and the players association filed a grievance forcing a public investigation into the allegations.

After the offseason, I would be required to testify in the collusion investigation in New York before three or four lawyers, including Gene Orza, the principal attorney for the players association. Orza was a very capable attorney, who could be a tough negotiator on behalf of the association and yet at times was very reasonable and conciliatory. I had always had a cordial relationship with him, but you never had any doubt that he was on the other side of the table.

The attorneys representing the players association would hammer away at me as I testified for nearly three hours, asking why I had not made an offer to sign free agents Jack Morris, a pitcher, and Tim Raines, an outfielder. Their argument would be that Morris and Raines were two players who have helped the Red Sox, and yet we had not made the slightest attempt to sign either one. I would reply that I was attempting to sign Clemens, Hurst, and Gedman, who had all contributed greatly to our American League championship and had helped lead us to the World Series, and to sign both free agents would have dramatically impacted our entire payroll, especially my contract negotiations with those current Red Sox players. I was never certain that they accepted my reasoning.

Another issue that the association's attorneys really continued to hammer away at would be the manner in which we released our offer to Gedman once we had reached a stalemate with Gedman and his agent, Jack Sands. Because Gedman was a local boy and fan favorite, Haywood had recommended that we make the most extensive distribution of the press notice as possible to let the fans and media know that we were making a good faith effort to sign the beloved starting catcher. And so because we knew that once we released the news locally, it would routinely be picked up by the wire services and disseminated nationally, at which point in time every major league club would get the terms of the contract as well, we went ahead and sent it to the other teams at the same time we dispatched it to the local press. I would explain to the attorneys that Gedman's was a special case and that this was not the standard procedure. However, the association's attorneys would zero in on the fact that we had sent this information directly to the other teams in the league and wouldn't buy my argument that the teams would have eventually gotten the information from the wire reports. They also would not accept the overall responses and reasoning of every major league organization questioned in the proceedings.

Baseball would lose the case and would be charged with collusion. It was a huge financial penalty—some $290 million—for the ball clubs to collectively have to pay and an enormous victory for the players association.

With Clemens not ready and Seaver retired, manager John McNamara made the decision that Dennis "Oil Can" Boyd would be his opening-day starter. On March 26, however, just four days prior to breaking camp to open the season, Boyd was pitching his last outing before opening the season against the Dodgers in Vero Beach, when in the sixth inning he experienced some tightness and soreness in his right shoulder and was forced to leave the game.

We flew him back to Boston to be examined by our team physician, Arthur Pappas. The decision was made to place "Oil Can" on the disabled list and put him on a special rehab program in hopes of resolving his shoulder problems in a few weeks and avoiding surgery.

With Boyd out, McNamara made the decision to make Bob Stanley our opening-day starter. Stanley had been used primarily as a reliever, having saved 123 games in his career to date, although on occasion he had been a spot starter and had been a starting pitcher in his early years in our minor league system. By starting Stanley he would keep Hurst in his customary role as the number-two starter on the ball club. McNamara felt that Stanley, as a veteran, could handle the transition until we got Boyd and Clemens back.

Stanley lost the season opener in Milwaukee 5-1, and we proceeded to lose the rest of the series—3-2 and 12-11—and opened at home with an 0-3 record. However, Hurst shut out Toronto 3-0 before another sold-out opening day at Fenway Park, and the best news of all was that we now had Clemens back from Florida and in our rotation. I was concerned that we might have rushed him back too quickly, but he insisted he was ready.

Despite the addition of Clemens, we still continued to struggle. By the end of April we were 9-13, and Clemens didn't win his second game of the season until May 1.

Up until this point in the season, we still had not signed Gedman. Marc Sullivan, the son of owner and managing partner Haywood Sullivan, had been the backup catcher, and so he stepped in to replace Gedman. Sullivan had been the Red Sox's number-one pick in the June 1979 free agent draft. He was an All-American catcher from the University of Florida, and his defensive skills and makeup were excellent. He was a quality young man with a great work ethic, but his offensive talents were very limited. In a brief appearance in the big leagues in 1985 and in 1986, for a total of 70 games, he hit .174 and .193. He just couldn't hit, but he had character and guts. Being the son of an owner and a local high school phenom out of Canton High School, there was enormous pressure on him, night after night. Despite his struggles with the bat and the constant fan and media criticism, which at times were unbearable and unkind, he took it all with dignity and class.

The first week of May, Gedman, Sands, and I were finally able to come to an agreement. When I look back, I regret that I didn't find a way to get him signed because the gap between what he was asking for ($3 million) and what we were willing to give ($2.6 million) was small, but ownership felt that our contract offer was extremely fair and so we held our ground.

Gedman told me that he had been working hard all winter long to stay in shape and implored me to let him re-join the ball club right away arguing, effectively, that he could play and contribute right away. Against my better judgment, I agreed. It was a mistake.

He got off to a very slow start, going one for 31 in his first at-bats. It became immediately apparent that the pitchers were way ahead of him and his lack of a normal spring training was impacting his performance. I began to second-guess myself for letting him talk me into joining the ball club immediately without going to Florida to face some live pitching.

He suffered some minor injuries early in the season, and Sullivan took over for several games until he was benched. We brought in Danny Sheaffer, a 26-year-old catcher who had been in our farm system for six years, hoping that at some point we'd get Gedman physically sound and back behind the plate as our regular catcher. Sheaffer caught in 25 or 30 games and hit only .121. The combined offensive production of the catching staff for the season was a pathetic 29 runs driven in.

On July 30 our hopes of getting Gedman back in the lineup faded forever because he tore the ligaments in his left thumb and his season was over. He would appear in only 52 games, hitting only .205. His career would begin to unwind from that point on even though he should have been a Red Sox starting catcher for a number of seasons. In the next two seasons he would hit .230 in 85 games and .212 in 93 games with four home runs and six RBIs. I can only speculate as to what he might have been, and I will always regret that we did not get him signed and to spring training on time. It well could have changed his career and our season.

Our season continued to go downhill as we became a miserable road team, with a 28-54 away record. I had no idea why we were so bad on the road, and at home we held a decent winning percentage. There is an old baseball adage: Win at home and split on the road, and you'll contend for a title, but we failed miserably in that regard. On numerous occasions I would travel with our ball club, and I would meet with McNamara and our coaching staff and attempt to see if we could find a way to improve on our road record. We never came up with any productive solutions. Hurst was the perfect example of our road dilemma. Hurst was 12-4 in a tough left-hander's ballpark like Fenway Park, and yet on the road he was 3-9. (One of the remarkable accomplishments by a Red Sox left-handed pitcher was the fact that lefty Mel Parnell had 72 wins out of his 123 career wins at home in Fenway. Hurst would end up a close second.)

Clemens also got off to a slow start, and by the time of the All-Star break he had a 4-6 record. A mini-controversy came up involving Clemens and the contract I had negotiated with him months earlier. Unfortunately the local media uncovered the fact that Clemens had the $150,000 incentive in his contract that he received if he was selected to the All-Star team. (There were numerous occasions where I began to wonder whether our local media had been trained by the CIA. At times they would uncover facts or information that were absolutely strictly confidential and known to only a few.) Because we had won the pennant the previous season, McNamara would automatically become the manager of the American League All-Star team, and he was already concerned about not being able to justify Clemens's selection to the All-Star team given the hurler's current record. But when word reached McNamara about the financial clause in Clemens's contract, he was even more concerned that should Clemens not be selected, it would hurt his relationship with the hurler and cause the local media to revisit the incident that had occurred in Game 6 when Clemens left the game with a blister problem. He immediately called me to ask if it was true. I verified the fact but told McNamara that it should have no bearing on his selection. I suggested that he visit with Clemens and discuss the issue with him man to man and let him know that the league president has a primary role in selecting the pitchers for the All-Star Game. I told McNamara that I was convinced Clemens would recognize that his won-lost record made it difficult for him to be selected. I have always felt that Clemens is a consummate professional, despite the media's negative portrayal of him. Clemens understood, and that was the end of the issue, even after he was not selected for the All-Star team.

After the All-Star break the Red Sox continued to struggle. We were above .500 only once during the entire season, and we went 28-54 on the road, which was the second worst road record in the league. Our disappointing season really allowed the media to go on the attack. At one point the pressure and the criticism reached a boiling point. We were in Detroit for a three-game series when Steve Finnerau, a beat writer for *The Boston Globe* had written a story with some scathing comments about one of our pitchers, Al Nipper.

(Finnerau was a very intelligent and talented writer. He was exhaustive and constantly questioning, almost to a fault. He would confront a source and bombard him with question after question, almost like the person was at the Inquisition. It almost seemed that with his persistence he was attempting to permeate the interviewee's very psyche or soul. He was that thorough, detailed, and zealous in pursuit of a story.)

About 10 minutes before game time, I happened to be in the clubhouse. Finnerau was still in the clubhouse, finishing up a lengthy interview he had conducted with one of the players. As the reporter was leaving, he ran directly into Nipper, who had been in the trainer's room getting a rub down on his right shoulder. Nipper was still smarting from Finnerau's story, and he began a loud verbal tirade against the man he felt had attacked him personally in print. His face just inches way from Finnerau.

Suddenly a shoving match ensued that I could tell was about to escalate into a more serious confrontation because Finnerau held his ground. I stepped into the breach, grabbed Nipper, and pulled him back into the trainer's room. Charlie Moss, the trainer, got between Nipper and me and Finnerau and insisted that the reporter leave. As Finnerau left, Nipper continued to shout at him, and I had my hands full restraining him. Finally, I was able to quiet Nipper down, and the incident was over.

The media has always been able to stir up a lot of controversy—especially when a team fails to meet expectations. They will conjure excuses and point fingers at everyone and anything. Whispers of a lot of nonsense, such as that "The Curse of the Bambino" has haunted the Red Sox franchise since Babe Ruth had been traded to the hated Yankees, began to surface as the reason for all of the disappointment. It was wonderful fantasy that made for good copy and fiction, but it was also utter nonsense. Sometimes a baseball will take a funny bounce or you'll get a bad call or a ball lands fair or foul by inches. It is all a part of the game, and no mystical force of power makes it happen. It just does. An event or player transaction, however sensational, that happened some 70 years ago has no impact whatever on the events and performances of today. The present players could care less about the past and care primarily only about the present. A season is a long, long marathon of 162 games. So many factors can impact it, not the least of which is injuries to key players. We would painfully find that out this season.

In 1987 we had as many as nine or 10 players disabled at various times during the season. "Oil Can" Boyd, who had won 15 games in 1985 and 16 games in 1986, would struggle all season long and pitch in only seven games the entire season because of injuries. On July 31 he would undergo a right shoulder surgery and his season was over, leaving a big void in our starting rotation. Gedman, our starting catcher, would be limited to only 52 games. The ineffectiveness of Boyd and Gedman, not to mention the late start of

Clemens, had more to do with our demise than "supernatural memories from the past."

Another injury and the subsequent trade that followed did not help our ball club's performance or standing with the Boston media. When shortstop Glen Hoffman went down, his disabling led to my realization that Hoffman was nearing the end of his playing career so I decided to see if I could make a trade that would keep him in the major leagues for a few more seasons because he had always been a loyal positive contributor to the clubhouse. I made numerous phone calls to just about every other major league general manager of the behalf of Hoffman, but to no avail. I then placed him on waiver. He cleared waivers, and so I out-righted him to our Pawtucket Triple-A club. Before Hoffman went down to Pawtucket to play, I promised him that I would continue to do whatever I could to get him back to the big leagues.

A few days later I was down at Pawtucket to take a look at our young talent when Mike Tamburo, the Pawsox president, told me I had an urgent phone call from Fred Claire, the general manager of the Los Angeles Dodgers. Claire wanted to know whether Hoffman was still available.

"Yes, Fred, in fact I'm watching him play now in our ball game here in Pawtucket," I told him.

"I've had some injuries to my middle infielder and I need a replacement right away," he replied. "What would you want for Hoffman?"

"Fred, in all fairness I was probably going to release him at the end of the season," I confessed. "But he's a great kid, and he can still fill in and do a decent job for a short time." I paused and then said, "If Hoffman does a good job for you for the rest of the season, you'll owe me a prospect out of your farm system. I'll give you three or four names to consider. If you release him at the end of the season, you owe me $10,000."

"We've got a deal," he answered right back. "I'd like you to get him into Philadelphia tomorrow afternoon and report directly to Tommy Lasorda, our manager. He'll play for us tomorrow night."

When I hung up the phone, I went into our dugout, got the attention of our Pawsox manager, Ed Nottle, and told him that Hoffman had been traded to the Dodgers so I needed Nottle to take him out of the ball game and tell the shortstop to shower and come to see me in the executive offices. When Hoffman came to see me, I told him of the trade, and Hoffman was elated. I told him we'd make his flight arrangements tomorrow and he was to report directly to Lasorda because he was scheduled to play tomorrow night against the Phillies. I wished him a great deal of luck.

When the Pawtucket game was over, the local media asked me about the trade and I told them that Hoffman had been traded to the Dodgers for a player to be named later or cash. I also notified the American League of the trade and the details. The story immediately went on the wire services and made all of the Boston morning newspapers and talk shows.

When I awoke the next morning, I suddenly realized I was in deep trouble. It dawned on me that because I had out-righted Hoffman to Pawtucket when he cleared waivers I had to get reverse waivers on him to trade him. I immediately called Claire at home but finally reached him at Dodger Stadium. I told him of my error and told him I'd immediately placed Hoffman on reverse waivers. I was confident that he would clear waivers and be ready to play for them by the end of the week. Claire was understandingly upset at my mistake and told me that Lasorda and his boss Peter O'Malley would be very upset over the delay.

Hoffman was already on his way to Philadelphia so I suggested to Claire that we would pay his salary and expenses until he cleared waivers. Claire was still upset and said he'd have to talk to Lasorda.

"Fred, Hoffman can work out with your second baseman in pregame workouts and get adjusted to working with him," I assured him. "When he clears waivers, he can step right in and take over at shortstop."

There was a long pause on the end of the line and then finally Claire said, "I'll call you back."

Later that day he called back and said the Dodgers would go ahead with the deal. I thanked Claire and told him I'd notify him immediately when Hoffman cleared the reverse waivers.

Within a few days Hoffman cleared waivers and he became the Dodgers' shortstop for the greater part of the remainder of the season.

When the story of my mistake broke, the Boston media besieged me with questions about the transaction and justifiably rebuked me for my oversight. The talk shows had a field day for a few days criticizing my error. One beat writer in particular, Mike Shalin of the *Boston Herald* really took off on me. He would imply that my incompetence in this situation was embarrassing to the organization and that other major league general managers would refuse to ever trade with me again. He wrote a blistering column that really took me to task with no holds barred. In his column criticizing me he quoted the waiver rules, but he quoted them incorrectly.

The pounding the organization and I were taking in the press really got to me, and for once I could not resist the impulse to respond. I wrote a letter to the paper in which I took total responsibility for my error but I indicated it had not caused the demise of the Red Sox franchise. I went on to state that because Shalin himself did not understand the major league waiver rules, I questioned his capability to criticize my error and I put in question his competency and expertise as a sportswriter.

My letter appeared on their sports page a couple of days later. I was certain that Shalin probably would come in for some rebuke from his sports editor and I probably lost whatever little favor I might have had with Shalin from that day on.

In addition to the injuries and the media frenzy the Hoffman situation had created, I was also facing the realization that some of the major offensive producers on our ball club who had contributed enormously to our American League championship the past season fell off dramatically and played a major role in our dismal season.

Jim Rice, who I truly believe should be ensconced in baseball's Hall of Fame fell off dramatically from his .324 batting average with 39 doubles, 20 home runs, and 100 RBIs. In 1987 he would fall to .277, 13 home runs, and only 62 RBIs. His age was now beginning to erode a brilliant career. He would undergo surgery on both knees after the season.

I believe that other than Clemens, Rice was the most misunderstood and unappreciated Red Sox player in the last two decades. Rice was not a "holler guy," someone who had a lot to say, pro and con, to the media after a ball game. That wasn't his temperament or his personality. He just went out and played the game with intensity, 100 percent effort, and great skill. When he had little or nothing to say to the media, he began to get criticized constantly. He felt his performance on the field, which over his career with the Red Sox was brilliant, was his answer to the media and to the fans, but in Boston that wasn't enough. Eventually he withdrew and refused to deal with the local media, and to ignore the media, even though there is often great cause to do so, unfortunately courts disaster.

One of my biggest disappointments out of the bullpen was Wes Gardner. To show how poorly our bullpen performed, Gardner led our pen staff with 10 saves. He also gave up 17 home runs and 98 hits in 90 innings and finished with a 5.42 ERA. It was a basic formula for disaster.

I was with the Mets when we drafted Gardner out of Central Arkansas State. Our reports indicated he had a real live arm with a well above-average fastball. When I first saw him throw in a rookie league game, he faced the first nine batters and struck out seven of them. In his second year in professional baseball pitching for Lynchburg, Virginia, in the Carolina League, he went 6-13 with 15 saves, a 1.87 ERA, and 67 strikeouts in 62 innings. In Triple-A Tidewater he saved 18 ball games out of the pen in one season and 20 another. From every indication he had the potential to become either a front-line starter or an outstanding reliever at the major league level; neither would ever materialize. There were occasional bursts of excellence, but they were too few and far between. In 1986, he suffered torn cartilage in his right shoulder and underwent arthroscopic surgery. There is no question that the shoulder injury he suffered played a major role in his demise and was the reason he never became the pitcher the scouts all felt he had the ability to become.

Another disappointment in pitching was Calvin Schiraldi with his 4.41 ERA despite the fact he struck out 93 batters in 83 innings. The previous season, between our Triple-A club at Pawtucket and his performance on our big league ball club once I recalled him, he had a combined 8-5 won-lost record with 21 saves a 2.14 ERA and 104 strikeouts in 95 innings. For whatever reason, his level of performance would never again consistently approach that quality.

I liked Schiraldi a great deal, and I was one of his biggest boosters. Joe McIlvaine, who was our scouting director with the Mets (and later became the general manager of the Mets and the San Diego Padres) and whose scouting judgment I had enormous respect for, felt that Schiraldi had the ability to become a solid front-line starting pitcher. When I later looked back on Schiraldi's career and attempted to pinpoint his shortcomings, the one factor that kept coming to mind was his lack of intensity. Clemens was a bulldog on the mound. He had one goal once he walked onto the field to compete—to win at whatever the cost. You had the feeling he would knock down his mother if it was necessary to win. Clemens was a warrior. With Schiraldi, I never had that feeling. He never seemed to have that same passion or intensity, which is so often the quality of the great athletes. It constantly separates greatness from mediocrity, because greatness demands passion, intensity, and commitment. And so Clemens will go on, one day, to be enshrined in baseball's Hall of Fame, while Schiraldi, who was a much greater collegiate pitcher, will be at home watching the induction.

Dave Henderson, the hero of the 1986 season, had also been a big disappointment. His star had fallen considerably in the opinion of McNamara and his coaching staff. As I sat with McNamara and his staff on a regular basis week by week and talked to McNamara daily, I could detect their disenchantment with Henderson's performance. As we talked more about Henderson, I kept asking McNamara and Walt Hriniak, our batting coach (and one of the most dedicated and hardest working baseball coaches and instructors I've ever been associated with), whether they felt that Henderson could develop into an above average power hitter. The answer was always no. They also told me that they felt that Henderson was a bit too lackadaisical and didn't seem to feel that he had the intensity on a regular basis to become a productive player despite what he had done the previous season.

Don Baylor, one of my all-time favorites from my days with the Orioles, also struggled offensively, and his production fell off dramatically. In 1986 he had hit 31 home runs and had driven in just shy of 100 RBIs, but in 1987 he hit only .239 with 16 home runs and 57 RBIs.

There was also a decline in Bill Buckner's performance. Buckner had been a major factor in our success the past season with his 18 home runs and his 102 runs driven in. In his 17th season as a major league player, he was a .292 career hitter with 164 home runs and more than 1,000 RBIs, and he had won Gold Gloves for his outstanding defensive play at first base. But in the last few weeks of the 1986 season he had re-injured his right ankle—when he was with the Los Angeles Dodgers he damaged the ankle's bone structure while sliding into a base—and although he continued playing, the injury and his age had begun to take a toll on his career. His range, mobility, and speed, which he had been known for, were greatly limited, and although the long recuperation period of the winter months helped Buckner somewhat in his recovery, he never seemed to fully regain his former mobility and agility. Buckner played in only 75 games, hitting .273 with only two home runs and grounding into 10 double plays, and he had extremely limited mobility at first base.

I was considering releasing Buckner. I held Buckner in such great esteem. His career records speak for themselves. Buckner was an intense competitor and a consummate professional, who led by his performance on the field. He had a great deal of guts and an intense desire to win.

I had made the trade for Buckner when he was playing for the Cubs. Midway through the 1984 season, we had had Mike Easler playing first base because Dave Stapleton had been seriously injured. Easler was an asset in the clubhouse and with a bat in his hands, but with a glove on his hand at first base, he was a liability, so I had to find a way to replace him at that position or we'd set a league record (maybe world record) for infield errors at first base.

I called Dallas Green, the Cubs' general manager, and inquired about Buckner, because our scouting reports indicated that despite his age and the earlier injury he could still play effectively. Green indicated that he would trade Buckner and that he was looking for some pitching. Dennis Eckersley was a starting pitcher in our rotation whose contract would be up the following season and was having basically a mediocre season. I felt we could move him, particularly because we were desperate to resolve our problem at first base. I told Green we were willing to make the trade.

We had, however, some major obstacles to overcome before we could consummate the trade; both Buckner and Eckersley had no-trade clauses in their contracts, Buckner's applied to the Red Sox and Eckersley's to the Cubs. Green and I agreed to notify both leagues that we had agreed in principle to a trade, and the leagues gave us 48 hours to work out our problems and consummate the trade.

Green was able to get Eckersley to agree to the trade by paying him $100,000 in "moving expenses," but my negotiations with Buckner were much more complicated. I called Buckner personally and told him how much we wanted him. Buckner had heard about Eckersley's deal with the "moving expenses"—I assume that Eckersley's agent had informed Buckner's agent about the commitment—and at first would not agree to the trade unless I paid him the same amount. I knew, however, that ownership would never approve a payout and the salary of Buckner's current contract.

I continued to talk to Buckner, but time was running out. I told him that because the Cubs had the young Leon Durham, who they considered their next great power hitter, Buckner's chances of playing were extremely limited; whereas if he came to Boston, he would be our starting first baseman the day he set foot in Fenway Park. Buckner lowered his request to $50,000 to rescind the no-trade clause, but I was still unable to get the approval.

With time running out, Green called me to check on the progress of the trade. I explained the situation and told him that I thought that we might not be able to make the trade. We hung up.

With less than two hours remaining, Green called me back and said, "I'll trade you Buckner and the $50,000 for Eckersley. If that's agreeable, we've got a deal."

"Thanks, we've got a deal," I replied. "I'll notify the American League office immediately. I'll talk to Eckersley and get him on his way to Chicago. Let's hope it helps both our ball clubs."

It was a trade that dramatically impacted the careers of both players. Buckner would go on to help us win an American League championship and finally near the tail end of his career play in a World Series. Eckersley would eventually be traded to the Oakland A's; be converted from a starter to a reliever, thanks to a brilliant decision by either Tony La Russa, the A's manager, or Dave Duncan, their pitching coach; and went on to become one of the most dominant relievers in Major League Baseball.

The deal had worked for us, but now with Buckner struggling and our team buried in the standings, it seemed like the time to act with the team being 14½ games out of first place and with little apparent hope of climbing back into contention. After a lengthy discussion with McNamara and the coaching staff, I made the decision to release him. I knew this would be one of the most difficult and personally distasteful unconditional releases of a player I would ever have to make, and it was, without question, one of the most difficult, if not the most difficult decision, that I ever had to make in my Red Sox career.

For me, releasing a player—any player, rookie or veteran, minor leaguer or big leaguer—has always been a most difficult task to perform either as a general manager or a minor league director. As a youngster I had been signed by the Philadelphia Phillies, and after a few months of playing on their Appleton, Wisconsin, team in the Wisconsin State League I was released and sent home. It was a traumatic and personally devastating experience to suddenly be told that at age 17 your sole ambition in life—to become a big league player—is shattered. You're told you are just not good enough and to go home. It was an experience I would remember for the rest of my life.

Whenever I had to release any player, that memory would come back to mind and I would deeply empathize with the player I was about to release; it made it much more difficult for me. I came to abhor that part of my job. Having to call Buckner into my office and inform him that I was going to place him on waiver for his unconditional release was extremely difficult. I greatly admired him as a player and as a person, and it was almost as much of an emotional moment for me as it was for him. If he were not claimed, it could well be the end of his outstanding baseball career. To leave the game after so many, many excellent seasons and in all probability to be remembered for the game-ending error that highlighted the Mets' dramatic come-back Game 6 win of the 1986 World Series and not for his great career, would be so unfair.

Around the same time as we released Buckner, I finally made the decision to see if I could trade Henderson. That decision caused a great deal of personal regret because I had originally drafted him as a top draft choice out of Fresno State College when I was with the Seattle Mariners. He had been a favorite of mine from the first day I met him. I called Henderson into my office to talk about the situation. He was upset and doubtful about the concerns the coaching staff had in terms of his motivation. He told me he felt he played hard every time he stepped onto the field and that he always gave 100 percent on every play. I told him I believed him completely and I never doubted his intensity, but others did. When Henderson left my office he was upset and dismayed, but he was also now resigned to the fact that his days with the Red Sox were limited.

I was mildly surprised that the interest in Henderson was all but nonexistent when I went from team to team in an attempt to move him. I felt he could still play and contribute to a ball club at the major league level despite the fact that he was struggling at present. I talked at length to Al Rosen, the general manager of the San Francisco Giants. Rosen was a longtime friend, a former major league player, and a highly respected baseball executive, and I kept trying to convince him that Henderson could help him. He told me his interest in Henderson was marginal at best because his scouts had rated him as "questionable." After a number of phone calls I finally convinced Rosen to take a chance on Henderson, but when Rosen offered me so little in return, I was tempted to withdraw my offer and go back to the drawing board and start all over again. But I finally agreed to the trade in light of Henderson's performance. Of the limited pool of fringe-type players who the Giants offered in return, our scouting reports suggested a utility-type player named Randy Kutcher. Kutcher was a journeyman nine-year minor league player, who had a limited number of games at the major league level. He was 27 years old and had hit .355 in Triple-A in some 60 games before being called up to the Giants where, in a limited role, had hit .237 in 1986 and .255 in 92 games in Triple-A. But his appeal was his versatility. He had played all three outfield positions, second and third bases in the infield, and behind the plate in an emergency. I felt at worst he would give us a 25th player to hopefully fill a role on our ball club; whereas if I released

Henderson, we got nothing in return. It was the principal of diminishing return at work.

Henderson would go to the Giants and struggle, and by the end of the season the Giants would release him unconditionally. Rosen would call me when Henderson was released and told me that he felt Henderson's career was about over. He also would voice the same consensus judgment of our staff that "he didn't display much intensity on the field."

The Oakland A's would sign Henderson as a free agent and he would go on to play for seven more seasons. In his first season with Oakland he hit .304 with 38 doubles, 24 home runs, 94 RBIs and win the award as the American League Comeback Player of the Year. He would play in three World Series and three league championship series for Oakland, and despite some injuries that would make him miss most of the 1992 season, he would end up hitting 105 home runs for Oakland while playing excellent defensive in center field. It was somewhat of a validation for Henderson and in his belief in his own ability. I was quietly delighted with his ability to prove the naysayers wrong.

Releasing Buckner on July 23 and trading Henderson in early August foreshadowed the moves we would make in mid-August when we were 14½ games out of first place. I made the decision to start reaching into our farm system and rebuilding the ball club. Our future now rested with a number of youngsters from within our minor league system. The challenge ahead, however, was the strengthening of our bullpen, adding some depth to our starting rotation, getting Gedman healthy, and adding some power to our lineup. It was a tall order to fill.

I had to find a way to add a third and/or fourth starter behind Clemens and Hurst and strengthen our bullpen, which had been a disaster. The total number of saves, 16, out of the bullpen was dismal. The overall performances of Schiraldi, Gardner, Joe Sambito, and Steve Crawford were a total disappointment, and our team's combined save total and ERA of 4.77 was last in the league.

With that kind of pitching out of the bullpen we were in deep trouble and weren't going to win many ball games in the late innings. The necessity to move Stanley out of the bullpen as our stopper and make him a starter had dramatically impacted the bullpen's performance. Nonetheless, I had a major challenge before me to revamp and strengthen the bullpen if we were to compete once again in the future. No ball club without a strong bullpen can ever be competitive, and the key to a solid pen is strong middle relief and an exceptional stopper. The Yankees, recently and in the past, or the great Oakland A's ball clubs of the past with Dennis Eckersley, have been proof positive of the value of a quality stopper. There have been many theories proposed in the past regarding the methods of creating a bullpen, some dissimilar with conventional thinking, but I have always been a strong believer in the absolute necessity of a veteran stopper to close a ball game. When a ball club gets into the ninth inning with a lead, I want a proven established closer coming out of that bullpen to close out the ball game if I am managing that ball club. If you don't have one, you do whatever it takes to find one—a Lee Smith, a Jeff Reardon, a John Smoltz, a Mariano Rivera, a Jeff Shaw, a Billy Wagner, etc. You obviously need decent setup relievers to get your stopper, but if you don't have a quality stopper, all else is in vain. I have never believed in bullpen by committee. For me it is absolutely essential that the bullpen has to be structured with a stopper.

Late in the season when we were 15½ games out of first place, Baylor came to see me in my office and told me that he was aware we had some young outfield prospects (Ellis Burks, Mike Greenwell, and Brady Anderson) in our farm system who were ready to take over by next season. He asked me if I would trade him to another ball club to keep his career alive in the big leagues. He recognized that we had to start re-tooling our ball club, particularly in light of our current struggles and the age of some of our veteran players like himself. I told him I would make every attempt to work out a trade if at all possible. Baylor was 38 years old with 17 years in the big leagues. I felt that he could still fill a role on a contending ball club, but I was surprised to find that there was not a lot of interest in him by those ball clubs. When the story broke after Baylor told the beat reporters who covered us on a daily basis that he had requested a trade, Dwight Evans, another personal favorite of mine and a staunch Red Sox loyalist, called and asked to talk to me in the clubhouse before pregame workouts.

When I went to the clubhouse to meet with Evans, he asked if we could go into the manager's office, which was empty, so we could speak in private. Evans had a deep love for the Red Sox and was always very sensitive the club's image and its future.

When we went into the office and shut the door, Evans said to me, "Lou, you can't trade Baylor, he's the leader on our ball club and we need him."

"Dwight, Don Baylor has asked me to trade him; it's his request," I paused before I continued. "Dwight, furthermore, Baylor has only been with us for two seasons; you've been here for 16 seasons. Why aren't you the leader on this ball club, not Baylor?"

Dwight was taken back by my response. He stared at me and without saying a word, turned, and walked out of the office and into the clubhouse.

I would eventually trade Baylor to the Minnesota Twins for a young 21-year-old right-handed pitcher named Enrique Rios, a youngster from Venezuela who our scouting reports from winter baseball called a prospect with a live arm. With the Twins Baylor would go on to win a world championship and receive a World Series playoff check. When his playing career was over, Baylor became a manager in the major leagues.

There were some bright spots in the disappointing season. Clemens, after a very slow start, went on a tear and was arguably the best pitcher in the league for the remainder of the season. He was brilliant as he went 16-3 with a 2.60 ERA to finish 20-9 with a final season ERA of 2.97 and 256 strikeouts in 280 innings. He was absolutely awesome down the stretch, at times dominating and overpowering. It was a testimony to his enormously competitive nature and makeup. Rounding out the stronger pitching performances were Hurst, who finished 15-13 with a 3.77 ERA, and Al Nipper, who was 11-12 and a 5.43 ERA.

We also had Evans coming off a career season in which he hit 34 home runs, batted .305, and knocked in 123 RBIs. Second baseman Marty Barrett led the league in fielding percentage, and Wade Boggs at third base hit .363 with an all-time high of 24 home runs and 89 RBIs, but he would undergo surgery to his left knee in early October at the conclusion of the season.

Because of the many trades, releases, and injuries, we were also able to use this miserable season to identify a large section of potential talent from our farm teams. I brought up a young 24-year-old outfielder named Mike Greenwell to open the season in left field. In his first full rookie season he hit .328 with 31 doubles, 19 home runs, and 89 RBIs. He was named to the Topps and *Baseball Digest* All-Rookie team and was selected by *The Boston Globe* as the co-winner of the Red Sox Outstanding Rookie of the Year at their annual awards dinner.

Greenwell shared that Co-Rookie of the Year honor with another outstanding product from our farm system named Ellis Burks. In late April, I brought Burks up from Pawtucket and inserted him into our starting line-up as our regular center fielder. In 133 games he hit .272 with 30 doubles, 20 home runs, 59 RBIs, and 27 stolen bases. He was the first rookie in Red

Sox history to hit 20 home runs and steal more than 20 bases during his first season of major league play and also the first rookie since Fred Lynn (21) and Jim Rice (22) to hit 20 home runs as a Red Sox rookie.

Although I was not certain nor did most of our baseball staff believe that Burks was ready to contribute at the major league level next season, we all felt he was not far away. It was the unanimous opinion of everyone that Burks was maybe just a season away from becoming our regular center fielder. He was an excellent defensive outfielder with an outstanding range, good speed, and a chance to become a good hitter with some power. I had always been impressed with his defensive skills and his speed, and I liked his quiet and yet positive inner determination. He was not a talker, just a doer. In 1986 Burks had played at New Britain, our Double-A club in the Eastern League. He had hit .273 with 14 home runs and played outstanding defensive in center field. The New Britain ballpark was probably the most difficult ballpark to hit a ball out of; it was definitely a pitcher's ballpark with the prevailing wind. (Jeff Bagwell, who went on to become a perennial National League All-Star for Houston, hit only four home runs in 140 games he played for New Britain.) Burks hit 14 home runs there; he had also stolen 31 bases. Scouts from every organization who covered the league talked about Burks and his potential. Although he had been injured the previous season and had undergone offseason shoulder surgery, he had bounced back extremely well, and based on his fine season at New Britain, our hopes were now that he might only be one year away from the major leagues.

Another potential big leaguer was a 24-year-old outfielder–first baseman named Todd Benzinger. He had been a high school sensation in Ohio and had been selected to the High School Coaches Association's All-American team his senior year. After we drafted and signed him, I had an opportunity to see him perform in our instructional league and I had been impressed with his hitting mechanics, level swing, and bat speed. To my disappointment, he went through a couple of tough seasons battling various injuries and seemed to be standing still in terms of progress. I still felt, however, if we could keep him physically sound, he could play a role on our major league ball club in the future as a solid utility player and pinch hitter or possibly, as a regular.

I brought him up to the Red Sox club during the 1987 season after he had hit .323 with 13 home runs and 49 RBIs in just 65 games at Pawtucket.

In the big leagues he had hit .278 with eight home runs and 43 RBIs in 73 games.

Our number-one draft choice in the 1982 draft and the 16th player drafted in the nation was a huge six-foot-five, 240-pound power-hitting first baseman named Sam Horn. He had once in a single high school game hit four home runs. In his rookie year playing on our Elmira, New York, team in the short-season New York-Pennsylvania League, he batted .300 in 61 games, hit 11 home runs, drove in 48 runs, and was named to the league All-Star team. In his third season in professional baseball playing for our Winston Salem ball club in the Carolina League, he had hit .313 with 21 home runs and 89 RBIs in 127 games.

This past season on July 25, we brought him to the big leagues, and he made quite a debut against the Mariners. He hit a towering game-winning two-run home run. The very next day he went three for five, including his second home run. In early August playing against the Blue Jays, he hit a grand slam. He would play in 46 games at the major league level, hitting .278 with 14 home runs and 34 RBIs. It was an extremely auspicious start. On his combined season record at both Pawtucket and Boston, Horn had hit 44 home runs and driven in 114 RBIs. His rookie performance was spectacular and extremely encouraging. His defensive skills were adequate at best, but his power potential was exciting. It was the consensus of our minor league staff that he had the potential to become a productive left-handed power-hitting designated hitter.

Brady Anderson, who had not yet turned 24, had hit .294 in some 50 or 55 games in Double-A New Britain, and when I moved him up to Triple-A Pawtucket late in the season, he hit .300. Andersen had excellent speed and was a very talented outfielder with good range and arm strength. He had not demonstrated above average power—although he had hit 12 home runs at Winter Haven in 1986. But in three seasons he had averaged just eight home runs per season. When he came to major league spring training at the start of the 1987 season, his speed and defensive skills along with Burks's obvious talents and defensive skills had extremely impressed our coaching staff. Whenever we sat in a meeting to talk about ways to turn the team around in the future, Anderson's name was brought up.

It also became very obvious that the staff now felt that Burks, Greenwell, Anderson, and Benzinger should become the nucleus of our future outfield crop. My concern was the lack of power that this quartet could bring to bear upon our offensive production, but there were no questions about their defensive skills and their speed, particularly in the case of Burks and Anderson.

(In order to use this new crop of outfielders, we made the decision to move Evans to first base from right field. Evans would continue to be a major force on our ball club. Despite our disappointing season, he had still been extremely productive, hitting .305 with 34 home runs and 123 runs driven in. With Evans at first base, we made Horn a designated hitter, giving us, hopefully, another power batter.)

After we had lost Gedman for the season, we brought up our Triple-A catcher John Marzano, our first-round draft choice in the June 1984 free agent draft. Marzano had had a sensational career at Temple University in Philadelphia where he was a first-team All-American and hit .448 his senior year. He was the MVP in the USA/Korea International Series in 1983. In Triple-A Marzano had been hitting .282 in 70 games with 10 home runs. He would catch in 52 games for us, hitting .244 with five home runs and 36 RBIs. He gave us hope for the future with his performance, and at the time we projected a solid catching rotation featuring a physically sound Gedman and Marzano. Unfortunately, in time, this projection never came to fruition.

Our Double-A club also had an outfielder named Carlos Quintana, who at age 22 had shown enough potential to project him as a definite major league prospect and who was maybe just a season or two away from the big leagues. At six feet two inches and 190 pounds, Quintana had solid basic skills except for running speed, which was slightly below average. He had been signed out of Venezuela by our scout Willie Paffen. During the past two seasons he had hit .325 with 81 RBIs in 120 games with our Greensboro, North Carolina, club and .311 in only some 60 games—his season was cut short by a broken right leg—with our Double-A New Britain club. His overall physical skills in the outfield projected him to be a left fielder, but it would be his bat potential that could well carry him to the big leagues as a regular. We would have to wait and see how he rebounded from the broken leg, but if physically sound, he might be able to contribute at the major league level after another full season in Triple-A.

In the sixth round of the 1980 amateur draft, we had drafted a six-foot-four, 210-pound left-handed first baseman named Pat Dodson from UCLA. He had, ever so slowly, worked his way through our farm system, but in 1986 at Pawtucket he hit right at .270 with 27 home runs and 102 RBIs, which led the International League. He was named the league MVP and won the Star of Stars award presented annually by the Howe News Service. He was also selected to the International League All-Star team. Some of our people felt that he just might be ready to contribute at the big league level now. I intended to give him every possible opportunity to make the big club during spring training.

We also had a young shortstop in our farm system (whose physical skills I always felt were better suited to play at second base, not shortstop) named Jody Reed. Most of our minor league staff felt that we should leave him at shortstop and let him play himself out of that position. Reed had been signed in his junior year by one of our more talented scouts named George Digby at Florida State University. He had played at Pawtucket in 1986 hitting .282. Many of our staff felt he was ready to make the transition to the major leagues. There were a couple of other players in our farm system who were question marks but might have an outside chance to help us in the future, but we would have to see how things unfolded.

One advantage the Red Sox could look forward to in developing these players' skills was that our organization had a special hitting instructor—the greatest hitter who ever lived—who worked with our minor leaguers. Ted Williams was at the Winter Haven complex every day during spring training to observe, teach, and train our prospects, whom he felt were much more receptive to instruction than our established major leaguers, and I treasured the contact I got to have with him when I was the Red Sox general manager.

The very first week I arrived in Winter Haven, Ted asked me to spend some time with him down on the lower fields where the minor league players train. In Winter Haven the major league stadium and practice field was all but contiguous and just a few feet away from the minor league training facility. It made it extremely convenient to walk between both facilities.

I went down to the minor league facility to visit with Ted. It was difficult for me not to outwardly display my excitement over meeting my idol, even though now I was in essence his boss as the Red Sox general manager. I shook hands with Ted and told him I was thrilled to have him working with our young hitting prospects.

As we sat and talked, Ted said to me, "Have you read my book on hitting?"

"No, Ted, I have not."

"I think you should read it. I'll get you a copy," he replied.

We spent some more time talking about some of the young prospects in our farm system that he would be working with that spring. After a 40-minute meeting we parted. About two or three days later Ted dropped by my office on his way down to the minor league complex and handed me a copy of his book on hitting entitled, *The Science of Hitting*.

"When you get a chance, read it. That's what I teach," he said.

I thanked him.

A week or so later, I was down on the minor league complex because Ted had called me down to look at a couple of our young prospects whose hitting potential he was excited about. One of the young players was Burks, who impressed Ted with his bat quickness. He asked me to come behind the batting cage with him where Burks was hitting and watch him hit. As Burks would swing at a pitch, Ted would keep offering advice and instruction to Burks.

At one point in the middle of Burks taking his cuts in the batting cage, Ted turned to me and said, "Did you read my book?"

"Yes, most of it."

Ted began to grill me on some of his theories in *The Science of Hitting*, critiquing my answers and correcting me if I missed a point and responded incorrectly.

Ted finally said, "What is the most important point I made about hitting a baseball?"

I began to stammer, stalling for time to respond with the right answer.

"God damn it, Gorman, it's 'Look for the one good pitch to hit,'" he blurted out.

"Oh, now I remember," I sheepishly responded.

Ted gave me a disdainful look and we continued to watch Burks swing the bat in the cage. I was suddenly back in college in a course in hitting with Professor Ted Williams. It suddenly made me understand how passionate Ted was about his theories of hitting a baseball.

"Gorman, remember this. Hitting a baseball is a special skill, it's almost an art form," he said as we watched Burks hit. "It doesn't matter how long you play the game, you can keep learning about hitting and playing this game forever."

I nodded in agreement, but I also knew that I had better finish reading his book. He wouldn't take too kindly to my lack of knowledge on his theories of hitting a baseball.

For Ted it was a crusade, the passion of his life, and unquestionably one of the great loves in his life. On occasion during different seasons, he'd pick up one of our games on television and he'd call me on the phone and give me a discourse as to what I should tell our hitting coach to help Mike Greenwell, Mo Vaughn, Tim Naehring, or Rich Gedman improve their contact, swing, or overall approach to hitting. These were a few of the many young hitters he had previously worked with in our minor league spring training camp in the past, and he felt they were his personal pupils, whom he wanted to do well.

I was constantly awed by Ted's enthusiasm, his drive, and his absolute passion and love of learning and teaching the art of hitting a baseball. It was difficult to be around Ted for any length of time and not be caught up in his same passion and enthusiasm for hitting a baseball. During the All-Star Game in Fenway Park in 1999, Ted's appearance on the field prior to the start of the game became one of the most memorable events in All-Star history. As he was wheeled into the middle of the infield, the All-Star players poured onto the field in spontaneous tribute to him. One by one the greatest stars of Major League Baseball came out to shake Ted's hand. As each one came forward, he would have a word or two with every player and always about hitting. The greatest players in the game in modern Major League Baseball were paying homage to the "Greatest Hitter Who Ever Lived." It was a classic and unrehearsed moment for all time.

I recall one day after a spring training workout, I was sitting outside the minor league clubhouse with Ted.

He turned to me and said, "In your Navy days did you see action in the Korean War?"

I told him I had served on the aircraft carrier USS *Hornet*, and by the time we got off the Korean coast, the war was basically over and most of our time there was mop-up duty. I asked him if he had done any flying after he left active duty as a Marine fighter pilot during Korea. He said he hadn't.

"If I hadn't had baseball to come back to though, I would have stayed in the Marine Corp. as a Marine pilot. I loved flying and really truly loved the Marine Corp.," he replied.

That enthusiasm and deep love was reflected in his contact with servicemen. During the 1999 All-Star Game at Fenway, I had arranged through my Navy contacts for a flyover by a squadron out of the Naval Air Station at Virginia Beach, Virginia. The flyover was spectacular, because they came in formation right over the top of Fenway Park with a tremendous crescendo of power and they thrilled a sold-out crowd. We brought the pilots and aircrew back to Fenway after they landed at Hanscom Air Force Base to entertain and feed them in the 600 Club, which is today called the .406 Club in honor of Ted's batting average.

Ted was up in a private luxury box inundated with a huge crowd of friends, VIPs, and well-wishers. The pilots requested a meeting, and I happily brought them into the box and squeezed them through the throng. Ted was gracious and enjoyed talking to them about flying. When I ushered the Navy pilots out of the seats, the captain in charge of the Marine color guard approached me and asked if his men could meet Ted.

The Marine color guard comprised a young Marine captain and six veteran career Marines, mostly staff sergeants or sergeant majors, who had served in Vietnam, Desert Storm, or Bosnia. Because once you are a Marine, you always are a Marine, Ted Williams was still a hero to all Marines. I went back into the suite and told Ted the Marines would like to meet him.

"Gorman, bring in those Marines. I want to meet them," he bellowed.

As the Marines filed in, Ted sat them down and one by one asked them where they had served and saw action.

As they concluded their visit, Ted said to them, "Gentlemen, I was proud to be a major league ballplayer and be elected to baseball's Hall of Fame, but my proudest moment was becoming a United States Marine."

As I stood there and looked into the faces of the veteran Marines, I could recognize their enormous pride. Ted had just paid them their greatest honor.

Besides building up those around him—whether minor league batters or fellow servicemen, Ted had a witty sense of humor that could charm a room. I recall one offseason when Ted was in Boston to attend a benefit function and dinner that was attended by Mrs. Yawkey as well. Ted never liked to make formal speeches, so at this particular event Ted agreed to take some questions from the audience.

Over the course of the question-and-answer session, I recall one fan asking Ted, "Mr. Williams, if you were playing today, how much do you think the Red Sox would be paying you?"

Ted smiled, turned to Mrs. Yawkey, and said, "I'd be her partner."

It brought the down the house, and in light of players' salaries today, he just might have been right.

My days and memories with Ted were special. His genuine enthusiasm, gregarious personality, and love of baseball were so inspiring that I felt rejuvenated every time I found myself in his company.

As our Red Sox struggled through the last few weeks of the 1987 season to finish 78-84, 20 games out of first place, after winning the American League championship the previous season, I had a monumental task at had. The disappointment of our demise was ever so much more painful and discouraging. I now had to find a way to retool our ball club, once again, into a legitimate contender. The sooner the better.

CHAPTER 3

1988

"Morgan Magic"

As I sat with Eddie Kasko, Eddie Kenney, Wayne Britton, Eddie Kenney Jr., and our entire baseball operations staff to pinpoint our failures of the past season and to brainstorm what we had to do to turn our ball club around, it was readily obvious to all of us that we had a great deal of work to do that winter. I was convinced that one major hole we had to fill, regardless of whatever else we did, was to somehow obtain a legitimate stopper for our bullpen. It's one thing to take a lead into the ninth inning, but if you can't close it out, all else is for naught. We were also in agreement that we should attempt to add some depth to our starting pitching. I had a definite concern over Dennis "Oil Can" Boyd's status and whether he could still contribute in our starting rotation after his season-ending surgery.

In December 1987 the winter meetings were held in Dallas, Texas, and I went there determined to shore up our bullpen and, if possible, add depth to our starting pitching. During the course of the winter meetings, the general manager of the Chicago Cubs called me and asked to set up a meeting. Jim Frey was a longtime friend, having worked for me many years before in the Baltimore Orioles organization. He had managed in our minor league system and also served as a supervisory scout. Frey eventually went on to serve as a coach on our major league club under Earl Weaver. Over the years we had stayed in contact and remained good friends. During his minor league career as an outfielder, Frey had been an outstanding minor league hitter. He had won numerous minor league batting titles, yet other than brief stints with major league ball clubs in spring training, he had never reached the major leagues as a player. Frey had a solid baseball background, and when he left the Orioles organization, it was to become the manager of the Chicago Cubs. After managing the Cubs for a few seasons, he left the field and moved into their front office to become the general manager.

Our scouting intelligence determined that the Cubs were unhappy with their closer, Lee Smith, and they would be willing to consider trading him. Smith had been their ace the previous five seasons, having saved 162 ball games. He had, however, fallen out of favor in the past season or two with the manager and front office.

At the annual winter meetings we had established a policy, one that is employed by just about every major league organization, of having our scouts work the lobby of the hotel headquarters. The scouts would attempt to gather as much information, rumors, and data about players who could be available for trade. They would also determine which organizations were looking to fill specific needs. It was a system that had been productive for years.

To me, the annual winter meetings were critically important to an organization. What an organization would, or would not, accomplish at the meetings might well impact the success or failure of a ball club next season or in future seasons to come. I established a command headquarters in a suite in the hotel to work from with our entire staff during the entire week of the meetings. It reminded me of my Navy days; on ships there would be a combat information center (or CIC in Navy terminology) that would serve as the intelligence-monitoring center for the entire ship. Once we set up our headquarters in the hotel suite, I spent day and night living and working out of the suite. We had all of our scouting reports on every other organization in the suite. They represented well over a year's work of scouting intelligence. We started each day with an early morning meeting of our entire baseball staff and we set up our modus operandi for the rest of the day. We would pinpoint ball clubs with which we could possibly do business. I would assign our scouts to spread out in the hotel lobby and seek out the scouts from other organizations and set up times to meet with their front offices to explore trade possibilities.

When the reports and rumors filtered back to me via our scouting sources that it was possible that Smith might be available, I picked up the phone in our suite and returned Frey's call. The Cubs manager was former Red Sox manager Don Zimmer.

I had known Zimmer for many years. I had developed a casual relationship with "Zim" when he managed the Red Sox and I was the general manager of the Seattle Mariners. He was a lifelong baseball man who was held in high esteem and respected by everyone in the game for his knowledge and experience.

The past six seasons, Smith had averaged close to 30 saves a year. In 1987, he had saved 36 games for the Cubs. He was a premier reliever. In my mind, I was still extremely skeptical that the Cubs really wanted to trade Smith despite the reports he might be available.

I was able to set up a meeting with Frey, Zimmer, and their staff. I brought Eddie Kasko (our scouting director) and Frank Malzone (one of our chief scouts) with me to our meeting with the Cubs. It was common practice to open the meeting with the normal friendly conversation. It was an opportunity to break the ice before getting down to the nitty-gritty and the real reason for the meeting, exploring the basis of a trade. I was initially cautious not to bring up Smith's name. I talked about our needs and asked Frey what his needs were and who might be available from his ball club.

Frey at first looked over at Zimmer and then back at me and said, "We might consider moving Lee Smith in the right situation."

I was still stunned that they would consider trading Smith. In the back of my mind I began to wonder if he had some sort of injury we were not aware of. I had read our scouting reports on Smith in depth, and there was no indication that Smith had physical problems whatsoever. He was still throwing free and clear with velocity. It has always been the basic and underlying axiom that applied to any and all trades, *caveat emptor*—or buyer beware. In other words, when you make a trade you take total responsibility for the physical condition of the player you acquire.

In a very unemotional tone of voice I replied to Frey, "Jim, we might have some interest in acquiring Smith. What are you looking for in return?"

Frey replied that they were looking for pitching, possibly starting pitching in return. I proceeded to go over the roster of pitchers on our 40-man under control list and indicated which pitchers we might consider moving. As I went down the list, both Frey and Zimmer expressed an interest in Calvin Schiraldi. I turned to Kasko and Malzone.

"Would you both consider moving Schiraldi in a trade for Smith?" I asked.

They both indicated they would consider doing so. I turned to Frey and told him we would consider trading Schiraldi for Smith.

"I would want another pitcher beside Schiraldi for Smith," he replied.

I paused for a few minutes and briefly caucused with Kasko and Malzone and then turned to Frey.

"Jim, one pitcher we might consider trading along with Schiraldi for Smith would be right-hander Al Nipper," I responded.

Frey asked for 10 or 15 minutes to meet with Zimmer and two of his scouts. After 10 minutes, they returned from the other bedroom in the suite.

"We're willing to trade Lee Arthur Smith for Schiraldi and Al Nipper. If that's agreeable to you, we have a deal," he announced.

I stood up and shook hands with him.

"Jim, we have a deal."

I was elated, and I felt that Smith was the absolute perfect answer to solve our problems for a stopper. I was anxious to get out of the suite before they changed their minds. I then called the players involved and the league office and announced the trade to the media. In the best of all worlds, a trade that helps both clubs is a win-win scenario. I knew that Smith would be a great addition to our ball club. I was sincerely hopeful that a change of environment for Nipper and Schiraldi would help the Cubs and an old friend, Frey.

From our standpoint, the acquisition of Smith to our bullpen, one that had a total of 16 combined saves, would be a huge addition. When I talked to Nipper to inform him of the trade, he took it hard. He was heartbroken to leave the Red Sox organization where he had spent his entire baseball career. He also idolized Roger Clemens and had become Clemens's close and constant companion. Schiraldi took the news of the trade in stride and was nonplussed. I wished him the very best of luck in Chicago and meant it. I obtained Smith's phone number from Frey and called Smith to welcome him to the Red Sox organization and tell him how thrilled we were to have him in a Red Sox uniform. After talking to Smith, I called Frey to arrange and coordinate a press announcement. We agreed to meet in the pressroom, which had been established each year at the winter meetings where clubs would come to announce trades, player moves, or personnel moves to the combined media from all over the nation. As soon as we made the initial announcement, we then met with our own local media individually. As I talked to our media from all over New England, they were in almost disbelief that we had acquired Smith for Nipper and Schiraldi. Overall they were elated and positive about the trade, but there were the usual doubting Thomases who were suspicious that there must be something wrong with Smith for such a trade to happen.

As the Chicago media began to talk to our media, a rumor began to circulate that Smith had some physical problems. Our media now began to be convinced that the Cubs had possibly unloaded damaged goods. The rumors about Smith were almost mystical in nature. There was one rumor that he had fallen down the dugout steps in Shea Stadium when the Cubs were playing the Mets and injured his knee. All of the rumors would prove to be false.

When I got back to my suite, I once again called Smith and told him how thrilled we were to have him with the Red Sox. I also asked Smith to come to Boston for the Annual Baseball Writers Dinner, meet our media, and undergo a general physical checkup with our team doctor, Arthur Pappas. Smith was extremely personable and agreed to meet all of my requests. Smith told me he was committed to working extremely hard over the winter months on conditioning, because he had not been pleased with his past season. He told me he was prepared to have a great season for us. His prediction would prove accurate.

In 1988 he would save 29 games for us, with a 4-5 record and a 2.80 ERA. In 83 innings of pitching he would strike out 96 batters and walk only 35. In the following season he would save 25 games in 30 chances and finish 6-1 with a 3.57 ERA. He would strike out 96 batters in 70 innings of pitching.

His physical with Dr. Pappas revealed no serious physical problems, and it finally squelched all of the rumors. In his days with our ball club his only negative was simply that Smith didn't have the best work ethic in the game. He pushed himself at his own pace, yet when you gave him the ball in the eighth or ninth inning of a game to save, he got the job done. He was always equal to the challenge. He just didn't like a regimented workout, and he hated the running program. When his career was over, Smith would rank among the all-time great relief pitchers in the history of the game. His contribution out of the bullpen was a major factor in our turnaround from the disappointments of the 1987 season.

Over the winter the media kept indicating, directly and indirectly, that John McNamara was still emotionally impacted by our disastrous loss to the Mets in the 1986 World Series and that the pressure from our ownership was intense for him to produce a winning season or he was gone. Although McNamara had no idea of Jean Yawkey's conviction that he had caused us to lose the World Series, I was well aware of her attitude toward McNamara. I made every possible attempt to keep any additional pressure off of his shoulders by always being extremely positive and supportive of him. The intensity and the criticism of McNamara, however, increased daily. I was fully aware that if he got off to a slow start, McNamara's job was in serious jeopardy. I felt strongly, however, that it was my responsibility to protect him as much as possible from the media pressure and criticism. There was enough pressure and challenge in just managing in Boston with the constant scrutiny and criticism of the local media, as well as having only one year left on his contract. McNamara was well aware of his tenuous position. The media, particularly Dan Shaughnessy of *The Boston Globe*, began to be critical of me for protecting and defending him. The simple fact of the matter was that I had no other choice. If the general manager of the ball club is publicly criticizing his manager, how can he justify allowing him to continue managing his ball club?

Also, if I were to publicly criticize the manager of our ball club, it would obviously undermine his position of authority and credibility with his players. If the general manager was critical of his field manager and questioned his competence, why should the players respond to his authority? As long as McNamara, or any manager working with me, was wearing a Red Sox uniform and running the ball club, it was my responsibility to defend him or remove him. To do otherwise would be a total disservice to the manager, the ball club, and the organization. It would also exacerbate a difficult situation.

I still wanted desperately to add more depth to our pitching staff, particularly starting pitching. I continued to contact other ball clubs in the hope of finding some help via a trade. Despite all my efforts I came up empty handed.

Most of the national media and a few of our own beat writers picked us to win the Eastern Division title. In light of the fact we had only added Smith to our bullpen—even though he was a great addition, we still had questions about our starting pitching and other positions, and I found it slightly baffling that we were odds-on favorites to win the East. We had finished last season in fifth place, 20 games out. We were improved, but to predict we were the favorite to win the Eastern Division was, I felt, reaching.

However, despite the fact it was really putting pressure on McNamara and me to win, it went with the territory and we both understood that well.

The hype and media coverage touting us to win the Eastern Division title and quite possibly the American League championship was helping to sell tickets and to create an enormous amount of interest in the ball club.

Spring training in 1988 turned out to be a much more uneventful camp than the previous year. I had every player in camp under contract, and no one was threatening to walk out. The one major concern I had was the physical condition of "Oil Can" Boyd. His arm was still giving him trouble. He was having some discomfort just throwing lightly. He was concerned about the discomfort and soreness he was still experiencing, and so were we. For us to seriously contend, we needed Boyd sound and in our rotation. The age-old axiom that "Good pitching will always get good hitters out" is ever so true, because you simply need pitching depth to win. No ball club can consistently score eight to 10 runs a ball game. Good pitching will always keep you close, and championships are won with good pitching.

We got off to a slow start in the regular season. By April 16 after a 2-0 loss to Texas, we were just 6-5 and not playing like a contending team. Bruce Hurst started the next night against Texas and he pitched a four-hitter. Our offense exploded for 20 hits and 15 runs, and we buried the Rangers 16-3. It was our first big victory of the early season. Mike Greenwell was now established as our regular left fielder, following an impressive 50-year line of Ted Williams, Carl Yastrzemski, and Jim Rice. Greenwell led our offense in the rout of Texas with three hits, including his fourth home run of the season, and six RBIs. We went on to win seven of the next eight ball games and post a 14-6 won-lost record to move within one game of first place. Boyd continued to have shoulder and arm problems, and Rice continued to struggle at the plate.

Just when it appeared we had turned the corner, by the end of April we proceeded to lose six of the next seven games and drop back to fourth place, three and a half games out of first. Fortunately for us, no one in the division was playing well or had put together a winning streak. It appeared that no club in the division would run away with the pennant. With any sort of a concerted effort on our part and a healthy pitching staff, we could contend, if not win it all.

I was constantly in touch with McNamara, and he was always aware of my thoughts and of our scouts' reports, evaluations, and recommendations. I was a strong believer in an open line of communication with the manager throughout the season to provide him with support, confidence, and timely scouting intelligence.

As the season moved into May, McNamara began to sense the pressure of the media and the urgency for him to win this season. He began to make major roster and lineup moves in an attempt to jumpstart the ball club into a winning streak. He juggled the starting lineup on a daily basis. He moved Wade Boggs from third in his batting lineup to leadoff, and then a day or two later he moved Boggs back to third in the order. He inserted Jody Reed into the lineup at shortstop. He was hoping to catch lightning in a bottle. By the end of May, however, we were still just a few games above .500, in fourth place in the division, some seven games behind the leader.

Then on June 3 a stunning announcement out of Costa Mesa, California, became front-page news throughout the sports world and took some of the focus off the action on the playing field. A woman named Margo Adams announced she had filed a $6 million breach of oral contract suit against Boggs. She alleged that she and Boggs had been carrying on a four-year affair and that Boggs had made definite promises to her, which he had refused to honor. The story instantly became a major topic of discussion throughout New England and in clubhouses throughout the major leagues.

My first concern was Boggs and his family and how it would impact their lives. I was also concerned how it might impact our ball club and what serious implications it might bring to bear on Boggs's playing performance. It would obviously be traumatic for his wife and children to deal with the problem and the crush of media attention. It was not going to be easy for Boggs and his family or for the Red Sox organization. It would be an issue in the tabloids, in gossip columns, and on talk shows throughout America. I was greatly concerned with what we could do to minimize the impact of the entire issue on Boggs, his family, and the Red Sox. He and the Red Sox would be dealing with the media hype and mania that were sure to follow in the weeks ahead; it might become overwhelming.

As time passed, the national media now began to follow our ball club on an almost daily basis. The torrent of abuse and off-color comments and epithets that Boggs would have to endure throughout the season would be all but unbearable, not only on the road, but at Fenway Park as well. Oftentimes in Fenway, Boggs's wife, Debbie, and their children would have to endure the fans' cruel and inhumane abuse that was showered upon Boggs. Yet Debbie stood by her husband in total support and unwavering loyalty. She grew in stature enormously in my personal view. Her support was remarkable and extraordinary. Boggs himself endured the constant, almost unbearable taunts with what seemed like total indifference. You had to feel that the indignation he was suffering on a daily basis had to be affecting his psyche, concentration, and inner being, yet he never for one moment gave in to his tormentors. He continued to play and perform despite the media maelstrom that engulfed him daily.

Whether the Boggs affair and the overbearing amount of media coverage and hype would negatively impact our ball club was something only time would tell. At one point in the season the incident did begin to cause some problems within the clubhouse. Some of the other players on the ball club were dragged into the scenario and tempers began to flare on some of our road trips. One time during the season, Boggs got into a shouting match with some of his teammates, and Boggs and Dwight Evans ended up in a shoving match that had to be broken up by the coaches and some of the players. The clubhouse began to divide into separate camps and various opinions over the issue. I'm certain that some of the players' wives had a lot of questions for their husbands regarding the Boggs–Adams incident and what went on during some of the road trips. The tension and strain that seemed to permeate the clubhouse became a definite concern for both McNamara and me.

On June 13 Clemens had his worst outing in many a season, and we were routed by the Yankees 12-6. We were now 10 games out of first place in the division. It was an ugly performance, and the media began to intensify their campaign to get McNamara fired. The talk shows in Boston and throughout New England were full of "Sac Mac" talk, and they continued to second-guess every move he made. Once the media, in particular the talk shows, took hold of an issue, negative or positive, they were like an angry dog with a bone in its mouth. Their attack would be relentless.

The negative criticism began to affect McNamara, and he gradually began to withdraw from the media and the beat writers as often as possible. The constant criticism was getting to him even to the point of physically affecting him. I was in McNamara's office at one point after a ball game in Fenway, which was routine after a game, and as McNamara came out of the shower to dress, I noticed his entire body was covered in red blotches. I asked Mac whether he had the mumps or an infection; he indicated he had neither. I began to realize it was probably the effect of the stress, the pressure of the job, and the constant media criticism.

I now became seriously concerned about his health and well being. I vividly recalled how former Red Sox manager Don Zimmer had been tormented and infuriated by the media criticism, at times so unfairly, and how it impacted his psyche.

In our next series we took two out of three from the Yankees, but we then proceeded to lose the next two games to the Baltimore Orioles. We remained eight and a half games out of first place. With the increasing criticism of McNamara, I somehow thought back to Mrs. Yawkey's comments to me after our tragic loss in Game 6 of our World Series battle with the Mets. I was confident it was on her mind now, and I was certain if we continued to struggle, she was going to insist that I fire McNamara. Publicly, I kept defending McNamara.

Just prior to the All-Star Game, we lost three games in succession to the Chicago White Sox; we remained nine games out of first place with a 43-42 record. During the All-Star break, Mrs. Yawkey called for a meeting with John Harrington, Haywood Sullivan, and me. I knew that her request for a meeting had ominous overtones for McNamara. The day after the All-Star Game we met at Fenway Park in one of our conference rooms. The sole issue was McNamara.

When we got seated in the conference room, Mrs. Yawkey said, "I'm disappointed in our ball club's performance, and I feel it's time to make a change in the manager."

"I still feel this ball club can turn itself around the second half," Haywood responded immediately.

I knew when the meeting was called that my chance of saving McNamara was impossible because Mrs. Yawkey had made up her mind on the issue a long time ago. Maybe it was best for the ball club, because it didn't appear we were heading in the right direction, nor did it appear that McNamara could right the ship. In one sense it would be a bitter pill for Mac to swallow that he was being fired, but the media pressure and criticism had begun to take its toll upon him. They had become mean spirited in their criticism of him and to be free of that might be a blessing in disguise. I liked McNamara a great deal, but the reality of the situation was that he was being perceived as incapable of leading the Red Sox out of its funk and that he had lost the confidence of his players.

"I feel McNamara has to be replaced for our team to improve," Mrs. Yawkey said.

After a little more discussion of the issue, the decision was finally made to dismiss McNamara.

I knew who I would suggest for the job—Joe Morgan. I had never understood why the Red Sox had never even considered making Morgan a coach, let alone their manager, after he had done a great job managing their Triple-A ball club at Pawtucket for nine seasons. I felt he was an excellent baseball man with great credentials, and I wanted him involved with our major league club. I felt his talents had been overlooked, and he belonged in uniform on the field. That was his forte, and I was determined to get him back in uniform.

When I joined the Red Sox organization in 1984, I made up my mind to promote Morgan to our coaching staff, and one year later I convinced McNamara to add him to his coaching staff.

Mrs. Yawkey told me, as our meeting was concluding, to meet with McNamara prior to the next evening's ball game and inform him that he was being replaced as the team manager. If Morgan was my recommendation to manage the ball club, I should go ahead and give him the job on an interim basis. Haywood responded that he would like to break the news to McNamara first himself, and then I could meet with him. Haywood and McNamara went way back from the days they had managed together in the old Kansas City Athletics organization, and they had established a close personal relationship over the years. I fully understood his request and had no problem with Haywood talking to McNamara first.

McNamara generally arrived at the ballpark for home games around 2 or 2:30 p.m., and on some days around noon. At 3 p.m. on July 15, Haywood called me and told me he was on his way to talk to McNamara, and he would let me know as soon as he had finished talking to him. When I entered McNamara's office in the clubhouse, he was already beginning to pack his personal gear prior to departing the ballpark.

Before I began to talk to him, he looked up and said, "Lou, Haywood has already broken the news to me and I understand, even though I don't agree. I know you were always in my corner, and I thank you for your support and the opportunity to manage the Red Sox." He came forward and shook my hand and said, "Let's always stay in touch."

He picked up an equipment bag filled with his personal belongings and left his office and the clubhouse.

I knew he had to feel some sort of relief from the constant media criticism, and yet I knew in his heart he was still very upset at leaving his job as the manager of the Red Sox. I had mixed emotions as I watched him shut the door of the manager's office behind him.

Shaughnessy in his book *The Curse of the Bambino* called McNamara, "a good old baseball man." He went on to write, "that good old baseball men like Johnny Mac had many friends in high places throughout baseball… McNamara kept getting jobs because he knew the game and didn't rock the boat. He would ingratiate himself with the people he needed and ignore everybody else."

Shaughnessy's portrayal—which sums up the Boston media's general sentiment of McNamara—was unfair. He had been hired in baseball to manage in the big leagues not because he was a "good old guy," as the media labeled him for his tenure as manager, but because most people in baseball respected him as a "good baseball man," something the local columnists and talk shows never acknowledged. He was a hard worker who was knowledgeable and loyal to his players and to the organization he worked for. He had his faults, as we all do. He oftentimes allowed his emotions to sway his judgments, and he wasn't Earl Weaver in making tactical decisions in a ball game, but then few managers are.

When McNamara departed, I walked out into the clubhouse. The players were all sitting around, half dressed, and you could sense the tension and emotion that permeated the entire area. The players were aware that McNamara was under the gun, and they knew something was imminent. Despite the media perception of McNamara, he was liked by most of the players. I turned to Morgan and asked him to step into the manager's office with me.

I closed the door behind Morgan and told him that McNamara had been fired and it was my decision to have him take over the ball club. At first he was stunned at the news and my decision to have him manage the ball club. It was a dream of a lifetime for Morgan to manage the Red Sox, his hometown team. I knew inwardly he was overcome with a sense of elation and joy that had to be the thrill of a lifetime, but once he realized the job was his, he was in total command of himself. I told him he would be the interim manager of the ball club for the rest of the season. We discussed a salary increase for him, which I felt was fair, but Morgan hardly paid attention; he just wanted to step out into the clubhouse and get started, whatever I offered him was inconsequential. He accepted immediately. He wanted to prove to the organization and to the fans in New England that he could manage a big league club. It was a challenge he had spent his whole professional life waiting for.

We discussed the ball club at some length and then I told him I'd address the ball club first about the change, turn the team over to him, and depart the clubhouse. I shook his hand and wished him the best of luck. As I shook his hand, I somehow felt his mind was already at work preparing for that night's ball game.

I walked into the clubhouse from the manager's office and asked the players for their attention. I told them that the organization felt that we needed to make a change in the manager and I had great respect for McNamara, but I felt that we had to do something to turn the ball club around; we had talent, but we weren't playing up to our potential. I told them that I also felt that all players in the clubhouse had to look within themselves to accept that they also shared responsibility for their failures to date and McNamara's departure. I then told the players that Morgan was now the manager of the ball club. I asked them to give Morgan their total support and commitment so that we could then turn this season around. I then turned to Morgan.

"Skipper, the ball club is now yours. Good luck," I said before leaving the clubhouse.

I then met with the media who were outside the clubhouse waiting for my pronouncement about the managerial change. I had the feeling that some of them felt a certain vicarious pleasure in McNamara's demise.

I personally had experienced the harshness of the media—sometimes for no apparent reason. When I first came on board with the Red Sox, I made it a policy to be as upfront and open with them as I could be—provided it did not interfere with my responsibilities as general manager or my relationships with the players. I felt our fans, who had invested more than 70 years of passionate support to the Red Sox, deserved to hear from the club's general manager on certain issues. My responses were always factual, candid, and frank. I knew of no other way to respond but to answer the media questions or a fan's question in a sincere and straight from the hip manner. I might have been too available or too open, maybe to a fault. It might have worked against me, but my nature was too people oriented to do otherwise.

It seemed that when it came to the local talk shows, sometimes it was more about the host generating controversy and higher ratings than discussing the issues themselves. Bob Lobel, an extremely popular and talented sports anchor for WBZ, seemed to feed off the more sensational stories in his sports talk show. His impish personae and his showmanship made him very appealing and interesting and could overshadow the issues themselves, and because of this, his ratings were always exceptional. Meanwhile, the majority of the TV sports anchors on the local Boston stations—John Dennis, Mike Lynch, Mike Dowling, and Gene Levanshy—seemed to rely upon the issues themselves to carry their shows.

Still in all, most of the TV sports media, including Bob Lobel, were extremely positive in their coverage of the Red Sox and more often than not upfront and reasonable in their dealings with me personally.

There were some exceptions where I felt that certain local talk shows took advantage of my availability by using it to criticize me in ways that I often thought were unfair and unwarranted.

For example, in my early years in Boston I had been invited by Eddie Andelman, a legendary local talk show host, to appear on his show as a regular guest. He offered to compensate me financially, which was the common practice for regular guests by most of the radio stations. I graciously refused to be compensated because I did not want to be committed to regular appearances—so as to not interfere with my workload for the Red Sox—and more importantly I did not want to be under an obligation to the station or Andelman because I was receiving a fee. My first obligation was to the Red Sox, and I did not intend to compromise my position in that regard because of a financial commitment. In time and for a number of reasons, I decided to terminate my association with Andelman and the radio station. I would be on Andelman's show, but only on very special occasions in future years.

Many years later a fan called his show and asked Andelman why he no longer had me as his guest on his talk show.

"When I had Gorman on my show, I never got straight answers on any interesting or factual information from him," Andelman replied.

I did not happen to hear that particular show but one of our top executive officers of the Red Sox did and told me about Andelman's response to the fan's questions. I was absolutely infuriated at his response. I was deeply upset that he would make such a statement about me. Even though I had not personally heard the exchange between Andelman and the caller, I contemplated what action I should take to respond to such an unjustified libelous statement. After sleeping on the issue I decided to recognize the source and ignore it. I was confident that anyone who knew me personally or who had dealt with me in the past, would readily recognize that there was no basis in fact regarding the statements about me.

I recall another occasion when a fan called into one of the local talk shows and stated that he had been to a Red Sox game at Fenway with his son and he met me coming out of the clubhouse just before game time. He asked me for an autograph for his young son, who was there with him.

"He graciously signed my son's scorebook, spent a few minutes talking to both of us before departing," the caller said. "I thought it was a very kind gesture by Mr. Gorman."

The talk show host after listening to the gentleman's comments retorted, "I'd prefer he was up in his office checking the waiver wires, but thanks for the call."

(Well, the irony of the whole scenario was that I had been going over what players were available on the waiver wires in a discussion with our manager and coaching staff before I had left the clubhouse.)

The negativity of the media in Boston could be cruel and debilitating. They seemed, to a great degree, to feed off controversy or crisis, personal or professional. They tended to analyze and re-analyze every issue, sometimes through logic and reason but more often than not through opinions, criticism, and mean-spiritedness. As I left the press conference where I announced the managerial change, I felt some relief that the scrutiny and derision McNamara had endured in print would finally come to an end. As I headed to my stadium box to watch the game, however, I had a slight reservation in my mind about how the ball club would react to the managerial change. I had a great deal of confidence in Morgan's ability, but I also recognized that if the ball club did not make a dramatic turnaround by the end of the season, I would have to reconsider Morgan as our manager and possibly look in a different direction. I liked Morgan and I wanted him to succeed, but I had to be a realist.

The first manager I had in mind was Joe Torre. I had been associated with him in my tenure with the Mets, and I liked him a great deal. I actually called Torre on the phone and told him that we had hired Morgan as our interim manager. If, however, it didn't work out, I wanted Torre to know he would be my first choice to manage our ball club. I felt he had the ability to develop into an outstanding manager.

I also had been very close to Lou Piniella throughout his career, having first been associated with him when he was a player in the Baltimore Orioles' minor league system and I was the Orioles' director of minor league operations. I later spent six or seven years with him in the Royals organization as the director of baseball operations and Piniella was on our team. We became close, and I had a great deal of respect for his intensely competitive nature and his character. He would have been high on my list also, but he had just been hired to manage the Cincinnati Reds and was obviously not available. I was hopeful, however, that Morgan would succeed because he had paid his dues and deserved the opportunity to prove he could manage a major league club.

The change in the ball club's intensity and attitude was truly dramatic. Morgan's first game as the Red Sox manager was the day after the All-Star break on July 15. Clemens took the mound at Fenway to face the Kansas City Royals and Bret Saberhagen. It was a classic matchup of two outstanding Cy Young award winners. Clemens pitched a brilliant game, scattering five hits and striking out 16. Evans hit a two-run home run in the first inning, and it was all Clemens needed. It was a 3-1 win, and it gave Morgan his first major league victory. On that date our overall won-lost record stood at 44-42. The Red Sox proceeded to sweep the Royals four straight, scoring 27 runs in the four games. It would be 12 games later before the ball club would lose, finally dropping a 9-8 loss to the Texas Rangers. By that point in the season we had moved into third place, but just two and a half games out of first.

The team continued its spectacular run as it closed a nine-game gap to move into a tie for first place on August 4. In the process of this remarkable and stunning revival, "Morgan Magic" had inspired the ball club to establish an American League record by winning 24 straight games at Fenway Park, and Morgan became an overnight folk hero in New England.

Morgan's debut was absolutely sensational as he managed the Red Sox to 12 straight wins and 19 victories in his first 20 games. It was one of the most remarkable starts by a rookie manager in Red Sox history. I was delighted. It was "Walpole Joe," the local hometown boy, who became the talk of the town. It was a classic tale of the local boy making good, and no one deserved the adulation more than Morgan. He had labored for years in the minor leagues as a player and manager, often driving a snowplow in the offseason for the Massachusetts Highway Department to earn extra money to raise his family. He was one of the most likeable and personable managers I had ever been associated with. What you saw was what you got when dealing with "Walpole Joe." He was dead honest in his dealings with his players and with me. He was devoid of any ego and a joy to work with.

Morgan had a favorite expression that he would use whenever he was quizzed by the media with an innocuous question; he would respond, "Six two and even." I never determined what this meant, and I'm not even sure that Morgan did either, but it became a Morgan trademark. As his ball club continued to win, Mrs. Yawkey told me to remove the interim from Morgan's title and make him the manager with a contract extension, which I proceeded to do.

It was difficult to pinpoint what ignited our ball club under Morgan, but his approach to the game and to his players was a major factor in the team's dramatic resurgence. He totally changed the atmosphere in the clubhouse. The tension disappeared, and the players seemed to be totally relaxed. His style was exactly what the ball club needed. Despite the club's phenomenal turnaround, Morgan's demeanor never changed. He seemed to relish the challenge and the pressure of the job. His personality was also even keel.

When Morgan assumed control of the ball club, one of his first managerial moves was to replace Spike Owen at shortstop with Jody Reed. It was an astute move by Morgan, because Reed went on to become one of the top rookies in the American League. Reed hit .293 in 109 games, and in Fenway, he hit .309. He struck out just 21 times the entire season and played well at shortstop. I felt, however, that Reed was still best suited tool-wise to play second base.

Todd Benzinger found more playing time under Morgan and he appeared in 120 games at first base, left field, and right field. He hit only .254 but drove in 70 runs with 28 doubles and 13 home runs while making only six errors in the 109 games he played at three different positions.

The media never questioned Morgan's knowledge of the game; he had spent his life in baseball, and he was an astute student of the game. He wasn't afraid to go against the grain, so to speak, or act contrary to conventional and traditional policy of how the game should be played. If his gut instincts told him to do something differently in game strategy, he did so, regardless of the critics or tradition. He was his own man.

The first major challenge that Morgan faced was an incident that occurred early in his managerial career. In the midst of his remarkable winning streak late in a ball game and with the Sox down by a run, Rice, one of the Red Sox all-time greats but now late in his fabulous career, was advancing from the on-deck circle to the batter's box to go up to hit when Morgan made the decision to recall Rice and send up Owen to pinch-hit for Rice. Morgan was sending Owen up to bunt and move the runners into scoring position. Rice was insulted and furious at Morgan's move to send up the .250 hitter to replace him, not realizing that Morgan had sent Owen up to bunt.

Rice felt that Morgan had intentionally embarrassed him by letting him get almost into the batter's box before calling him back, and for Rice the final indignity was sending up the weak-hitting Owen to hit for him. When Rice got back to the dugout, he went right at Morgan, grabbing him and shoving him down the dugout stairs. Morgan attempted to protect himself but did not back down. Immediately a number of players and others intervened to break up the scuffle.

It was a major challenge to Morgan's authority and control of the Red Sox ball club. As soon as the ball game ended, the media couldn't get to the clubhouse soon enough to confront Morgan about the incident. Morgan's response was classic.

"I'm in charge of this nine," he said.

He was not about to back down to any player, whatever his stature. This was his ball club, and he was in charge, make no mistake about that. Morgan had won over the hearts of Red Sox fans everywhere and in the process the respect of his players.

After the ball game was over, I went down to Morgan's office to visit with him and discuss the Rice incident with him. I asked him whether Rice should be fined for his action.

Morgan had a great deal of respect for Rice and his career accomplishments with the Red Sox.

"No, Lou, I want to handle this in my own way," he said.

I knew the challenge by Rice had upset him greatly, and he wasn't going to back down, but because he had such respect for Rice as a player, he'd handle the incident in private.

Although the media did not question "Morgan Magic," in some insistences they kept implying that one of the principal reasons for firing McNamara was the Boggs–Adams scenario. I was well aware that Mrs. Yawkey was very upset at the entire incident and the distasteful national publicity that followed, which reflected adversely upon the Red Sox organization. There was no question Mrs. Yawkey was dismayed by the entire situation and scandal, but McNamara's fate had been sealed long ago after we lost Game 6 of the 1986 World Series.

Boggs, however, continued to be impervious to the insults and to the national attention and derision as he stayed hot at the plate. He would finish the season hitting .366 with 214 hits, his sixth straight season with 200 or more hits. He only struck out 34 times in 584 at bats.

I recall one incident when a reporter from a national media publication called me and asked if Boggs was emotionally distraught over the negative media attention he was receiving and was it impacting his performance on the field. At the time the reporter called me, Boggs was hitting right at .370. I asked the caller had he recently looked at the current American League batting averages. I don't recall his response, but the conversation ended quickly after my remark.

After we lost to Texas 9-8, our ball club won the next day, led by an Ellis Burks grand slam. Bob Stanley picked up the win in relief, and Smith notched up his 16th save of the season. The next day Hurst beat the Milwaukee Brewers, raising his record to 11-4. Greenwell hit a two-run home run, and Reed went four for five to give us a 6-4 win. Smith would come on to close the game down for his 17th save of the season. We were now 57-43, and "Morgan Magic" continued to become a household phrase.

Even though we were winning, I still felt that in order to get back to the World Series this season we needed one more hurler. I took a chance. That same day I traded Brady Anderson and Curt Schilling from our farm system to the Orioles for right-handed pitcher Mike Boddicker.

The first time I personally saw Schilling pitch was in the Winter Instructional League right after we had signed him. I loved his arm strength and his makeup. He had pitched at the Single-A level in 1987 in the Sally League at Greensboro, North Carolina. He was 8-15, but his strikeout ratio was excellent. In 184 innings he had struck out 189 batters. We had projected his advancement to the major leagues as possibly four or five years away. I liked his toughness and aggressiveness. At six foot four and 210 pounds, he was also an impressive specimen.

I had reservations about parting with him. I felt, however, with Clemens, Hurst, and Boddicker we would have three front-line starting pitchers capable of combining to win 55 to 60 games and lead us back to postseason glory. Schilling was still possibly five years away (and that projection proved accurate) from becoming a big league pitcher.

Anderson was also a good young prospect with excellent defensive skills. He had hit .294 at New Britain, our Double-A club in 1987, with six home runs, 35 RBIs, and 24 stolen bases. Our reports indicated that Anderson would become a solid center fielder, with good speed and very little power but could hit for a decent average.

It was the consensus opinion, however, that Burks should be our regular center fielder over Anderson. Burks hit .277 with 20 home runs with our major league club the previous year and had superior fielding skills. He had great speed, range, and arm strength and gave every indication he would hit with some power. With Rice in left and Evans in right field, Burks was the perfect anchor in center field. It would give us one of the better defensive outfields in the league.

Schilling went to the Orioles' Triple-A club at Rochester, New York, winning 13 and losing 11 with a 3.21 ERA. He pitched briefly with the Orioles' major league club. The following season the Orioles sent him back to Triple-A where he was 4-4 and had a 3.92 ERA. He was recalled to the major league club and appeared in 35 games. He finished with a 1-2 won-lost record and a 2.54 ERA. On January 10 the Orioles traded Schilling with pitcher Pete Harnisch and outfielder Steve Finley to the Houston Astros for infielder Glenn Davis. He would spend a part of the season at Triple-A Tucson with a 0-1 won-lost record and 3.42 ERA; he then was recalled to the Astros' major league roster, and he went 3-5 with a 3.87 ERA appearing in 56 games. The following season on April 2,1992, Schilling was traded to the Philadelphia Phillies for pitcher Jason Gremsley. In his first season with the Phillies Schilling finally established himself as a big league pitcher going 14-11 with a 2.35 ERA. He would follow it up with a 16-7 record in 1993 but then developed shoulder problems and a season later, elbow problems. He would struggle through three difficult seasons going 2-8, 7-5, and 9-10 before he was fully recovered and once again had a winning season in 1997. He opened the 2000 season on the Phillies' disabled list recovering from off-season arthroscopic surgery on his right shoulder. On July 20 the Phillies traded him to Arizona. He would become a 22-game winner in 2001 and, along with Randy Johnson, lead the Diamondbacks to a world championship and become a strong candidate to one day be inducted into baseball's Hall of Fame.

In retrospect, the acquisition of Boddicker gave us a solid major league starter who could be productive right away, and inserting Burks into our lineup as our starting center fielder dramatically improved our defense, our offensive production, and speed on the club. Burks stole a combined 52 bases in his first two seasons with our ball club.

I was hopeful that the addition of Boddicker as an integral part of our starting rotation, along with the addition of Smith as a solid dominant stopper would give us exactly what we needed to take us back to the World Series.

It had been my passion from the moment I joined the Red Sox organization to win a world championship on my watch. Having grown up in New England as a "dyed-in-the wool" Red Sox fan as a youngster, I had dreamed about playing for the Red Sox. That dream died abruptly after the Phillies released me after my very brief attempt at professional baseball. The thought, however, of one day becoming the general manager of my beloved Red Sox was beyond any possibility of my wildest imagination. Often I had to remind myself that it wasn't a flight of fancy or a pipe dream, that I was now the general manager of the Red Sox. It was real, and the challenge of fulfilling the ultimate dream for Red Sox fans everywhere was now my challenge and my responsibility. It was awesome to consider that possibility.

In my baseball career I had been personally involved in the development of highly productive farm systems in Baltimore, Kansas City, Seattle, and New York. I had grown up in this game committed to building the future of an organization from within. Some general managers will move developed talent at any chance they get to nab a key short-term component for their team and try to make a run to win it all. Despite my absolute obsession to win a world championship, I never lost sight of the critical need to continue to develop talent from within an organization's own system, and I continued to make our farm system a major priority.

In addition to acquiring Boddicker, I had signed a veteran player named Lance Parrish in late July, as a free agent, with the hope of giving us an experienced player whose bat might help us.

Parrish was able to fill in at first base and serve as a designated hitter, although he had spent most of his major league career at third base. He was able to contribute offensively while playing in 52 games. He hit eight home runs and drove in 32 runs, 13 of those RBIs either tied or won a ball game for us. At one point, he hit four home runs in a five-game series.

After Morgan's remarkable winning streak, the ball club began to play at a pace that was less sensational than during his debut as the manager, but that was to be expected. The ball club, however, was now 60-43 and in third place. After a losing road trip on August 12, our ball club returned home to Fenway, and Hurst beat the Detroit Tigers 9-4 for his 13th win of the season with Stanley picking up a save. Evans (three RBIs) and Rice (a two-run home run) paced the offense. We then proceeded to win seven of the next 10 games to go 71-54 in second place, just two games out of first. Boddicker beat the Angels on August 23 for his fourth win, and Boggs and Greenwell paced the offense aided by a three-run home run by catcher Rich Gedman. The Fenway Park home record under Morgan was now a sensational 29-4.

I continued to marvel at Boggs's impenetrable demeanor as he continued to endure the taunts and insults in city after city about his affair with Margo Adams. It had to get to him, and yet he continued to swing the bat with amazing proficiency on his way to another outstanding season. I was absolutely amazed at his indifference. Most players might have retaliated or challenged their loud-mouthed detractors, but not Boggs. He just kept rolling along.

Morgan was indefatigable, and nothing seemed to diminish his enthusiastic approach to the game. He was truly having fun managing the ball club. His positive, outgoing nature continued to permeate the entire ball club. It was a happy, jovial, loose clubhouse and playing the game had become fun once again.

On September 1 we defeated the California Angels in Anaheim 4-2 to raise our overall record to 74-59, and we had moved to within one game of first place. Wes Gardner picked up his sixth win with help from Stanley, and Smith picked up his 21st save of the season with an outstanding ninth-inning performance, striking out all three hitters that he faced. Benzinger and Parrish both hit two-run home runs to lead the offense. Finally on September 4 we edged the Angels 6-5 to move into a tie for first place with the Tigers. After a shaky second inning Clemens settled down and allowed only two more hits the rest of the way. Stanley came in to pitch in the seventh with two outs but failed to hold the lead. Smith came in and pitched effectively into the 10th to pick up his 22nd save of the season. It was a lead-off home run by Parrish in the top of the 10th that won the ball game.

On September 5 we took sole possession of first place with a 4-1 win over the Orioles in Baltimore. Right-hander Mike Smithson picked up the victory with Dennis Lamp and Smith in relief. Evans won the game with a home run and three RBIs. Evans would finish with 21 home runs and 111 RBIs. We increased the lead to three and a half games on September 10 as Clemens spun a one-hitter over the Cleveland Indians to shut them out 6-0 at home. It was Clemens's 16th win of the season, and he was in total control, at one point retiring 15 straight batters. Evans was once again the offensive star going four for four, with a double, triple, and three RBIs.

It continued to be something special to visit with Morgan in his office after each ball game. His enthusiasm and confidence were contagious. You could not be in his presence or his office without being convinced that there was no way we could lose a ball game. I loved his enthusiasm, and I loved his positive and upbeat approach to baseball and to life. Whatever "six two and even" meant, I never found out, but it didn't matter; for Morgan it took care of all the problems of the day. Morgan's personality and upbeat approach to life were so much like my own. I just can't deal with negative people because they put you in a slump, but positive people lift your spirits in life's darkest moments and difficult challenges. Morgan was my kind of person.

Oftentimes in Morgan's office at Fenway, when I would go to visit him either before or after a ball game, Boston Bruins players would be there, talking hockey or baseball to Morgan. Cam Neeley was a frequent visitor to Morgan's office. When I first met Neeley, I was surprised to realize how big he was. He had the size and build of a pro football player. My remembrances of my days watching the old Bruins or the Providence Reds of the American Hockey League were that the players were much smaller in stature.

Morgan had been both an outstanding baseball player and hockey player at Boston College, and he still loved to lace on his skates and get out on the ice. On one or two occasions he had worked out with the Bruins and loved every minute of it. He was still a great hockey fan at heart.

If in all of my seasons with Morgan we ever had any disagreement over any one issue, it was mushrooms. Morgan loved mushrooms and grew them in his backyard. He was both a connoisseur and an expert on the subject, but I hated them and still do. Morgan would grow these special exotic mushrooms or purchase them at a specialty store and bring them to me for a special treat. I didn't have the heart to refuse them, but they never ended up going home with me.

By September 17 we had increased our division lead to five games with a 3-1 win over the New York Yankees at Fenway Park before another capacity crowd. Somehow it always seemed very special when you beat the Yankees any time in any season. Maybe it was a backhanded tribute to their dominance and excellence over the years. Hurst notched his 18th victory of the season and his 13th successive win at Fenway Park, the longest home winning streak for a pitcher since Mel Parnell went 16-3 in Fenway in 1949. Hurst spun a three-hitter, striking out nine for the win. Evans hit a two-run homer to give us an early lead and the eventual victory.

The win put us 20 games over .500 for the first time since our pennant-winning season of 1986. On September 23 we scored a dramatic win over the Yankees at Yankee Stadium. Hurst had one of his worst performances of the season. He left in the sixth inning with one out and behind 9-5. However, in the eighth inning, Boggs and Marty Barrett drove in two runs apiece to close the gap to 9-7. In the top of the ninth Reed singled in a run and then pinch hitter Owen singled up the middle with two men in scoring position to cap off a dramatic 10-9 victory. Lamp picked up the win in relief, and Smith recorded his 29th save to close out the game.

We actually won the division title while the ball club slept quietly in the Hollenden House Hotel in Cleveland on September 30 with two games remaining in the regular season. It was ironic that our ball club should be in the same hotel where supposedly the sexual hijinx involving Boggs, Adams, and others had taken place. We awakened the next morning to find that we were now the Eastern Division champions. "Morgan Magic" had taken the ball club from two games over .500 to 16 games over .500 at the conclusion of the season. It was an impressive turnaround. Our victory in capturing the Eastern Division championship became the first time since 1918 that a Red Sox ball club had finished first twice in a three-year period. We also finished the season drawing 2.5 million paid admissions.

We would now face a strong and very talented Oakland A's baseball club. They had won 104 games during the regular season. They would be odds-on favorites in the championship series. During the regular season they had gone 9-3 against us, yet in six of the losses we had lost by two runs or less.

Our big question now was whether "Morgan Magic" could once again pull off another miracle and handle the heavily favored A's and take us back to a World Series. Unfortunately, we had never played well in the Oakland Coliseum, and I had no answer as to why. Naturally our media had all the answers as to why, but I wasn't certain too many of them were valid.

We had spent a great deal of time the last month of the season scouting and following the Oakland ball club in preparation of meeting the A's in the playoffs. Our scouts were looking for the strengths and weaknesses of their personnel to give us whatever edge we might uncover. I had Eddie Kasko, our scouting director and an excellent judge of talent, and Joe Stephenson, one of our top major league scouts, covering the Oakland club in the weeks preceding the playoffs. Kasko and Stephenson were extremely talented scouts with years of experience. Their input and scouting intelligence on the A's would be turned over to Morgan and his staff to analyze in depth before taking on the Oakland ball club. The reports from Kasko and Stephenson were thorough, in depth, and complete.

When I met with Morgan prior to our first ball game against Oakland in Fenway Park, Morgan as always was upbeat and confident that we could handle the A's. His confidence was encouraging, but realistically I knew we had our hands full with this Oakland ball club. They were a solid club without many holes. We had hit .283 to the A's .263 team average, but they were second in the American League with 156 home runs, and they led the American League with a 3.44 ERA. They also had the most dominant reliever in the league in Dennis Eckersley, a future Hall of Famer. He had 45 saves as compared to our team total of only 37. This was the same Eckersley whom I had traded to the Chicago Cubs for Bill Buckner a few years earlier.

The A's pitching staff was headed by right-hander Dave Stewart. Stewart was 21-12, followed in the rotation by Bob Welch at 17-9 and Steve Davis at 16-7. Their bullpen was also solid, anchored by Eckersley and a middle relief core of Eric Plunk, Gene Nelson, and left-hander Rick Honeycutt, a player I had acquired and brought to the major leagues while I was the general manager of the Seattle Mariners. Their pitching strength was impressive.

The Oakland offense was powered by Jose Canseco, at .307 with 42 home runs and 124 RBIs. Dave Henderson (our former Red Sox hero who many felt was lacking) hit .304 with 24 home runs and 94 RBIs, and Mark McGwire had 32 home runs and 99 RBIs. Their offense also included former Red Sox third baseman Carney Lansford and my old friend Don Baylor as a designated hitter.

We had struggled the last few weeks of the season and had not finished strong. Adding to our problems, "Oil Can" was suffering with what appeared to be a blood clot in his arm. We were seriously concerned about Boyd. After consulting with Dr. Pappas, I made the decision to place him on the disabled list. He had ended the regular season with 18 wins, and so his absence from our rotation would hurt greatly.

Somehow I had a premonition that either Eckersley, Baylor, or Henderson would come back to haunt us. Whenever the A's had a lead in late innings, Eckersley was nearly invincible. I often wondered what motivated the Oakland brain trust of La Russa and Dave Duncan to convert Eckersley from a starter to a reliever. Whatever their reasoning, it was a stroke of genius because it transformed the Oakland bullpen from average to dominant.

Hurst would be our Game 1 starter against Stewart. Clemens had pitched just three days earlier against the Indians, and Hurst had four or five days' rest. Hurst was the logical starter for Game 1.

Hurst pitched extremely well, giving up only a solo home run to Canseco on the first pitch in the fourth inning. It would remain a one-run game until the bottom of the seventh when we were able to tie the ball game 1-1 on a sacrifice fly by Boggs.

With one out in the top of the eighth, Lansford doubled off Hurst and then our former hero of a few seasons ago, Henderson, singled to score Lansford with what eventually proved to be the winning run. As soon as Oakland scored in the eighth to take a 2-1 lead, Eckersley was summoned from the bullpen to nail down the victory for the A's. That scenario would haunt us the rest of the series.

In the ninth inning we put two men on base and with two outs. Boggs came to bat with an opportunity to tie or win the game for us. It was a classic confrontation. The American League batting champion faced the American League's best reliever. Every single fan in Fenway Park was on his feet, and the din of noise emanating from the stands and reverberating throughout the ballpark was deafening. The count went to two and two, but on the next pitch Eckersley struck Boggs out. Boggs in a postgame interview admitted he had taken a bad swing on the pitch that he struck out on. He said, "Eckersley had fooled him" on the pitch.

"I blew it in the ninth inning, and it was my fault we lost the game," he said. It was to Boggs's credit that he uncharacteristically accepted the blame for the loss.

In Game 2 we started Clemens against Steve Davis of the A's at Fenway Park. We desperately needed to leave home with at least one victory. Clemens and Davis hooked up in a great matchup, and the game was scoreless until we took a 2-0 lead in the bottom of the sixth on a line drive single by Burks.

In the seventh inning the A's got to Clemens as they scored three runs on four hits highlighted by a towering two-run home run by Canseco. They now led 3-2. However, in the bottom of the seventh, Gedman hit a solo home run to tie the ball game. Stanley had relieved Clemens to start the eighth inning. The game remained deadlocked at 3-3 going into the top of the ninth. Smith took over for us in the top of the ninth, and another capacity crowd of more than 35,000 were on their feet at Fenway.

"We've got to win this ball game. We can't go out to Oakland down two games to none," I told myself out loud.

My wife turned to me to ask what I had just said, and I told her I was just thinking out loud. I desperately hoped that Smith could hold the A's at bay until we could retake the lead and even the series at one game apiece.

After retiring the first batter in the top of the ninth, catcher Ron Hassey reached first on a walk and advanced to second on a ground out. Then weak-hitting shortstop Walt Weiss was up next. With two outs he singled into left-center field scoring Hassey, and Oakland had a 4-3 lead. Once again it was Eckersley, relieving Gene Nelson in the seventh inning, coming into the game, and slamming the door shut on us. He picked up his second save in two games.

In Game 3 we had Boddicker facing Welch. We jumped off to an early 5-0 lead against Welch, scoring three runs in the first inning, thanks primarily to a two-run double by Greenwell and scored two more runs in the top of the second. With Boddicker on the mound and a 5-0 lead, I turned to Haywood, but before I could say a word, he spoke.

"Let's just hope we can hang on to this one. We need it badly."

I turned away without saying a word. I knew he was absolutely right.

Too often ball clubs will get off to a lead only to allow their opponent the opportunity to get right back into the ball game in the bottom or top of the very next inning. I banished such a thought from my mind.

Our worst nightmare, however, came back to haunt us in the bottom of the second inning. Boddicker took the mound with a comfortable 5-0 lead, but the bottom fell out. McGwire led off with a solo home run, and a few batters later, Lansford drove a line drive two-run homer over the left-field fence to carry the A's right back into the ball game. For me that was the defining moment of the entire series. We lost a commanding lead, and the momentum of the ball game now changed dramatically.

We failed to score in the top of the third. In the bottom of the third as we clung to a one-run lead, Hassey hit a two-run homer to drive Boddicker out of the ball game and put Oakland in front 6-5 to stay. The ball game went downhill from that point on. Gardner relieved Boddicker and pitched decently, allowing a single run in the bottom of the fifth. We battled back to score a single run in the top of the seventh to make it a 7-6 ball game. It gave us a slight glimmer of hope.

We went to the bottom of the eighth trailing still by only a run. We had played the A's for 25 innings of the American League Championship Series having lost 2-1 and 4-3, and here we were once again losing by only a single run. The specter of Eckersley, however, was always looming in the background. In the bottom of the eighth Oakland would take us out of the ball game for good. Maybe it was justifiable retribution for Henderson as he slammed a two-run homer off Gardner to propel the A's to an eventual 10-6 win and a commanding 3-0 lead in the series. Eckersley took the mound and shut us down once again. He picked up another save, and we were now in deep, deep trouble.

It was a major disappointment for Boddicker to pitch so poorly in Game 3. He had pitched extremely well down the stretch after we had acquired him, winning seven ball games with a 2.69 ERA. With the odds stacked squarely against us now, it would be difficult to climb out of the hole we had dug ourselves into.

As I walked into Morgan's office the next day before Game 4, it was still classic Morgan, upbeat, confident, "six two and even." Not a negative thought in his mind. It was impossible to be negative around him, no matter what the odds. I loved him for his eternal optimism.

Hurst would start Game 4 for us. Oakland would bring back Stewart, their ace. Hurst gave up a solo home run to Canseco, his third of the series, and they would get another single run in the bottom of the third. In the top of the sixth, we closed the gap to 2-1 on a solo home run by Gedman. Hurst was relieved by Smithson in the fifth inning. It remained a 2-1 ball game until the bottom of the eighth when Oakland scored two runs to take a 4-1 lead. Like death and taxation, once again, Eckersley came out of the bullpen in the ninth to close us down for his fourth save of the series. It gave Oakland the American League championship. Eckersley was rightfully selected as the Most Valuable Player of the series.

Oakland had scored an impressive sweep. Yet we battled them throughout in nearly every game, except for the 10-6 loss, of the series and that was a one-run game until the eighth inning. But unfortunately close only counts in horseshoes.

As I reviewed the entire season in my mind, it became obvious to me if we were to win it all, I needed to add some more punch in our offense, one more starter, and get "Oil Can" sound. If Boyd was healthy, a starting rotation of Clemens, Hurst, Boddicker, and Boyd might well be the best starting four in Major League Baseball. A more solid middle reliever would shore up our bullpen. If we were able to address these needs over the winter, we would enhance our chances to get back to the World Series.

It was also obvious that Rice, after 16 brilliant seasons as a .298 hitter with 382 home runs and 1,500 RBIs was now beginning to show signs of slowing down both in the field and at bat. Rice had had a brilliant career for the Red Sox, playing in 14 seasons and went into the 1988 season as a .302 hitter with 364 home runs and 1,351 RBIs. He had been selected to the American League All-Star team in nine successive seasons, in testimony to his outstanding career.

I was also hoping that the Wade Boggs–Margo Adams scenario would fade away for good, and that distraction would be gone. It proved to be only wishful thinking on my part for the local Boston media wouldn't let the story die. There was also a story circulating that *Penthouse* magazine was planning to run a tell-all feature story in the spring. The local media were salivating over that possibility.

Our farm system had been highly productive, and our major league ball club now had 19 players from our system on the 40-man roster. We had an excellent scouting staff, although the staff was beginning to age a bit. We might have to, in time, begin developing some younger scouts to complement and replace our older scouts. The quality of their judgment honed over a lifetime of experience, was exceptional and extremely difficult to replace, if that was at all possible.

As I looked back on the first five years of my tenure as the Red Sox general manager, we had won two Eastern Division titles and an American League championship, and we had come within one pitch of winning a world championship. We had also drawn more than two million paid admissions for three straight seasons, actually averaging more than 2.2 million per season, and that was only the second time in Red Sox history that had ever happened. Still in all, the disappointments of not winning "the big one" made whatever we had accomplished to date unfulfilling and unfinished.

Another major disappointment to me was our failure to sign two young players we drafted. I felt they would have been tremendous additions to our major league ball club and to our organization.

The first such player was one we drafted in the third round of the 1985 free agent draft, out of Jefferson High School in Tampa, Florida, Tino Martinez, the same Tino Martinez who would go on to play for the Mariners and become a standout performer on some great Yankees world championship ball clubs. George Digby, a superior grassroots scout, with excellent judgment was extremely high on Martinez, who was an outfielder in high school. When Digby recommended a player, you took heed. His track record and reputation were that good.

Digby told me that he felt Martinez would hit with good power in time. He loved his overall tools and potential. He had been following him for more than two years and was extremely anxious to have us draft him. We had him double checked, and our reports all came back positive. I told Digby that I was confident that we'd draft him in the first three or four rounds.

We drafted Constantino "Tino" Martinez in the third round and then attempted to sign him, but unfortunately we were unable to do so. At age 17, his mother felt that he was too young to leave home, and she rebuked our constant financial offers. His family was a very close-knit Cuban family, and Martinez was the apple of their eye. Not only was he an outstanding baseball talent, he was also an outstanding student in the classroom.

Martinez ended up attending the University of Tampa right in his own backyard. He became a three-time Division II All-American and the MVP in the World Amateur Championships in Parma, Italy, his junior year. He set the University of Tampa's all-time record for home runs and RBIs. He was selected to the *Sporting News* College All-American team in 1988 and led the USA baseball team to a gold medal in the Summer Olympics. He was also selected as an academic All-American. The Mariners drafted Martinez in the first round of the 1988 draft and signed him shortly thereafter.

Had I been able to convince his parents, and primarily his mother, to allow him to sign with the Red Sox out of high school, he would have been a tremendous addition to our ball club in 1988, 1989, and 1990. He was an outstanding young man from a wonderful family, and his talents and leadership qualities would have been assets. My failure to sign him despite my best efforts was a huge loss to the club.

A second major disappointment to me and to the Red Sox was our failure to sign our 1986 first-round draft choice. We drafted Greg McMurtry out of Brockton, Massachusetts. McMurtry was an extremely talented athlete. He was big and strong at six foot three and 195 pounds and had outstanding speed. As a center fielder on his high school team, he had hit over .400 and led the Boxers to a 22-1 record. He was also a brilliant football player having caught 58 passes and scored 20 touchdowns. He was heavily recruited by every major college in the nation for football and heavily scouted by professional baseball.

His football coach at Brockton was the legendary Armond Colombo. Coach Colombo was a fellow alumnus of Stonehill College in Easton, Massachusetts, and we had been teammates on our college baseball team. The principal of his high school was also a classmate. Dr. Daniel Kulick, the assistant superintendent of schools, was my roommate and teammate on the basketball team at Stonehill. They were all of a mind that we had a definite chance to sign McMurtry.

If you were able to create the absolutely perfect intelligence scenario to obtain information on any player, we had it. From multiple sources I was told he was an outstanding young man, highly competitive, intelligent, and tough. I felt that the appeal of playing for the local team, the Boston Red Sox, was a huge plus for us. There was, however, a fly in the ointment named Bo Schembechler of the University of Michigan.

I brought McMurtry and his family to Fenway Park for dinner and a ball game and to negotiate a contract. We offered him a signing bonus in excess of $200,000 plus a full college scholarship. It was the largest cash bonus ever offered to a Red Sox free agent player at that time. They asked for a day or so to consider our offer. I tried to press home our offer and the allure of playing for the Red Sox in his own backyard. I was concerned if McMurtry left Fenway still uncommitted to us, he would be under a full-court press from Schembechler and the Michigan football program. I was right.

We never were able to dissuade him from going to Michigan to play football. He went on to play in the Rose Bowl and become an All-American, and he spent a five-year career in the National Football League. He never played a day of professional baseball. I am still convinced to this day that had McMurtry signed with the Red Sox, he would have become an out-standing major league center fielder with a long and productive career in a Red Sox uniform. I am also convinced that had we signed both Martinez and McMurtry and added the mix of talent we had on our big league club already, they well could have been the catalyst that carried us right back to the World Series.

But it was time to look to the future. Morgan and I would spend a great deal of time along with our overall baseball staff brainstorming every aspect of our ball club and our organizational talent as we began the process of retooling our ball club for the upcoming season.

We had won the Eastern Division title, but it was a hollow and unsatis-factory victory. We ran up against an Oakland ball club that was better, and we would have to go through them again next season if we were to get back to the World Series.

The constant challenge is to get there, but once you're there, you have to take your chances. Certainly Red Sox fans had suffered long enough for 70 seasons of frustration. I desperately wanted to be the one to break that spell.

CHAPTER 4

1989

A Season of Mediocrity

Coming off a division championship season and with Joe Morgan now riding a crest of huge popularity as the field manager right from the start of spring training, Red Sox fans were looking forward with optimism and eager anticipation to the upcoming season. The thought of "Morgan Magic" for an entire season was exhilarating.

That December, once again, I went to the annual baseball winter meetings in search of some additional offensive help. Our starting rotation consisted of Roger Clemens, Mike Boddicker, Bruce Hurst, and Dennis "Oil Can" Boyd, and the nucleus of our bullpen was Bob Stanley and Lee Smith. It was obvious, however, that we needed one more solid starter and more depth in our bullpen while adding some offensive power. There was still concern about Boyd's health. Should he go down, it would greatly increase our need for pitching depth in our starting pitching rotation.

But while I was working on reinforcing our pitching, I was also trying to finalize Hurst's contract. Hurst, his agent, and I had been in negotiations since before the beginning of the 1988 season. I had offered him a multiyear deal, but we had still been unable to reach an agreement. During the December meetings we—John Harrington, Haywood Sullivan, and I—met with Hurst and his agent, who was also in talks with the San Diego Padres at the same time, to seriously try to solidify Hurst's future with the Red Sox.

After a day and a half of negotiations, we finally agreed upon a dollar amount for a multiyear contract. The Padres came right back, however, and matched the financial package we had tendered. An hour after our meeting ended, Hurst's agent called us back and asked for a special incentive where the Red Sox would have to pay Hurst's contract should there be a players' strike or a walkout and no baseball was being played. John, Haywood, and I told him that we could not agree to that proposal even though I wanted to retain Hurst because he was vital to our ball club. Shockingly the Padres agreed to the incentive, and Hurst signed with them. I was devastated.

Hurst would tell me years later that a short time after he signed with San Diego, he realized he had made a mistake leaving the Red Sox and would regret doing so for the rest of his career.

With the loss of Hurst, I turned my attention to talking to other general managers about trade possibilities. I had been exploring the options before this time in order to see what might be available to fill our needs. I had indications that Montreal would be willing to trade a right-handed starting pitcher named John Dopson. I had decided to take a chance on the 26-year-old, providing that I could acquire him as a first-year player on my terms and his contract terms would be extremely reasonable. With only one year of experience, he was not eligible for salary arbitration. We could basically have control of his salary for the next few seasons, and hopefully he could prove to be effective for us as a starter.

When we got to the winter meetings, I made contact almost immediately with the Expos' general manager, Bill Stoneman. After some negotiation, I agreed to trade shortstop Spike Owen and right-hander pitcher Dan Gakeler to Montreal for Dopson and shortstop Luis Rivera.

Spike Owen had been a steady, solid, but not spectacular performer for us, but he was a factor in our reaching the 1986 World Series. Owen was a competitor and a solid team player, but his overall physical skills were not great. His drive and intensity made him play beyond the level of his physical skills. We'd miss his competitive nature in our clubhouse. I felt that based on our organization reports, the pitcher we traded, Gakeler, was not a future major league prospect. On the other hand, I had acquired a serviceable shortstop in Rivera. He had decent physical skills and could also do a more than adequate job at shortstop with a decent range. But more importantly I had acquired Dopson, who hopefully could contribute as a starting pitcher. Dopson had pitched for Montreal at the major league level the previous season after six years in the minor league system and had struggled, going 3-11 with a 3.04 ERA. Most of our reports considered him a fringe major league starting pitcher, but one considered Dopson a definite

FROM THE DESK OF
LOU GORMAN

My love for the Red Sox started at a young age and continued up through my college years at Stonehill College, a liberal arts school in Massachusetts. I followed every game and every season religiously.

LOU GORMAN COLLECTION

Many of the leadership skills I used as a general manager, I learned from my time in the Navy.

Until 2004 the 1986 Red Sox team was closer to winning a World Series than any team in Red Sox history after 1918. We were one pitch away from the world championship and I always wanted to bring the title to Boston on my watch.

PHOTO COURTESY OF THE BOSTON RED SOX

PHOTO COURTESY OF THE BOSTON RED SOX

Roger Clemens was our ace throughout my tenure as Red Sox general manager. Clemens and I faced a long drawn-out contract negotiation following the 1986 season and he left spring training in protest. However, I have greatly admired him for his tenacity on the mound and his competitive nature. He is a definite Hall of Fame pitcher.

In 1987 the Boston media, known for their constant negativity and love of controversy, made a big deal over a mistake I made in a trade with Fred Claire, Tommy Lasorda, and the Los Angeles Dodgers.

I agreed to send shortstop Glen Hoffman to L.A. for a future prospect or cash, but I forgot to get a reverse waiver I needed to make the trade. The press rightly criticized me for my error but continued to besiege the Red Sox and me for days after the incident occurred.

LOU GORMAN COLLECTION

One of the highlights of being a member of the Boston Red Sox organization is being able to meet and work with former Red Sox greats, such as Ted Williams (top left and middle left), Bobby Doerr (middle center), and Johnny Pesky (bottom right).

As a child I idolized Ted Williams (top left and middle left) and as general manager I was able to see him at spring training every year when he helped to coach our prospects in hitting.

Prior to the 1988 season I traded Calvin Schiraldi and Al Nipper to the Chicago Cubs to obtain Lee Smith (right), who was an outstanding hurler. I later traded Smith to the St. Louis Cardinals for Tom Brunansky.

One of the most difficult decisions I had to make as a general manager was to release Red Sox great Jim Rice (far left) after the 1989 season. Rice spent his entire career in Boston and was inducted into the Boston Red Sox Hall of Fame in 1995.

Red Sox third baseman Wade Boggs was a very talented hitter and a major offensive producer on our ball club. Unfortunately in 1992 Boggs and I were unable to reach an agreement on a new contract and he left Boston for the New York Yankees.

PHOTO COURTESY OF THE BOSTON RED SOX

LOU GORMAN COLLECTION

I selected Joe Morgan (right) to take over as manager of the Red Sox in 1988 after John McNamara was fired. Morgan brought to the team a never-ending optimism that ignited a streak of success the media labeled "Morgan Magic."

We drafted Curt Schilling in the second round of the 1986 amateur draft, but two years later I traded him and prospect Brady Anderson for Mike Boddicker, a move that helped us win our division that season.

PHOTO COURTESY OF THE BOSTON RED SOX

LOU GORMAN COLLECTION

The early 1990s brought a lot of changes for the Red Sox organization. In the spring of 1992 Jean Yawkey passed away, ending the family's longtime ownership of the club. The next spring the Red Sox dedicated (above) and opened their new spring training facility in Fort Myers, Florida.

Dan Duquette (right) took over as Red Sox general manager after I was fired in 1993. Because of a change in ownership, he actually had more autonomous control of baseball operations than I did.

LOU GORMAN COLLECTION

In 2002 I was inducted into the Boston Red Sox Hall of Fame. It is such an honor to be a part of the legacy of this great organization.

The current ownership of the Red Sox—Larry Lucchino (far left), Tom Werner (middle right), and John Henry (far right)—and general manager Theo Epstein (not pictured) did an amazing job to bring to Boston a world championship that has been 86 years in the making.

prospect who could be a solid third or fourth major league starter. If Dopson could help our team, it could be a big plus for us.

Our scouts working the lobby of the hotel headquarters heard rumors at the meeting that the Cincinnati Reds were looking to move first baseman Nick Esasky. Our scouting reports on Esasky were positive. They indicated that Esasky was a player who could hit with power from the right side of the plate and who could be especially effective in Fenway Park. He was defensively sound and a quality person on a ball club. He was coming off a season where he hit only .243 with 15 home runs and 62 runs driven in. I made a call to Murray Cook, the Reds' general manager, and we set up a meeting with them.

After one or two meetings with the Reds, who had expressed an interest in Todd Benzinger and a right-handed pitcher from our farm system named Jeff Sellers, I brought up Esasky. I could tell from our conversation with Cook and his staff that Esasky could be available.

As we continued to talk about attempting to work out the terms of a trade that would hopefully help both ball clubs, I recalled a report from Larry Thomas, one of our scouts in the Midwest, who had submitted a favorable report on Reds left-handed reliever named Rob Murphy. I suggested to Cook that we take a break to allow us to caucus, but I felt we had a basis to work something out. Cook agreed.

When we broke off our meeting for an hour or two, I met with our staff to get their total input. Eddie Kasko, our scouting director, who was an excellent judge of talent, also brought up Murphy's name for consideration. Kasko indicated that Murphy was a workhorse and could be very effective in short relief, particularly against left-handers. Finally after everyone had their say, I suggested that I propose trading Sellers, who was a fringe prospect going 7-8 with 5.28 ERA in 22 major league starts, and Benzinger, who was considered a productive extra player at the big league level and had been in our farm system for seven years, for Esasky and Murphy.

As I analyzed the possibility of the trade, I felt that Sellers and Benzinger could be expendable to acquire Esasky and Murphy. Esasky would potentially give us a power-hitting first baseman and Murphy would give us a needed and effective left-hander in our bullpen. I also knew that should I acquired Esasky, his contract would be up at the end of the 1989 season. I would have to negotiate an extension to his contract or lose him. If he gave us the productive season that I hoped he could give us, I'd take my chances.

I'd find a way to sign him to an extension and keep him in a Red Sox uniform.

We met once again with Cook and his staff. I proposed Benzinger and Sellers for Esasky and Murphy. Cook said they would need another player to make the deal, and I told him I did not feel that it would be equitable for us to include another prospect. Cook gave one or two names that they would take as a player to be named later—but no later than the end of the upcoming season. Once I had an indication of whom they had in mind, I asked for a few minutes to discuss those names with Kasko and scouts Frank Malzone and Wayne Britton, who said if I felt that Esasky and Murphy could help our ball club, I should make the deal. I went back to Cook and told him we had a deal. That following January I would deliver them the player to be named later—right-handed pitcher Luis Vasquez.

Sellers would never pitch effectively at the big league level, nor would Vasquez ever be a factor for the Reds at the major league level. Benzinger would play a limited role for the Reds but never developed into a front-line major league player. But Esasky and Murphy would dramatically impact our ball club in the upcoming season.

I continued to search for some help to shore up our bullpen but had little success at the winter meetings other than acquiring Murphy. I then began to turn my attention to the waiver wires in the hope of finding a veteran hurler who might be cut loose by some ball club because of financial restraints. On January 5 I decided to take a chance on a veteran right-handed pitcher named Dennis Lamp. He was 37 years old with 11 years of major league experience for the Chicago Cubs, the White Sox, the Toronto Blue Jays, and the Oakland A's. Lamp, who had had sporadic success after going 11-0 in relief in 105 innings for Toronto in 1985, had elected to accept free agency from Oakland after appearing in only 36 games in relief, finishing with a 1-3 in 1987 record. After he pitched for us in 1988 I signed Lamp to a Triple-A contract but invited him into our major league spring training camp with a conditional major league contract if he made the club after camp.

I signed Mike Smithson to a Pawtucket Triple-A contract and invited him to camp as well. Smithson was a former Red Sox prospect who had been traded to Texas and then to Minnesota where he had gone 15-13, 15-14, and 13-14, averaging more than 235 innings pitched each season. I was once again taking a flyer on Smithson, but basically, as with Lamp, the risk was minimal because they were both signed to minor league contracts.

If they had good springs and our staff felt they could contribute at the major league level, it would be a win-win situation all around. We just might get lucky with the two of them and fill two holes in our bullpen.

In addition to Lamp and Smithson, we also had Stanley, Murphy, Wes Gardner, Lee Smith as a closer, and possibly left-hander Tom Bolton from our farm system. We could be decent, if not better, but there were some big ifs. Bolton had been primarily a reliever in his minor league career, but we had nurtured him along both as a reliever and as a starter the past couple of seasons. He had pitched extremely well at Pawtucket the past season, going 12-5 with a 2.89 ERA as a starter, but when we had brought him to the big leagues in early August, we had struggled in short relief. He had also started one or two games with limited success. It was still a recommendation of our Triple-A manager, Ed Nottle, and our organizational pitching coach, Lee Stange, that Bolton could fill a role out of the pen to get left-handed hitters out and could spot start.

The rest of our ball club would be anchored by Wade Boggs at third; Marty Barrett at second; the newly acquired Esasky at first; Jody Reed at shortstop; Ellis Burks, Mike Greenwell, Jim Rice (but beginning to slow down offensively), and Dwight Evans in the outfield; and Rich Gedman and Rick Cerone behind the plate. I had picked up some bench and role players to give us some depth in Danny Heep, a left-handed hitting outfielder, who could also fill in at first; Randy Kutcher, a right-handed hitter, who could play just about all three outfield positions; utility infielder Ed Romero; and Luis Rivera.

We had our share of question marks. Our own local media collectively picked us to finish anywhere from first to fourth in the division. Were we good enough to catch and overtake the Toronto Blue Jays or the Baltimore Orioles, who appeared to be media favorites to capture the Eastern Division title? Only time would tell. We would have to stay injury free, our bullpen would have to hold up, and Greg Harris and Dopson would have to step up and perform well in our starting rotation.

When we finally got to Winter Haven for spring training, I met with Morgan and his coaching staff—Al Bumbry, Dick Berardino, pitching coach Bill Fischer, Richie Hebner, and Roc Slider. We spent a day evaluating our ball club. The consensus of our staff was simply that if our additions to the bullpen were solid and Dopson could win 14 or 15 games, we would be very competitive, barring injuries. Morgan, as always, was very optimistic and confident that we would be very competitive. I still didn't feel that comfortable, and I was determined to keep checking the waiver wires, talking to other ball clubs, and closely following the releases out of the various spring training camps.

The media made spring training a time of generated controversy for the team. Before we left Boston for camp, Morgan had mentioned two events he would like to be able to attend during spring training, which would require him to miss two and a half days of camp. One was the annual St. Patrick's Day parade in Walpole, his hometown, where he was to be honored as the parade marshall. The second was to be the speaker and honoree at a communion breakfast at his alma mater, Boston College. I agreed to let him attend both events, convinced that the coaching staff could handle the workouts and drills during it without any problems. I was wrong. The media made a big deal over Morgan's absences. In a practical sense his absence from one workout and one ball game had little or no bearing whatever on the ball club's conditioning or preparation for the upcoming season, but it did provide the media with the first chink in Morgan's halo of adulation, and they wouldn't let it die.

The Margo Adams–Boggs scenario also continued to be a disruptive influence in spring camp, especially after the *Penthouse* article where Adams told a reporter about Boggs, his sex life, and the sexual adventures of other players when they were on the road. After the story broke, many of the players and their wives were very upset. On one or two occasions, Boggs and some of the other players got into unpleasant shouting matches. I was worried about the clubhouse morale because we could not afford to break from camp as a house divided. We had enough question marks in terms of the club this season, and an erosion of morale could be potentially very harmful. I discussed the issue with Morgan, but he told me he could deal with it. After talking to him I was convinced he would handle the problem, and I dismissed the issue from my mind.

In reaction to the national media exposure regarding the Adams–Boggs incident, a request was made for Boggs to appear on national television with Barbara Walters to discuss the issue and his alleged affair with Adams. It was one thing to face a horde of local and national media on a daily basis searching, probing, and questioning Boggs, (if he would speak to them, which he did not desire to do), or any member of the organization who was asked to discuss the issue, but for Boggs to appear on national television I felt was too perilous for Boggs to even consider. When I heard that Boggs was seriously considering appearing on the show, I asked our vice president of public relations Dick Bresciani to talk with him and find out if he was serious. Bresciani came back and told me that Boggs was definitely intending to go forward with the interview, I decided I had better have a personal talk with Boggs.

After a workout one day, I asked Boggs to come visit with me in the office. After he showered and dressed, he dropped by my office. I asked him how he and his family were handling things, and if there was anything that the Red Sox or I could personally do for him. He told me that he and Debbie were handling it okay. I told him I had heard that he was considering going on national television with Walters to discuss the Adams incident.

"Wade, do you really think that's a good idea? Why put yourself in such a precarious position on national television and subject yourself to more critical exposure that can't help you or your family?" I asked.

"Lou, I've talked to Barbara Walters personally and she told me she would send me her questions in advance of the interview. That I could review the questions and discard any that I did not want to answer, and that she would only ask me the questions that she would send me."

"Wade, once you're in that studio on national television, you're at their mercy. I'm certain Miss Walters is well intentioned, honest, and sincere, but I just don't understand why you want to exacerbate the problem any further. Wade, it's your call, but I think it's a mistake."

Before the meeting concluded, Boggs told me that Walters was coming to Winter Haven in the next few days to tape the interview. I told Boggs I wished him well and that I hoped it was the right decision.

About two or three days later, Haywood was sitting out on a small veranda outside his office on the second floor watching the pregame infield practice. We were playing a spring training exhibition game against the White Sox. From his vantage point, he could see the entire ballpark at Chain O' Lakes Stadium, and he also had a commanding view of the main entrance. As his gaze wandered to the main entrance, he spotted a team of television cameramen and Walters making their way through the turnstiles into the stadium. Because my office was adjacent to his, he called me to come out to the veranda immediately. I rushed over, assuming something had happened to one of our players during the infield workout.

"That's Barbara Walters and her camera crew coming into the stadium," he said as he pointed to the main entrance. "I don't want them filming or interviewing Boggs or his family in the stadium. You had better go down there and talk to her."

I went down into the stadium and asked the ticket-takers at the main turnstile if they had recognized Walters when she came through a few minutes ago.

"Everyone recognized her, and we all asked for her autograph," one of them told me.

"Did they purchase tickets?" I asked.

"Yes," they answered in unison.

I then proceeded to locate where Walters and her crew were seated and took a seat right behind them. I felt like an undercover CIA agent on a spying mission as I slipped into my seat. My mission was not to allow Walters to interview Debbie Boggs, her family, or anyone in the stadium. I attempted to be as inauspicious as possible, but as some local fans from Boston passed by my seat, they recognized me and addressed me with comments about the ball club or some personal greetings. After this personal attention continued from different fans, Walters and her crew now turned to pay attention to me, unaware of who I was or what my position with the ball club might be. My cover was blown.

When the ball game ended and most of the fans had left the ballpark, the camera crew began to set up their cameras. I assumed they planned to have Walters conduct the interview with Boggs right there. At that point, I stepped forward and told her we could not allow any interviews in the ballpark. She asked me who I was, and I introduced myself and my position to her. She was extremely gracious and charming. She then told her camera crew to dismantle the cameras, and they proceeded to leave the ballpark. The interview with Boggs was held at the local Holiday Inn. In the interview, Boggs came across in a sympathetic and humane manner, and true to her promise, Walters stayed with the prearranged script.

Around this time, Jim Baker, the veteran radio/television columnist for the *Boston Herald*, made mention in one of his columns that I would be filling in on the next Red Sox spring training televised game in lieu of Sean McDonough, who was off on a network assignment. In talking about my participation in the telecast that he said that I would most likely ignore Boggs's upcoming television interview with Walters.

During the telecast, I criticized Baker's statement that I would intentionally not mention the Boggs interview because I felt the commentary was uncalled for. And because Boggs was not playing in the game, any comment on the interview would be out of place.

"Unless an incident or an event has a direct impact on a ball game in progress, I feel it does not deserve mention during the course of the broadcast," I said on the air.

(It has always been my personal opinion, and I feel strongly about this issue, that play-by-play announcers often spend too much time yakking about insignificant or unrelated subject matter that has little or no bearing on the game in progress. As a baseball fan, I want to hear about what is happening on the field, not about an incident that does not affect the action. Some play-by-play announcers inundate you with too much information and technology and make the simplest play sound like the final out of the seventh game of the World Series. They will make a routine play sound like a dramatic game-saving event.)

My comments either were relayed to Baker or he had been listening to the broadcast because the next day in his regular radio/television column, he proceeded to take me to task. I was incensed because I felt his criticism of me was unfair and inappropriate. In response I wrote a letter to the *Boston Herald* that evening and faxed it off the next morning. I might have been a bit too harsh in my written reaction to Baker's criticism, but I felt so strongly about the issue. The *Herald* printed my letter in a special manner to highlight my comments about Baker.

Baker was livid when he read my letter and he proceeded to call me in a very emotional and agitated state. He continued to berate me for my letter and my criticism. As he continued to rant and rave at me, I felt I'd heard enough so I proceeded to tell him I was going to hang up the phone, and I did.

(The strained relationship with Baker continued for a while but as time passed I would run into him at various events—press conferences at Fenway and social events—and gradually we began to let bygones be bygones. We have developed a very cordial and friendly relationship. The incident, in time, became ancient history for good.)

With all of the distractions, our spring exhibition season was lackluster because we went 12-19, but we weren't overly concerned because it is often impossible to gauge a team's final record based on what they do during the spring. Individual performances will give you some indication, but I have always been concerned primarily with the following factors in spring camp: 1) getting your veteran players, the heart and soul of your ball club, in top physical condition, staying injury free, and getting them the needed maximum playing time in competition, particularly the last 10 days before breaking from camp; 2) giving your younger players and major league players who are recovering from injuries from the past season maximum exposure in the early competition of spring training; 3) having a well-organized camp with emphasis on conditioning, fundamentals, and instruction; 4) conducting consistent staff evaluations of your talent in camp and investigating ways to maximize the performance of that talent; 5) working to build a positive attitude throughout the entire organization but specifically among the 25 men who will open the season on the major league roster.

Besides the leadership of the manager, a talented coaching staff is absolutely essential to the success of any camp and the performance of a ball club during the season. In the past players spent many years honing their skills and the fundamentals in the minor leagues, but with the expansion that has occurred in present-day Major League Baseball, players are now promoted to the big leagues when they are still learning the ropes after only two or three seasons of minor league competition. That teaching must continue when they reach the big leagues in order to maximize their talent and potential.

We opened the regular season with four losses, two to Balitmore and two to Kansas City, but we won our home opener 5-2 against Cleveland behind Mike Boddicker. Then "Oil Can" Boyd struggled in his first start of the season and lost to the Indians 10-6. But Dopson and Clemens won their first three starts. By the end of the first month, we were 10-12 and tied for third in the American League Eastern Division.

The first hint of future problems came in early May when Boyd's shoulder problems from the past reoccurred, and we had to put him on the disabled list. (He would end up making only 10 starts, half of them late in the season, and would win only three games.) We continued to play right around .500, winning one and then losing one. We were unable to put together any sort of a consistent winning streak. By the end of May we were 24-24 but remarkably in second place because no one in the division was playing much better.

On occasion during the roller-coaster of wins and losses, the media would refer back to Morgan's absence and some of the players' rumblings late in spring training when Morgan held a clubhouse meeting to criticize them for, what he considered, a lack of intensity and emotion and being a "dead ass" team. Supposedly, according to the media, the resentment carried over into the season. I spent time with the club to try to get a reading on the rumors. Morgan continued to assure me that there was no morale problem. He was convinced that we could make a run at the division title once again, and the more time I spent with the ball club in the clubhouse, around the batting cage, and in the hotel, I also became convinced there was no morale problem.

But there was one complaint. Stanley became critical of Morgan, complaining that Morgan misused him in the bullpen by letting him sit for stretches as long as 10 days and then not pitching him enough. Morgan used Stanley primarily as a reliever, although he did start one or two games. It was not like Stanley to be critical of his manager because he had always handled criticism and problems in the past with class and character, but his complaint against Morgan was answered by Morgan saying simply, "I utilize whoever can do the job for us, period." That did not sit well with Stanley, and he spoke out publicly against the way he was being treated.

I contemplated talking to Stanley personally about the situation, but then realized I would be interfering with Morgan's authority over the ball club, and once a manager's control is undermined, he's lost the respect of his players and control of his clubhouse. I decided instead to discuss the matter with Morgan directly and let him handle the problem in his own way, which he did.

By the end of June we were 36-39 and continuing to struggle. We were really never able to break away from the pack in our division.

In the beginning of July one small incident occurred that involved Lee Smith and our participation in the annual exhibition game in Cooperstown, which this year was between the Red Sox and the Reds. The game coincided with the induction of Carl Yastrzemski, a former Red Sox great, and Johnny Bench, a former Reds great, into baseball's Hall of Fame.

We had played at home on July 9 against the Yankees and won 10-5 with Smith picking up the win in relief. After the game I went into the clubhouse and commended the ball club on their performance. I told them that everyone was required to be at the clubhouse at 7 a.m. the following day to make the trip to Cooperstown for the exhibition game. Clemens asked if he could bring his sons to the ball game with him—he was always extremely close to his family—and I told him he could.

When the ballplayers showed up at Fenway Park right before 7 a.m. to board the buses and head to Logan Airport to pick up the charter flight, only Smith was missing. Right on schedule, the buses departed for the airport without him.

When we arrived at Cooperstown, there were some travel complications for the Reds that made it impossible for them to play the game. Because the exhibition game was sold out, I arranged for us to get enough players from our rookie Elmira, New York, club. The game would be delayed only an hour, and all of the fans waited to see the game. When the Elmira club arrived, Morgan and the Elmira manager, Mike Verdi, got together and divided up the ball clubs, placing the major league pitchers with the Elmira club and the rookie pitchers with the big league ball club. All of our pitchers would pitch one inning apiece.

During the game, Morgan came up to me to ask me about the Elmira catcher Eric Wedge, who was on the field. I told him that we had drafted him in 1989 from Wichita State and he looked very promising. Morgan agreed but noted that Wedge might lack the arm strength needed for a major league catcher. I made a note of his assessment in the back of my mind.

On the flight back to Boston, I discussed with Morgan how we'd handle the situation regarding Smith. He was the only player who missed the trip, and we had made it eminently clear to the ball club it was a command performance. Morgan suggested that we fine him a substantial amount to set an example for the ball club. I finally agreed to fine Smith $5,000 for missing the trip, although Morgan felt I was much too lenient.

When Smith showed up at the ballpark the next afternoon, I met with him and asked him why he had missed the trip to Cooperstown. His excuses were weak, and so I told him in person and then in writing that he was being fined $5,000 for missing the trip. He was not too happy with my decision to fine him.

Two days later I heard from his agent that they were going to appeal the fine. Eventually the appeal went to an arbitrator, the fine was reduced to $3,000, and the issue was resolved and forgotten.

By the All-Star break we were still hanging on as a .500 ball club with a 42-42 won-lost record, but we were now six games out of first and showing no indication that we were capable of playing any better. Rice had begun to regress at age 37. After being forced to undergo elbow surgery, he was limited to playing in only 56 games. Rice would finish the season hitting .234, three home runs and 28 RBIs. At the end of the season I would face a major decision regarding his future career with the Red Sox.

Injuries would continue to impact our overall performance. Ellis Burks, a key to any success we might hope to have, suffered two separate shoulder injuries. It caused him to miss over one-third of the season. Despite that fact, he hit .303 in the 90 games that he remained healthy enough to play in. Another injury that hurt the overall performance of our ball club was the loss of second baseman Marty Barrett for over two months. His injuries required surgery. After his rehabilitation period he returned to our lineup, but he never regained his previous level of performance. He struggled badly with the bat, hitting only .256, his worst offensive year ever. His play in the field defensively was affected, and his range, which had never been great, was reduced even further, as was his overall quickness in getting to ground balls or in turning the double play. Gardner, who I had counted on to work out of the bullpen primarily as a middleman and an occasional spot starter, had shoulder problems and was disabled for over a month starting in late May. He did not return to the active roster until late June.

Into August we continued to struggle along at a break-even pace, winning two or three, losing two or three. On August 13 in Baltimore Bolton lost to the Orioles 6-1. We then came home to Fenway Park to face the Toronto Blue Jays and lost all three games to Toronto and three more to the Milwaukee Brewers.

It appeared that we had dug ourselves into a deep hole too difficult to climb out of. Our season might as well had been over because we went into New York to face the dreaded Yankees, our perennial nemesis, referred to by some as the "Evil Empire."

The fact of the matter, however, is simply that they have just been damn good for many, many years. Red Sox ball clubs have always had to claw their way over the Yankees to win a league championship or to get to a World Series. The rivalry between the Yankees and Red Sox may well be the greatest in all of professional sports and is for certain the fiercest in Major League Baseball. Many purists might argue that the Giants–Dodgers rivalry would match it, but I believe the luster of that series has long since been diminished.

We lost the first game of the series to the Yankees 6-4. Clemens started and struggled right from the start. It was a very bad sign.

When I came to Yankee Stadium the next evening, I went into our clubhouse to try to somehow project a strong positive attitude. I wandered through the clubhouse, coffee cup in hand, upbeat and enthusiastic, engaging in casual conversations with many of the players. I wanted my demeanor to be cheerful and confident, hoping it would send a positive message to the players. (I later theorized that the players might have thought I was a strange dude, because here the team was in the midst of a bad losing streak and I was walking around happy and smiling, like all was right with the world. But we desperately needed some inspiration or miracle to keep us from total oblivion.)

The same evening before another capacity crowd in Yankee Stadium, we eked out a 4-3 win with Murphy pitching brilliantly in relief, striking out four of the five batters he faced for his eighth save.

Boddicker came back the next night to pitch an outstanding ball game, and we beat the Yankees 4-1. Somehow beating the Yankees is always extra special and extremely satisfying, almost like winning two games in one.

We went home to Fenway Park to face the Detroit Tigers. Smithson, with Lamp in relief, won. Clemens pitched a five-hitter and won. Joe Price and Boddicker also won starts. (In the last game of the series against the Tigers, we lost Gardner again when he was struck just below his right eye by a batter's line drive, crushing some of the bone structure around the eye and impacting his future career.) We swept the Tigers in five straight. We had now won seven straight. Hope sprang eternal. We then faced the California Angels in Fenway and proceeded to take three out of the next four games with Clemens winning his 14th game to close out the series.

As we began the final month of the season, we had just won 10 of our last 11 ball games, and time was running out, but that didn't discourage Joe Morgan. I loved him for his enthusiasm. It was always, "six two and even" in the darkest of moments. We had closed the gap to within striking distance, but we would need a spectacular month to truly climb back into contention for the division.

On September 4 we opened a nine-day road trip to the West Coast to face the A's, the Angels, and the Mariners. It would make us or break us. Dopson, who had been out of our starting rotation for over a month with some shoulder problems, opened the road trip to celebrate his return with his 10th win of the season, defeating the A's with some help from the bullpen 8-5. Little did we realize that would be our last hurrah. We proceeded to lose the next eight straight games, three of them by just one run. It was the death knell, and our season was finally over despite the fact we would finish with a dramatic flourish, winning 13 of our remaining 16 games. Had we not taken a nosedive on our last road trip to the West Coast—losing seven out of eight ball games, it would have been a whole different story for the 1989 season.

We finished the season in third place in the division and six games out of first place with an 83-79 won-lost record. The Toronto Blue Jays captured the Eastern Division crown with an 89-73 won-lost record.

When I once again looked back at that disastrous West Coast trip it dramatically pointed out how it critically impacted our final standings in the division. With all of our combined injuries and some lackluster performances from some key players on our ball club, we still had had an opportunity to win the Eastern Division because there wasn't a dominant team in the division. Gedman, who was penciled in as our starting catcher coming out of spring training, never did get untracked, and had his worst season, hitting only .212 with four home runs and 16 RBIs. I had signed Rick Cerone as a free agent, a veteran catcher to give us some short-term depth at that position. Cerone came on strong, and with Gedman really struggling badly, Cerone became the starting catcher and did a decent job. Cerone hit .243 and drove in nearly 50 RBIs. My hope was that John Marzano, one of our former first-round free agent draft picks, would eventually challenge Gedman for the starting catching position.

Boggs got off to an extremely slow start, and after two months of the season was hitting only .290. From that point on he began to really take off on a tear. He finished hitting .330 but still well below his remarkable .356 career average. It was the first time in the past five seasons that he had failed to win the league batting title.

Greenwell also had a good season, playing well defensively at home and hitting .308 with 95 RBIs. His home run production, however, dropped off to 14, and he was also not as effective in driving in runs as he had been in the past.

Clemens had a sub-par season, going 17-11 and finishing with a 3.13 ERA. He did strike out 230 batters, but he was unable to sustain any sort winning streak because he never won more than three games in a row at any point during the season. It was not a typical Roger Clemens season where he would dominate the opposition every time he stepped on the mound. A dominating Clemens might well have carried us to the division title.

Boddicker got off to a very slow start, winning only three games in the first two months of the season. By mid-June Boddicker was only 3-6.

On the positive side, Esasky had a tremendous season for us and he was a bright shining star for us in a lackluster offensive year for our ball club. Esasky, whom I had acquired earlier in the season, hit 30 home runs, almost one-third of our entire home run output, and he drove in 108 RBIs. Esasky would be honored by the Boston baseball writers as the Most Valuable Player on the ball club in a unanimous vote, a vote that was well deserved and never in question. He had a sensational season, and my challenge was to convince him to remain in a Red Sox uniform because he was now a six-year major league veteran and eligible for free agency.

There were some other outstanding performances on defense and at the plate. Evans hit .285 with 20 home runs and 100 RBIs. He also gave his usual outstanding defensive performance in right field. Evans and Esasky combined for 50 home runs, approximately one-half of our entire team output. Reed was a big plus, hitting .288. He played outstanding defensively, adapting well to his new position at second base. Rivera did a very adequate job defensively at shortstop and hit .257. Our extra players—Danny Heep, Kevin Romine, and Randy Kutcher—did a decent job filling in defensively. Heep, whom I had signed as a free agent, hit .300 for us in a backup role, playing both in the outfield and on occasion as a designated hitter.

On the mound there were a couple of pitchers whose performances matched and exceeded expectations. Murphy, whom I had acquired in the trade with the Phillies along with Esasky, had a spectacular season for us. Appearing in 74 ball games strictly in relief, he struck out 107 batters in 105 innings, winning five games, saving nine ball games, and finishing with a 2.74 ERA. Lamp pitched in 112 innings in various roles and did a most adequate job finishing 4-2, with two saves and a 2.32 ERA. Smith was outstanding as always, winning five ball games, saving 25, and striking out 96 in 70 innings in 64 games.

Once again I would have to spend the offseason finding ways to improve our ball club by adding some more depth in our starting rotation, shoring up the bullpen, and trying to find some help for our ball club offensively. It was a tall order, and I did not want to trade away our future unless I absolutely felt we had a chance to get back to a World Series. The drought had been too, too long.

I would also have to re-sign a number of players on our roster whose contracts were up and probably face one or two arbitration cases. Fortunately, on my recommendation we had hired Elaine Weddington Steward as an associate counsel in 1988, and I had also promoted her to the position of assistant general manager. She would work closely with me in contract negotiations and salary arbitration cases. As a graduate of St. John's University with a law degree, she would prove to be a tremendous asset.

The media and talk shows were already gearing up to give us all the answers to our problems, and I knew I would receive the usual amount of criticism and second-guessing. But that had always been the way it was, and I was now totally convinced that it always would be that way. It goes with the territory in Boston, and I knew I had better learn to accept it or ignore it.

But I had to focus on what I had to do to improve our ball club. That was all that mattered. It was a big enough challenge in itself. As always it would be another busy offseason, but success never comes without a price.

CHAPTER 5

1990

Once More a Division Title

Now it was time to look to the future and the 1990 season. I had to find a way to re-sign Nick Esasky and also to deal with major decisions regarding the careers of Jim Rice and Bob Stanley. With a little less than a month remaining in the season I met with Esasky in my office to begin discussing a contract extension. I wanted him to know how much we desired to keep him in a Red Sox uniform and that we were prepared to offer him a multi-year contract. I told him I was prepared to begin contract negotiations. Esasky told me he would deal with me directly and not through his agent.

As we continued to talk over the next few weeks, I finally offered him a three-year contract extension for around $3.5 million a season. Esasky told me he was satisfied with my contract offer, and he had enjoyed playing in Boston. He told me that after the season was over the only other club he would talk to was the Braves because he and his family lived in Georgia. He kept his word despite the interest he received from other ball clubs.

The Braves met with Esasky and also offered him a three-year contact for slightly more than my offer. Esasky called me a day or two after the meeting and told me of the Braves' offer. I told him we'd match the offer dollar for dollar. He told me he wanted some time to talk with his family about the offers and he'd get back to me in a few days with his decision. I asked him if there was anything else we could do to convince him to stay with us in Boston.

"No, you've been great. The offer is fair," he responded. "I've just got to talk this out with my family."

I was convinced then there wasn't any point of pressing him any further. He had been upfront with me all along, and it was now a question of whether his family ties to the Georgia area would override our effort to keep him in Boston.

One week later he called me to tell me he had decided to take the Braves' offer and sign with Atlanta. He thanked me profusely for our offer, the opportunity to play in Boston, and my openness in dealing with him.

"Lou, the family pressure to sign with the Braves was too great for me to ignore," he stated simply. "I thank you for the way you dealt with me. Good luck next season."

I desperately wanted to retain him because he had been a great addition to our ball club and a class act for our clubhouse. I often pondered whether I could have handled the situation any differently to change his mind. I felt the family pressure to sign with the Braves was overwhelming for him, and only an unreasonable and overpriced contract might have kept him. But I was restricted by an overall budget for our entire payroll, and in the long run that would have been a costly mistake.

Esasky would go off to the Braves' spring training camp in West Palm Beach that next spring and play in a number of exhibition games. When the National League season opened, he began to have some serious physical problems. He would only play nine more major league games. He had developed some ailment that affected his vision and balance. It was a very sad ending for a quality individual at the height of his professional baseball career. However, his contract (like all baseball contracts) was fully guaranteed, so the Braves had to pay Esasky the full amount due him for the next three seasons. It well could have been the Red Sox's obligation had he accepted my offer instead of the Braves' offer, and I am most certain that had Esasky's injury happened while he was under contract with the Red Sox, I would have never heard the end of it from ownership and the local media.

My next difficult tasks were making decisions regarding the careers of Rice and Stanley. Rice had been one of the greatest players in Red Sox history, and in my judgment, he belongs in the Hall of Fame. Rice had spent 15 outstanding seasons in a Red Sox uniform. He had hit 382 home runs— third all-time in Red Sox history behind only Ted Williams and Carl Yastrzemski; he had driven in 1,451 runs and had 2,452 hits—also third all-time in Red Sox history; and he maintained a .502 slugging percentage—fourth all-time in club history.

But in 1989, Rice had only played in 56 games and had gone to bat just 209 times. His production was down, as he hit .234 with a paltry three home runs and 28 RBIs. It was an embarrassing performance and far below the usual brilliance of a typical Rice season. I also knew that Rice had been critical of Joe Morgan, feeling that Morgan had not handled him with the respect due him or utilized him more in his regular lineups. There would be no easy way to release a player of his stature with such an outstanding career.

Stanley had been a legendary workhorse for the Red Sox during his 13-year career. He held a number of all-time Red Sox pitching records, including saves (132), games (637), and relief wins (85). But in 1989 Stanley had a 4.88 ERA and struck out only 32 batters in 79 innings of pitching. He also had complained very publicly about how Morgan was using him in the bullpen.

When the season was nearing its end, I brought together our coaching staff and Morgan to discuss our entire ball club—the pluses, the minuses, what we needed to add or subtract to turn things around for the next season, and which future prospects on our Pawtucket club could be brought up to the major league level in 1990. We discussed what moves needed to be made at the annual winter meetings, and I came away with an in-depth understanding of our strengths and weaknesses. We also discussed current roster situations. The consensus opinion was that Rice had regressed greatly from his usual stellar performances of the past and could well be at the end of a great career. It was also the consensus opinion that Stanley was questionable and that he just might not be able to pitch effectively in the future.

It was apparent, however, that critical decisions had to be made regarding their contracts, and the buck would stop with me. I talked to John Harrington and Haywood Sullivan about the Rice and Stanley situations and told them that our staff was in agreement that Rice's career could be over, but Stanley might still have a couple of seasons in him, and that to re-sign them both would be expensive. Both John and Haywood said if that was also my judgment, I should do what needed to be done. Both John and Haywood also suggested that we consider offering Rice a job working in our baseball development area.

I recognized that I would personally have the unpleasant and distasteful task of telling one of the great Red Sox players that he was being released unconditionally. There just wasn't any easy way to do it. When I made contact with Rice to inform him that we were putting him on waivers, he did not take it well. I indicated that we'd like to keep him in the Red Sox organization and I'd like to discuss a position within the organization with him. He said he had no interest, and the conversation ended abruptly. I understood his anger at the release because he had been the consummate Red Sox player and an intense competitor; I was certain he felt he could still play. It was extremely difficult for him to accept his playing career was at an end.

In time Rice accepted a position in our organization. He remains an integral part of the organization to this day. His induction into the Red Sox Hall of Fame in 1995 was unanimous and a fitting tribute to his many great seasons in a Red Sox uniform.

Next on the agenda was Stanley. I decided to discuss his situation further with Morgan, and I suggested that despite his struggles the previous season, we consider giving him one more opportunity in our bullpen. It ended up being a moot point because Stanley decided to retire. In recognition of his great seasons in a Red Sox uniform, he was also a unanimous selection for induction into the Red Sox Hall of Fame.

I then turned toward building the team we'd field in 1990. There was much work to be done. Our pitching staff had, basically, only two solid starters in Roger Clemens and Mike Boddicker. It was a patchwork starting rotation; after Clemens and Boddicker, our starting rotation included Greg Harris (a relief pitcher for most of his career), Tom Bolton (a journeyman pitcher out of our minor leagues), and Dana Kiecker (a right-hander who had never pitched in the big leagues).

Harris was a player out of the Mets' farm system. I was familiar with him from my days with the Mets. I always felt that Harris could be an asset to a pitching staff because of his versatility. He could start or relieve, and his overall stuff was good enough for the majors. He was a good competitor and totally convinced of his own ability to pitch in the big leagues. At times he would appear to be a bit too cocky, but he never lacked for self-confidence. It seemed to work to his advantage and enhance his overall confidence level and performance.

Left-hander Bolton had pitched brief stints in parts of three seasons in the big leagues but with very limited success. He had actually only pitched a total of 61 innings in three appearances at the big league level. We had penciled in John Dopson as our third starter behind Clemens and Boddicker after he had won 12 games the previous season. He looked like he might be on the verge of developing into a solid front-line pitcher. Unfortunately, he ended up spending just about the entire season on the disabled list with elbow problems. Bolton replaced him in the starting rotation.

Kiecker was an eight-year minor league veteran pitcher. It was a desperate move on my part to bring him to the big leagues, but with a seriously depleted pitching staff, the 152 innings he pitched in 1990 were a blessing.

One of the real unsung heroes on the ball club was catcher Tony Peña. I had signed him as a free agent in November 1989, having always been enamored with his exceptional defensive skills. He was everything we had bargained for defensively, and he brought with him a dynamic and positive attitude into our clubhouse. His enthusiasm and his love of playing the game was a joy to behold. He brought a breath of fresh air and levity to our ball club. Peña did an excellent job in handling our pitching staff, in particular Harris, Bolton, Kiecker, and Jeff Gray out of the bullpen.

The bullpen, which I had envisioned would be one of the strengths of our ball club, became instead, a bit of a disappointment. I had signed Jeff Reardon, one of the premier relievers in Major League Baseball with 266 career saves and 57 wins, as a free agent the previous December. When we opened the season, we had Reardon and Lee Smith in our bullpen, two of the most dominant relief pitchers in the history of baseball. However, when we reported to Winter Haven for spring training, Smith came to me and told me that he did not want to pitch as a setup man out of the bullpen. He told me that I should go ahead and attempt to trade him because he would walk away as a free agent at the end of the season. I attempted to convince Smith that he would still get ample opportunity to work as a closer and that with Reardon and him, we had an opportunity to return to postseason play. He had no interest in my argument. His only concern was that he and he alone should handle the closer's role. Saves translate into dollars in a player's contract, and I fully understood his thinking in that regard, but, somewhere, somehow, it made you wonder, when did a sense of team loyalty and team values ever enter the equation? In today's world of professional athletics, sadly, I must say I don't think it is often enough. Too often the emphasis by the agent and the ballplayers is on personal achievement because it translates into dollars with the advent of free agency.

I began to attempt to trade Smith for hopefully a starting pitcher to add some depth to our rotation. I was absolutely convinced that there would be a great deal of interest in Smith and I would eventually be able to trade him for a starting pitcher.

I called every major league organization. To my absolute astonishment, the interest in Smith was slim to none. I found that difficult to understand. With nearly every club I talked to, they had some unfounded criticism and negative reports about Smith's attitude, physical status, or work habits, yet in truth Smith had issues with none of the above. He was great in the clubhouse and he was physically fine. When he came out of the bullpen and took the ball to close out a ball game, he was an intense competitor. He gave 100 percent of his ability. He never was overly dedicated to a tough daily physical workout schedule and he hated to run the normal wind sprints in spring training or during the season, but it never seemed to affect his performance on the mound however.

Trying to find a trading partner, I zeroed in on the Atlanta Braves. At that time Bobby Cox was the club's general manager. They had two fine young pitchers in their farm system at the Double-A and Triple-A levels named Steve Avery and Kent Mercker. Our scouting reports indicated they both had outstanding ability and that either one could help our starting rotation. I kept after Cox for close to two months attempting to convince him that Smith, in their bullpen, could really help them win a World Series. Cox would not budge on either young pitcher. He kept coming back to me offering just about every pitcher on the Braves' Triple-A pitching staff. Cox told me he had promised the fans in Atlanta that he was going to build the Braves into a contending ball club with his young prospects from within their farm system, particularly with his young pitching prospects.

Still unable to trade Smith, we opened the season at home against the Detroit Tigers before a sellout crowd. In a special moment to begin the game, Toni Giamatti, the wife of the late brilliant commissioner A. Bartlett Giamatti (who died so young and so unexpectedly), threw out the ceremonial first pitch. Clemens had a no-hitter into the sixth inning before giving up a single to Tony Phillips. He pitched brilliantly into the seventh before being relieved by first Rob Murphy and then Smith. In the ninth, Smith gave up a single to the first batter he faced and proceeded to load the bases before finally striking out the dangerous Alan Trammel to preserve a 5-2 win for Clemens.

It puzzled me that a pitcher of Smith's stature would not interest other clubs. During his last three seasons with the Chicago Cubs he had saved more than 100 games, and in his two seasons with the Red Sox he had saved

54 games and struck out 192 batters in 156 innings. He didn't appear to be fading.

I began to once again call other organizations in search of pitching. I called Dal Maxvill, the St. Louis Cardinals' general manager. In placing the call to the Cardinals, I was told by the switchboard operator that Maxvill was in the clubhouse in the manager's office. They forwarded my call to the manager's office, and Dorrel "Whitey" Herzog, the Cardinals' field manager, answered the phone.

"Whitey, this is Lou Gorman of the Red Sox looking for Del Maxvill; is he there?"

Herzog was a longtime friend and an outstanding baseball man. He had done it all in baseball and was highly respected in the game. He and I had worked together in Kansas City when Whitey was the Royals' field manager and I was the director of player development and assistant general manager.

"Lou, great to hear from you, what's up, man?" he responded heartily.

I told him I was attempting to trade Smith because I now also had Reardon in the bullpen as my closer. I told him I was calling Maxvill to see if the Cardinals had any interest.

Herzog, always direct and to the point responded, "Yeah, we've got some interest in Smith. What would you need in return?"

I told Herzog I was looking for pitching to help our starting rotation primarily.

Herzog responded that they did not have pitching available to trade, but he mentioned that he could move a starting outfielder.

"I have an outfielder named Tom Brunansky who could help your ball club. I could move him for Smith," he suggested.

I told Whitey I'd give Maxvill a call and for him to let Maxvill know I called.

After I hung up, I immediately checked our scouting reports on Brunansky and also his salary figures. The reports indicated that he was a decent defensive outfielder with an average throwing arm but very accurate. He had some power and was an excellent guy in the clubhouse.

A day later Maxvill called, furious at me for having talked to his manager. He began a tirade, berating me verbally for having gone to Herzog before talking to him. I attempted to explain that I had called his office for him, but the call was switched to the manager's office and it was Herzog who answered the call. It was to no avail however, because Maxvill continued on his tirade and finally hung up the phone on me. I assumed with this action the Brunansky for Smith trade was dead.

A few days later Maxvill called back and was deeply apologetic, telling me I had caught him at a bad moment and he would consider making the Smith trade for Brunansky. (I later learned that there were strained relations between he and Herzog and this probably was the basis for his anger.) Realizing I had very little choice available to me because the interest in Smith was all but negligible, on May 6 I agreed to the trade, and Brunansky became a Red Sox player.

Brunansky would go on to play in 129 games for us, hitting .267 with 27 doubles, five triples, 16 home runs, and 71 RBIs. Smith would go to the St. Louis Cardinals and have a brilliant season. He would finish 6-3 with a 2.34 ERA and 47 saves, leading the National League.

A few years later, we were at the annual baseball winter meetings when I ran into Cox, who had become the Braves' field manager.

"Bobby, if you had made the trade with me a few years ago for Lee Smith, could the Braves have won a world championship with him?"

Cox looked taken aback at first by my question, but then after a pause, said, "Yeah, Lou, I guess we might have."

(What was ironic was that in 1991 when Smith led the National League in saves, the Braves closer was Juan Berenguer, who was 0-3 and had only 17 saves compared to Smith's 47.)

We finished the first month of the 1990 season 11-8, nothing sensational. One of our losses was an embarrassing 18-0 shellacking by the Milwaukee Brewers at Fenway Park on Patriot's Day before another capacity crowd. It was a humiliating defeat and one of the worst shutouts in Red Sox history. A few days later we gained a measure of revenge by scoring an 11-0 shutout of the Seattle Mariners at home behind the pitching of Boddicker, with relief help from Murphy and Reardon. Peña had four hits, including a three-run home run, and Wade Boggs had three hits and drove in two runs.

Peña had always been impressive with his outstanding defensive skills and his enthusiasm. Our need for depth at the catching position was obvious, and I felt fortunate to be able to acquire him. He was ideal to fill our needs behind the plate, and his value to our club both on the field and in the clubhouse was special. He ended up hitting .263 with seven home runs and 56 RBIs and led all American League catchers in fielding with a .995 percentage. He caught in 142 games and the Red Sox were 72-61 in games that Peña caught. At the end of the season he was honored by the BoSox Club, a longtime Red Sox booster club, for his valuable contribution to the success of the team.

We continued to play up and down baseball throughout the season. By the end of May, through 45 games, we were in third place in the Eastern Division. On June 3, we beat the Indians 8-2 behind Clemens, who struck out 11 in eight innings. We pounded out 13 hits. Dwight Evans hit a two-run homer, Ellis Burks slapped a solo shot, and Boggs nailed a two-run home run to pace the Red Sox offense.

On June 7, Harris won his fifth game of the season, pitching eight outstanding innings against the New York Yankees at Fenway Park. He gave up only one hit and no bases on balls, and struck out seven. It was one of his finest outings of the season. Reardon pitched the ninth inning and picked up his seventh save. Jody Reed and Mike Greenwell had back-to-back RBI singles, and Boggs drove in another run in the seventh with a double. The victory completed a four-game sweep of the Yankees at Fenway, and we were now in first place by a game and a half with a 29-23 record.

By July 7 we were in first place with a 44-31 won-lost record, and we held a three-and-a-half-game lead in the division. Immediately after the All-Star break we lost five of the next eight games, but three of the losses were by one run.

Our loss to the Minnesota Twins on July 16, a 3-2 defeat, dropped us out of first place by a half game with a 47-40 won-lost record. We moved right back into first place the next evening by scoring a 1-0 win over the same Twins. Tim Naehring's first major league hit drove in the only run of the game. Naehring had opened the season at Pawtucket, where he hit .269 with 16 doubles and 15 home runs. He was an eighth-round selection in the 1988 draft out of Miami University of Ohio. Naehring had hit .391 and had a .639 slugging percentage while being named Player of the Year in the Mid-American Conference the year we drafted him. Naehring had the ability and potential to develop into a solid major league third baseman. A series of injuries unfortunately handicapped him throughout his career. Naehring is an outstanding young man and an intense competitor with solid leadership qualities. Had he not been handicapped by injuries, I felt he had the potential to become an All-Star performer.

On July 25, Clemens won his 13th game of the season, pitching a three-hit shutout in a 2-0 win over the Milwaukee Brewers; Carlos Quintana hit a two-run home run in the second inning off Chris Bosio for the win.

Clemens allowed only three singles and struck out nine for a complete game shutout. Greenwell chipped in with three hits in the win. We were now 51-46 and tied for first place.

Quintana was another product of the Red Sox farm system, who had played five seasons in the Sox farm system with brief stints in the big leagues. For the most part, his entire minor league career was spent in the outfield. In 1990, however, he made a transition from the outfield to first base and did an excellent job defensively while playing in 131 games at first base. He hit .287 with 28 doubles, seven home runs, and 67 RBIs. His offensive production was a welcome addition, and his solid defensive play at first base turned out to be a big surprise.

His promotion to our major league club was one more reason to intensify our scouting efforts in Latin America. I had been preaching to our scouting staff for the past two or three seasons at our annual organizational meetings that we needed to increase our efforts and scouting coverage in the Latin countries.

Other organizations, in particular the Dodgers and the Pirates, had been active in the Latin countries for many years. They were the pioneers in the area. In recent years other organizations were intensifying their scouting coverage in the Latin countries.

It had been fashionable for a number of organizations to develop baseball complexes in these countries. They would train, house, and feed youngsters in the hope of developing future major league talent. The concept had been productive and highly successful in the development of future major league talent for a number of organizations.

I had been a longtime personal friend of Pedro Padron Panza, the owner of the La Guaira Tiburones (Sharks) of the Venezuelan Winter League. I met him in 1964 in my early days with the Baltimore Orioles when Luis Aparicio played for his Winter League club. We developed a longstanding friendship and mutual respect for each other that lasted until his untimely death. Over the years of my career in baseball, I had worked with Padron in sending him ballplayers for his La Guaira ball club to play winter baseball. La Guaira was a major seaport town in Venezuela about 45 minutes from Caracas, a thriving metropolitan city with a population larger than New York. The La Guaira team played all of their home games in the University Stadium in downtown Caracas. It was a facility that could seat around 25,000. They would share the stadium with the home-standing Caracas Leones (Lions). Over the years I had sent him players such as Dave Johnson,

Lou Piniella, Mike Epstein, Dave May, Merv Rettenmund, Curt Motton, Mike Hedlund, Darryl Strawberry, Wally Bunker, Pat Kelly, Jim Rooker, etc. In the early years, many of the Triple-A players and a number of the major league players needing extra work on a particular phase of their game, or having missed a part of the major league season because of an injury, would desire to play winter baseball not only to help their game, but also to earn extra money that winter baseball would provide. (Today, with the astronomical salaries being paid to players, it is difficult to convince some players an extra few months of winter baseball could really enhance their careers. They don't need the money, and their incentive to play winter base-ball is all but nonexistent.)

In my last few years as the general manager of the Red Sox, Padron, on one of his annual visits with me in Boston, proposed that he was willing to purchase a plot of land in Venezuela and build a complex in conjunction with the Red Sox. We would mutually develop playing talent for the Red Sox and for the La Guaira ball club. Our investment was extremely reason-able in light of the total cost to build the complex and the promise of devel-oping some future major league talent. I took the proposal to Haywood. I recommended that we accept Padron's proposal. After some discussion, Haywood was lukewarm toward the concept. The proposal by Padron even-tually fell by the wayside. I sincerely felt that it would have, in time, paid huge dividends for the Red Sox.

(Since that time the Houston Astros have built a complex in Venezuela, and they are confident that in the future it will pay huge dividends for their major league ball club. When Dan Duquette took over as general manager of the Red Sox, he readily recognized the value of expanding and intensify-ing the Red Sox coverage in the Latin countries. With the blessing of John Harrington, the club's chief executive officer, Duquette went about enhanc-ing the impact and exposure of the Red Sox in the Latin countries and throughout Asian countries. The results have already begun to pay divi-dends for the Red Sox.)

On July 28 in an attempt to add more offensive punch to our lineup, I acquired veteran outfielder Mike Marshall from the Mets for two minor league players. Marshall was a career .270 hitter with 153 home runs in an eight-year career spent mostly with the Los Angeles Dodgers. Unfortunately, injuries would restrict Marshall's contributions to our ball club. He would appear in only 30 games, hitting .286 with six doubles, four home runs, and 12 RBIs. On July 31 the Braves released left-handed pitcher Joe Hesketh. I signed him immediately as a free agent to add some depth to our pitching staff. I felt he might give us a left-handed spot starter or reliever.

In August and early September, Jeff Gray, whose minor league contract I had purchased on June 5, literally became the sole savior of our bullpen. In April the Phillies had released him and I had signed as a free agent to a Triple-A contract with Pawtucket, because I had been impressed with his minor league stats. Our scouting reports indicated he was questionable and a fill-in at best, and he had only pitched nine total innings in the major leagues. At Pawtucket he was 2-4, but in 31 innings he struck out 35 hitters and walked only seven batters.

With Jeff Reardon as our regular closer, I felt Gray might give us some help in middle relief or as a setup man. When Reardon went down, however, with a ruptured disc in his back and had to be operated upon, the rest of our bullpen was also in total disarray. Gray stepped into the breech. He did a magnificent job with seven critical saves in his last seven trips out of the pen when the division title was on the line. Overall, he pitched in 28 games and prevented 21 out of 28 inherited runners from scoring. At one point Gray went 11 straight appearances without allowing a run to score. He finished 2-4 with nine saves and 50 strikeouts in 50 innings pitched. His saves kept us in contention.

On August 1 Bolton won his fifth game of the season, pitching eight innings, allowing only five hits, and beating the Chicago White Sox 9-5. Burks, Greenwell, and Brunansky paced the offense. The three-game series against the White Sox at Fenway drew more than 104,000 fans.

On August 19, Clemens won his 18th game of the season, beating the California Angels 4-1. Clemens went seven innings, allowing seven hits and striking out eight. It was the 11th time during the season that Clemens came back to post a win after a loss. Gray pitched the last two innings to pick up his third save of the season. Boggs, Reed, and Brunansky paced the offense. So we were now 64-55, but in first place.

We went to Toronto for a big series in the SkyDome against the Blue Jays, holding on to a one-game lead on August 23. We lost the first game 4-3.

Kiecker came back the next night and shut out the Jays 2-0 for his fifth victory of the season. Clemens would win his 19th game of the season shutting out the Jays 1-0, and Harris would follow the next day, also shutting out the Blue Jays 1-0.

On August 29, Clemens won his eighth straight start and 20th game of the season, beating the Cleveland Indians on the road 7-1. Clemens scattered eight hits, allowed no bases on balls, and struck out nine. We got multi-hit games from Quintana (four hits), Burks (three hits), and Luis Rivera (three hits, including his sixth home run of the season). We were now 73-57 and in first place by six and a half games.

The next day I made a trade that became the most controversial trade of my Red Sox career. Realizing we had a definite chance to win the Eastern Division title but staring at a decimated bullpen, I decided to go for broke. Reardon, our primary stopper, was all but through for the season after surgery on a ruptured disc on August 4. Murphy, who had pitched so well the previous year, had struggled badly all season long. He was 0-6 with a 6.32 ERA. In 57 innings he had allowed 85 hits and walked 32. Dennis Lamp, a right-hander, had pitched mostly in middle relief, was 3-5 with a 4.58 ERA in 105 innings pitched. Wes Gardner, who never fulfilled his enormous potential, was utilized out of the bullpen but was ineffective. He would finish the season 3-7 with a 4.89 ERA.

I felt our bullpen was in dire need of some immediate help if we had any chance at all to win the East. We could not, however, hold onto our lead in the division unless I could find a way to strengthen our bullpen. Certainly if we were able to hang on and win the division title and eventually face the A's for the American League championship, we would desperately need help in our bullpen to have any chance whatever.

I had alerted our scouting staff in mid-June to keep on the lookout for some bullpen help, realizing that Gardner and Murphy were struggling. When Reardon went down, it became critical to find someone to bolster our pen or our season was history. A number of our scouts, including our scouting director, Eddie Kasko, and senior scout Wayne Britton, indicated that Larry Andersen was probably one of the top relievers in the National League. For the Astros he had appeared in 50 games and went 5-2 with five saves and a 1.95 ERA. His ERAs the previous two seasons with the Astros were 1.54 and 2.94, and he struck out 151 batters in 169 innings pitched.

I called Bob Watson, the Astros' general manager, to inquire about Andersen's availability. Watson indicated he would move Andersen for a prospect out of our farm system. We discussed some names, and one of the names he brought up was a third baseman on our Double-A club at New Britain named Jeff Bagwell. I checked out our reports on Bagwell, a player Erwin Bryant had signed out of the University of Hartford. (Bryant was a former player in the Red Sox farm system and after playing for a few seasons, he was released. Our minor league and scouting staffs, however, were so impressed with Bryant he was offered a job within the organization as a territory scout. He turned out to be an excellent judge of talent.)

I read all the scouting reports on Bagwell in depth. Butch Hobson was managing Bagwell at New Britain. He indicated that Bagwell was a "definite prospect with excellent makeup." But the reports indicated that Bagwell would have to move from third base to first base, because his basic fielding skills were not suited for playing third base.

I also had reports on Bagwell from the previous season after we had signed him when he played in some 60 games at the Single-A level. I felt I had sufficient information on Bagwell to make a decision.

Bagwell had played in half a season after signing as a free agent in late June out of college. At Winter Haven in the Single-A Florida State League, he hit .308 in with two home runs and 19 RBIs. At New Britain, he hit .333 in 481 at bats with four home runs and 61 RBIs. His doubles (34) and his triples (seven) would seem to project him offensively more as a line drive hitter as opposed to becoming a power hitter. Each of our scouts who had seen and evaluated Bagwell felt he was a "definite prospect" with good makeup, but none of the reports projected that he would have above-average major league power. We were wrong.

Currently we had Boggs playing third base for the major league club. In our farm system we had additional third-base depth with Naehring and Scott Cooper. Naehring was highly regarded by our entire organization. We considered him a definite major league prospect, and potentially an All-Star performer. Cooper was also judged to be a major league prospect with solid defensive skills, but not in the same category as Naehring. It was obvious we had depth at that position. I was also hopeful that we would re-sign Boggs and retain him in our organization for the foreseeable future. On the other side of the diamond, we had a young first baseman in our farm system named Maurice "Mo" Vaughn. Everyone in the organization considered Mo to be the heir apparent to play first base in Fenway Park in the very near future. It was the consensus opinion of our minor league staff, and our scouting reports concurred. Vaughn would have above-average power from the left side of the plate and with the potential to hit 30 or 40 home runs a season.

There were some questions about whether Andersen would become a free agent as a result of the collusion ruling against baseball ownership.

There were supposedly 12 or 13 players who could be declared free agents as a result of some legalities resulting from the original collusion case. I called our player relations committee in the commissioner's office in New York to determine Andersen's status. The committee indicated to me that they were certain that Andersen would not be one of those players given his free agency. I was confident therefore, that if we traded for him, we'd have him in our bullpen for the foreseeable future.

It had been 72 years since the Red Sox had won a world championship. Mrs. Yawkey was not in the best of health, and the Red Sox had never won a world championship during the 40-plus years the Yawkey name had been associated with the Red Sox franchise. We now had a chance to win the Eastern Division title and hopefully get back to the World Series. The Oakland A's were a solid ball club and a formidable opponent that we'd have to face to get back to the World Series. I decided that after a great deal of thought that the best opportunity to get back to the world championships was now. I had to make that trade and take our chances.

But if I didn't strengthen the bullpen, we had no chance whatsoever. We had a power-hitting first baseman in Vaughn ready to come to our big league club, depth at third base, and no indication from our reports that Bagwell would give us a power bat. I recall an expression that singer Beverly Sills was quoted as saying, "You may be disappointed if you fail, but you're doomed if you don't try." I knew if I didn't go for broke now, I would, for the rest of my life, always wonder what might have been.

I talked to Haywood and John and explained to both of them our reports on Bagwell and Andersen. I told them it was my opinion that we should make the trade. They accepted my recommendation.

I called Bob Watson and made the trade, Bagwell for Andersen. Andersen would strengthen our bullpen and help us win the Eastern Division title, and we'd go on to face the A's. Andersen worked mostly as a setup man, pitching in 22 innings, walking only three and striking out 25 with a 1.23 ERA. He was exactly what we needed to bolster the pen at a critical juncture in our run at the division title. Bagwell eventually became a first baseman, but he also developed into an outstanding home run hitter and a National League All-Star.

Unfortunately, at the end of the season, when the arbitrator made his ruling on the special group of players who could be given their free agency, he ruled that Andersen would be one of them, and we lost him despite the information I had previously received. It was a trade I would be criticized for often in the future. Yet in retrospect I remain convinced it was a trade I had to make at that time or live to regret.

Just prior to the August 31 deadline that required players to be on the active roster of any ball club eligible for the playoffs in order to compete in postseason competition, Andersen was added to our roster.

Dan Shaughnessy, of *The Boston Globe*, would later write that it was "a trade that would ruin Gorman." There was also criticism that I personally had not scouted Bagwell at New Britain.

But because I had a number of in-depth scouting reports from two managers and three or four scouts, for me to take a look at Bagwell (or any player) in three or four games and assume that my judgment would override the consensus I already had from qualified professionals would be arrogant and unwise. If, as Shaughnessy claimed, the gamble I took in making the trade would ruin me, then so be it. I had to take a chance and live with the consequences. For too often in life we later regret most of the chances we failed to take.

Around the same time, the Oakland A's acquired outfielder Willie McGee from the St. Louis Cardinals on a waiver claim. I was immediately accosted by the local media, who were critical of the fact that I had not grabbed McGee to help our ball club.

At a press conference prior to our ball game on August 30, the media pressed me for my failure not to claim McGee. At the time Oakland made the waiver claim on McGee, Brunansky in right field had driven in 12 runs in the previous eight games. At Fenway Park that season, Brunansky hit .340 with 13 home runs and 51 RBIs, while playing extremely well defensively. Burks in center field hit .296 with 38 doubles, eight triples, and 21 home runs while drawing in 89 runs. He had played outstanding defense in center field. Greenwell in left field hit .297 with 30 doubles, six triples, 14 home runs, and 73 RBIs. He handled left field at Fenway Park in almost Gold Glove fashion.

In response to the media's criticism of my failure to claim McGee, I stated, "With the way that Greenwell, Burks, and Brunansky are playing, where would we play McGee?"

The media jumped all over my response. They kept taking my statement partially out of context and continually kept reporting that I had said, "Where can McGee play?" The inference being that I was didn't believe that McGee could play. This was never my position. I merely felt that Burks, Greenwell, and Brunansky were doing an excellent job for us in the outfield, and I didn't feel the need to alter that combination. McGee certainly might have been able to contribute off the bench for us, although we had Evans to serve as designated hitter despite a nagging back problem. I was not downgrading McGee's ability, I just felt the outfield we had in place was doing an outstanding job for us, and I just didn't feel the need for change.

McGee would go on to play for Oakland. He would appear in 29 games, driving in 15 runs and stealing three bases. It would be a long time before I would finally stop hearing on talk radio or reading it in the print media, "Gorman said, 'Where can Willie McGee play?'" It was par for the course in dealing with the Boston media, and after seven years of dealing with them, I had come to accept that it came with the territory whether you liked it or not.

What I really should have been criticized for was for not acquiring Harold Baines. He became available at the same time McGee was acquired by Oakland. Baines, an exceptional left-handed hitter, would have been a great addition for our ball club.

I had talked with Tom Grieve, the general manager of the Texas Rangers, just the week before Baines was traded. Baines's name was never mentioned by Grieve. I was totally surprised and taken aback by his availability. That was the player I should have acquired, and no one in the media ever questioned me as to why I hadn't acquired Baines. They only jumped on me about McGee.

On September 10 in the first game of a doubleheader against the Milwaukee Brewers, Harris won his 13th game of the season. Gray saved his ninth game of the season, his seventh save in his last seven appearances. Rivera's two-run double gave us the lead for good. After that, we proceeded to go into a slump, one of our worst of the season, and we went into Baltimore clinging to a precarious first-place lead.

On September 19 we fell out of first place for the first time since July 30. Harris gave up a wild pitch and a line drive single to Cal Ripken to put the Orioles in the lead in the third inning. Tony Peña's single in the fourth, however, tied the ball game 3-3. In the fifth inning, Sam Horn, a former number-one draft pick by our organization, hit a three-run home run off Harris to put the Orioles ahead for good. We were now one game behind the Toronto Blue Jays.

On September 28 the entire season was on the line. The Blue Jays came into Fenway Park tied with us for first. It proved to be one of the most exciting and dramatic series of the season. The first game would draw the largest crowd of the season, 35,735. Boddicker was our starting pitcher. He held onto a lead until the seventh inning when he suddenly seemed to lose his stuff. Toronto scored four runs off him to take the lead. In the bottom of the eighth, thanks to some sloppy defensive play by the Blue Jays, we bounced back to take a 5-4 lead. In the top of the ninth inning, Gray gave up a two-run home run (one of the very few times in pressure situations late in the season that Gray was ineffectual) to Jose Felix to put Toronto ahead 6-5.

I went down to the clubhouse to meet with Morgan before we faced the Blue Jays again and was told he was in the dugout. As I came into the dugout the first player I met was Reardon, who was in uniform despite having surgery on a ruptured disc a month earlier. I was stunned to see him there; I never expected him to be ready to play until next spring.

"Jeff," I said, "What are you doing here?"

He smiled at me and then with a wide grin said, "I'm ready to go. Dr. Pappas said I'm cleared to play and I'm ready to be activated."

I was just about speechless and I mumbled, "Jeff, that's great. I'll check with Dr. Pappas."

Without talking to Morgan, I made a beeline for the doctor's office in the clubhouse to find Dr. Pappas.

When I found him and asked him about Reardon, he said, "Lou, I've been looking for you to let you know that Jeff is recovered and can be activated."

"Doctor, is that some sort of a miracle he can come back that quickly from such a serious injury?"

"It's hard to believe he could come back that soon, but Jeff is something special," he responded.

Dr. Pappas was right. Reardon was special. It was all but inconceivable that he could come back that quickly, but more importantly that he wanted to come back and was willing to do whatever it would take to come back.

It was an absolute tribute to Reardon's tremendous guts, toughness, and competitive nature. I've known some athletes who would have cashed it in and called it a season, but not Reardon. He was a tenacious competitor and a winner.

I went to him and said, "We're thrilled you're back and thanks for such a great effort to come back."

That night Reardon came on in the top of the ninth to retire three straight and set up a dramatic bottom of the ninth. The Blue Jays brought on their ace reliever, Tom Henke, to close out the game. Reed opened the inning with a base on balls, Quintana's sacrifice bunt moved Reed to second, and Boggs walked. Burks was the next hitter, and he hit a line drive single to left, but Reed could only advance to third. Greenwell then followed with a looping single to right to tie the game. Finally an unheralded player named Jeff Stone, whom I had brought up from Pawtucket on September 4, made his first major league at-bat of the season, and he delivered a single to right to win the game 7-6. It was a dramatic win, and the 35,000-plus fans in attendance reacted like it was a playoff victory. Stone's hit set off a huge celebration in the stands. It was readily apparent that this huge crowd fully recognized the importance of this win.

On the very next night, Clemens returned after a 25-day stay on the disabled list due to inflammation and fluid in his right shoulder, which had sidelined him since September 4. He was 20-6 with a 1.98 ERA at the time of his shoulder problem. On the heels of our come-from-behind win the night before, Clemens pitched six scoreless innings, allowing only four hits for his 21st win of the season. Despite Clemens's successful return, it was the Brunansky show as he became the 11th player in Red Sox history to hit three home runs in one game and the sixth in Sox history to do so at Fenway Park. He hit a solo home run in the fourth, a three-run home run in the sixth, and another solo home run in the eighth. Thanks to Brunansky's heroics, we took a 7-0 lead into the ninth inning, but Lamp, pitching in relief with a huge lead, gave up a grand-slam home run and suddenly the score was 7-5. Reardon, in his fourth appearance after surgery, came on to retire Fred McGriff and earn his 20th save for the ninth straight season. He became only the second reliever in major league history to do so.

With a second straight win over Toronto on September 29, we were now 86-72 and in first place, holding a slim two-game lead over the Blue Jays. On October 1 we clinched at least a tie for the Eastern Division title with a 4-3 win over the Chicago White Sox. Kiecker pitched seven strong innings, allowing just six hits and one earned run. In the eighth inning, Andersen, pitching in relief, had his only poor outing since we had acquired him from Houston, giving up two earned runs before Reardon once again came on to retire four straight batters and pick up his fifth victory of the season. We were now 87-73.

On the final day of the regular season—October 3—with Fenway Park jammed to capacity, we scored a 3-1 win over the White Sox to capture the Eastern Division title for the third time in the past five seasons. Boddicker won his 17th game, holding Chicago scoreless until the seventh inning, when the White Sox scored their only run. Reardon came on once again, struggled in the ninth inning, but hung on to pick up his 21st save. Greenwell, Evans, and Brunansky paced the offense. However, it was a sensational diving catch deep in the right-field corner by Brunansky with two outs and two White Sox runners on base that saved the day and the game. It was the defensive play of the season. It set off a wild celebration in the dugout, on the field, and in the stands.

The season ended with a new home attendance record of 2,528,000. It was the fifth straight season that we had drawn more than two million fans at Fenway. It had never happened before in Red Sox history.

We would now have to take on the A's for the American League championship and the right to return to the World Series. They won 104 games. They were the defending world champions, having swept the Giants in the 1989 World Series, a Series that was memorable because of the great earthquake that severely damaged the Bay Area while the World Series was underway. The A's had sent Bob Welch, Rickey Henderson, Jose Canseco, Mark McGwire, and Dennis Eckersley to the All-Star Game. We had played the Oakland ball club 12 times during the regular season and had lost eight.

Their starting pitching was anchored by Dave Stewart, who was 20-11 with a 2.56 ERA, and Bob Welch, who was 27-6 with a 2.95 ERA. It was unquestionably the best one-two starting rotation in the American League, if not all of baseball. Welch would go on to win the Cy Young award in the American League, an honor he well deserved.

The club's middle-relief pitching was not sensational, but it was adequate, and at times very good. Their closer, Dennis Eckersley, was the best in the game. He was 4-2 with 48 saves in 50 attempts with a phenomenal 0.61 ERA. When the A's had a lead in the eighth inning and with Eckersley on the mound, it was all over; he was that damn good.

Their offense was built around the "Bash Brothers," Canseco and McGwire. Canseco had hit 37 home runs and driven in 101 runs and McGwire had hit 39 home runs and driven in 108. Dave Henderson had hit had .271 with 20 home runs and Rickey Henderson had hit .325, with 28 home runs and a league-leading 68 stolen bases. They were heavily favored to win the series and rightfully so.

Nonetheless, the opportunity was before us and we'd take our chances. If there was one thing the painful and nightmarish loss in Game 6 of the

1986 World Series taught us, it's that anything is possible in a short series; we knew that all too well.

Game 1 of the American League Championship Series was played at Fenway Park. Clemens started on the mound for us, coming off a 21-6 season with a 1.93 ERA and 209 strikeouts in 228 innings. The A's countered with Stewart, a 20-game winner for Oakland. It was only the second start for Clemens since coming off shoulder problems that had hampered him the last three weeks of September.

Clemens pitched well for six innings, shutting out the A's on four hits while striking out four. Boggs had given us a lead with a solo home run into the screen above the Green Monster in the fourth inning. The A's tied the game with a run in the top of the seventh off Andersen. The Oakland club took a 2-1 lead into the top of the ninth as Carney Lansford, a former Red Sox third baseman, had an RBI single off Gray, but in the top of the ninth our bullpen fell apart. Lamp and Murphy gave up seven runs to blow the game wide open and give Oakland a 9-1 win. Stewart had just allowed four hits in eight innings, and then Eckersley pitched a scoreless ninth inning to close out the win.

Game 2 was also at Fenway Park with Welch on the mound for Oakland facing Kiecker. Kiecker pitched into the sixth inning, allowing the A's only one run and six hits. The ball game would remain tied 1-1 until the seventh when the A's scored off Harris, giving them a lead and the eventual 4-1 win. The A's had a commanding 2-0 lead heading home to the Oakland Coliseum. It was going to be an uphill battle for us from that point on. It would test the very limits of Morgan's optimism.

On the flight to Oakland I sat and talked with Morgan, but always true to form, he was conceding nothing. His optimism and enthusiasm were infectious and uplifting. It was still difficult to obscure the fact that our backs were pinned against the wall, down two games to none and facing the defending world champions.

As I conversed with Morgan on the flight to Oakland, I was hopeful that somehow his inner toughness and optimism could rub off on our ball club and coupled with some Irish good luck (or a miracle), we just might battle our way back into this series. We resumed the series in Oakland Coliseum after a day off. Boddicker started on the mound for us, and right-hander Mike Moore, who won 13 games for the A's, was the Oakland starter. Some 50,000 A's fans jammed the Coliseum confident and boisterous. They had no reason to doubt that their heroes would trample the Red Sox on the way back to repeat as world champions.

Once again, we jumped out in front as Brunansky drove in a run in the top of the second to give us a 1-0 lead. However, in the bottom of the fourth, the A's came up with two runs to give them a 2-1 lead. It proved to be enough for the A's third straight win. Oakland scored two more runs to give them a 4-1 win, an overwhelming and commanding lead in the series. Boddicker pitched well enough, going eight innings and giving up six hits and only two earned runs. Our Red Sox managed only six hits off Moore and the middle of the A's relief staff. Eckersley, as always, pitched the ninth, once against shutting the door on our ball club, and gaining his second save of the series.

Our last hope now rested squarely on the shoulders of Clemens to at least keep our slim margin of hope alive. Once again a capacity crowd of cocky, confident, and very vocal A's supporters came ready to celebrate another return to the World Series. They were crammed into every nook and cranny of the Oakland Coliseum. While sitting in our dugout watching his ball club in the pregame workout, Morgan was surrounded by a totally negative media convinced of our impending demise. Morgan, however, refused to project a doomsday attitude and continued to be positive.

The image of George Custer at Little Big Horn flashed into my consciousness as Morgan, in response to a media question replied, "We've got our big man going tonight; he'll get us back in the battle."

The media could never seem to extinguish Morgan's enthusiasm. It was the only way that Morgan knew how to play this game; it was real, sincere, and typical Joe Morgan.

In the second inning of the ball game a dramatic and unprecedented incident took place. Clemens felt he was being unfairly squeezed on nearly every pitch by plate umpire Terry Cooney, and Clemens began to demonstrate his displeasure on nearly every pitch. On a particular pitch that Clemens was convinced was a strike, Cooney called it a ball. Clemens visibly demonstrated his displeasure with the call and directed some comments to the umpire with which Cooney took issue. Cooney ripped off his mask and began to shout at Clemens, feeling he was showing him up.

Clemens's competitive nature took over and he charged off the mound and confronted Cooney head on; then, in an unprecedented incident in playoff history, Cooney tossed Clemens out of the ball game. Normally in a playoff game, the umpiring crew is a bit more indulgent in dealing with player disputes. Cooney, however, was not about to be lenient, and Clemens was gone—so was our faint hope of staying alive in the ALCS.

Cooney would later state that Clemens had directed profanity at him, but Clemens categorically denied that he used profanity. In the course of the dispute between Cooney and Clemens, Marty Barrett attempted to intervene to protect Clemens, but in the heated confrontation, Barrett was also ejected from the ball game.

Clemens's ejection seemed to highlight our utter frustration during the entire series. We had faced a very good ball club, and we weren't equal to the challenge. I knew going into the series we were facing an outstanding and talented ball club and that we were definite underdogs, but I still had hope, however, that we'd show up and make a battle out of the series. It was wishful thinking. Oakland was just better, period.

In the second inning, the A's scored three runs, and basically the ball game was over. Stewart went on to pitch a four-hitter, allowing only a single run in the ninth inning. Left-hander Rick Honeycutt, a player I originally had brought to the major leagues a number of years before when I was with the Seattle Mariners, came on in relief to retire our hitters in order to save this ball game for Stewart. It was the third straight year that Stewart had won the pennant-clinching game for Oakland. Stewart was named the series MVP.

Reluctantly, Morgan would finally concede about the Oakland A's, "They are a helluva of a ball club and deserved the championship. No question they are the best team in the league."

We had scored only a total of four runs in the entire four-game series, and the Oakland pitching had shut down our offense completely. As a ball club we hit only .188 and our team pitching ERA was 4.50, while the Oakland ball club hit .299 as a team and had a spectacular combined staff ERA of 1.00. It was an overwhelming victory by Oakland.

Despite our disappointing performance in the ALCS, we nonetheless had a fairly successful season in winning the Eastern Division title, but it still wasn't enough. I would have my work cut out for me once again this offseason. Our season had demonstrated that we had little power and very little speed. These were areas of our ball club that I would definitely have to address this winter. Once again, I'd also have to address the end of a Red Sox legend's career.

At one point late in the season in the middle of a doubleheader, I was in my office for a few minutes to return one or two phone calls. I looked up and was surprised to see Evans standing in the threshold of my office in his civilian clothes. He had played in the first game as the designated hitter, and I was confounded as to what he was doing out of uniform, out of the dugout, and in my office.

Before I could question him, he said, "I want to retire. I can't play anymore. I just can't swing the bat, my back is too painful and it's time for me to hang it up."

I was really taken back by his statement. At first I didn't know how to respond.

After collecting my thoughts I said, "Dwight, you can't make that decision right now. Why don't you go home—sleep on it—and we'll talk about it tomorrow?"

I told Dwight we'd announce that he had a slight back flareup and would sit out the second game.

When he left my office, I went up to the owner's box to let John and Haywood know what had transpired. I also contacted Dr. Pappas in the clubhouse to let him know what Evans had said. I told him I'd get Evans to come out to Fenway the following afternoon for a meeting with all of us. I placed a call to the dugout to let Morgan know Evans's status and request.

The next afternoon Evans met with Morgan, Dr. Pappas, John, Haywood, and me in one of our conference rooms. I asked him to explain to everyone his conversation with me the previous evening.

"I told Lou, I just can't play any longer, my back is killing me and affecting my ability to swing the bat and I feel it's time to retire."

Dr. Pappas spoke up.

"Dwight, I really feel if we put you in traction for a few days, I believe we can alleviate the pain and clear up your problem."

Evans at first was reluctant to consider Dr. Pappas's suggestion because his back was seriously handicapping his performance.

I finally said to Evans, "If you will give it a try and it doesn't work, then you and I can discuss your request for retirement. Is that a deal?"

Evans agreed to give traction a try, and he reported to the UMass Hospital in Worcester the next day.

At that time, I had to make a decision regarding our team, as it would relate to Evans's condition. If I disabled him officially, he would be lost to our club for 15 days, but if I gambled that I might get him back on the ball club in five or six days, I would be ahead of the game, because a sound Evans was a plus over a temporary fill-in from Triple-A. I decided not to disable Evans and go one man short for a few days. I gave some thought to reaching down into our farm system to bring up a young 21-year-old outfielder on our Single-A ball club at Lynchburg, Virginia, in the Carolina League, named Phil Plantier. He had the potential to hit with power in the future but was still a year or so away defensively, so I might be rushing him to the big leagues too soon.

Five days into the treatment Dr. Pappas called me to tell me that Evans felt great and was ready to leave the hospital, test his back, and face live pitching. I arranged to have some college pitchers and a college catcher to come to Fenway for the next day or two to throw live batting practice to him. I also received a request from Evans to have Carl Yastrzemski fly into Boston to work with him while he was taking his batting practice, which I arranged. After two days of batting practice Evans told me he felt great and I immediately got him on a plane flight to re-join our ball club. I called Morgan to let him know that Evans was on his way.

Naturally, the local media chronicled the Evans saga daily, and when our batting coach Richie Hebner found out that Yastrzemski had been working with Evans, he felt he was being upstaged and was enraged. When the Red Sox returned from the road trip, Hebner made a beeline for my office and began to rant and rave, extremely upset and offended that I had allowed Yastrzemski, and not him, to work with Evans.

I tried to point out that Yaz had always been a guru to Evans and with Hebner on the road with the club, it made more sense to keep him with the team and bring Yastrzemski in per Evans's request. Hebner, who was an intense competitor and a very proud professional, was angry at Evans and also upset with *Boston Herald* reporter, Joe Giuliotti, who had written about the Evans incident. Hebner felt it reflected poorly on his job performance as the Red Sox hitting coach.

When Hebner left my office, he went looking for Giuliotti. Hebner confronted Giuliotti, a few heated words were exchanged, and I was alerted about the confrontation. I immediately went and separated the two of them before it escalated into an ugly situation. I got Hebner into our clubhouse to calm down and get dressed and go to work. It also took a little more tact and patience to smooth Giuliotti's temper and appease the entire situation.

When the season was over, the concern over Evans's physical problems would impact our decision whether to pick up the club option on his contract. The option was substantial, and the medical prognosis was not good.

Evans had a few idiosyncrasies, but he was by far one of my all-time favorites on the Red Sox ball club.

He was the consummate professional in every sense of the word with an honest and sincere love for the Red Sox and the game itself. He was conscientious, almost to a fault. At times he was sincerely concerned about even the minutest details in the clubhouse, in the ballpark, in the hotel, and on the charter flights. He was different, and he was special. Once he put his uniform on to compete, he gave you 100 percent every single day in every game, and I admired him greatly both as a person and as a professional.

After a lengthy discussion about the option on Evans's contract with John and Haywood, the decision was made not to pick up the option. In essence, he would become a free agent, no longer a member of the Red Sox ball club.

I was sincerely saddened to let him go, not only to see someone I personally admired leave, but also to bring to a close a brilliant career in a Red Sox uniform.

During my tenure at the Red Sox, it was one of the most difficult phone calls I had to make to let Evans know that we would not be picking up the option on his contract to bring him back.

When I thought back to the Red Sox outfield of Jim Rice, Fred Lynn, and Evans, all three of whom have been elected to the Red Sox Hall of Fame, I could not recall too many ball clubs in the last 40 seasons with an outfield that would surpass the quality of that Red Sox outfield. In Red Sox history, probably only the greatest Red Sox outfield of all time of Tris Speaker, Duffy Lewis, and Harry Hooper (with Speaker and Hooper in baseball's Hall of Fame in Cooperstown) would surpass the team of Rice, Lynn, and Evans in overall talent and brilliance.

With the Evans decision made, I turned my attention to planning for the winter meetings, finding new talent to bolster our lineup, and trying to further our quest for complete postseason glory. In the past seven seasons we had won three Eastern Division titles and an American League championship, and we came within one pitch of winning it all. But nothing—nothing—would ever matter until we won a world championship. The frustration and patience of everyone, media and fans alike, was wearing thin.

CHAPTER 6

1991 and 1992

An Attempt to Rebuild

The frustration of having been swept away by the Oakland ball club in the American League Championship Series the previous October was still a distasteful memory as I headed to Florida to attend our annual organizational meetings. I would always coordinate our annual meetings in conjunction with our winter instructional program, and we would schedule our formal meetings each day around the daily afternoon ball games of our instructional club. For me it was always a very special and unique opportunity to build morale and a deep sense of commitment and dedication to the organization. I would always schedule a social event or two in conjunction with the meetings to develop a sense of comradeship. I have always been an ardent believer that success is about people and not policies, because any policy is only as effective as the people who endorse it or implement it.

As I opened the first day of our meetings, I made a brief state of the union address.

"I want you all to know that all of us in the front office and ownership alike recognize that the success of this organization begins and ends with the people in this room today. The work that you people do, day in and day out, season after season, is absolutely essential to the success of the Red Sox organization. We are family, and we are an organization with one overriding goal to win a world championship that has been a long, long time in coming."

I paused for a brief moment and then continued, "I want you all to know I'm proud to be associated with you and personally grateful for all your sacrifices and hard work and dedication."

At our annual organizational meeting I always felt strongly that our baseball operations staff should understand my philosophy behind moves I had made over the course of a season. I had walked in their shoes as a farm director, player development director, and as a director of baseball operations for other teams, and I was personally aware of the enormous amount of sweat and tears that goes into the development of a prospect. Because I had traded away some of our good young prospects in Brady Anderson, Jeff Bagwell, and Curt Schilling, I wanted our baseball people to know my reasons for doing so. The Red Sox organization and our fans had waited 72 years to win the big one, and whenever we had an opportunity to get back to the World Series, I felt we had to go for broke. I would always have my critics whenever I made a trade that didn't work out or take us to the promised land, but success is always on the far side of failure and the greatest risk will always be in not taking one. I also made it clear to the scouts that their judgments would always play a major role in any decision that our front office would ever make.

A strong trustworthy scouting staff is integral to the success of any general manager, despite what the media would like the public to believe. There is no substitute for good judgment, and without question numbers and statistics do play a role in player evaluations and they are excellent additional tools in evaluating the whole player, but it is still the element of human judgment, in my opinion, that has to be the most essential factor in player evaluations.

The legendary veteran scout and president of the Negro Baseball Hall of Fame Buck O'Neil said, "If scouting were just a matter of signing guys who hit the home runs and pitch the no-hitters, anybody could do it. But the major league prospect might be the guy who is something special even though he struck out swinging or the outfielder who overthrew the third baseman on a throw from right field or the pitcher who walked nine batters. We call them *tools:* speed, arm strength, range, hands, bat speed, velocity, and quickness."

It is difficult to definitively define how one acquires good judgment, because there is something very intuitive about it. There is no question that experience, certain basic techniques, and methodologies apply and that learned knowledge acquired from working with and learning from other veteran professional scouts helps to develop scouting expertise. There are also those special individuals who seem to be born with extraordinary talents to scout and to consistently, with few exceptions, provide solid, accurate player evaluations.

Recently there has been an influx of new, young, and talented executives into the front offices of Major League Baseball, and they have introduced revolutionary new theories and techniques of evaluation, for example, the *Moneyball* approach. In some instances they have placed a greater emphasis on the overall statistical compilation of a player's performance vis-à-vis the "eyeball to eyeball" judgment of an experienced professional baseball scout. It is an "empirical approach to player evaluation" that stresses the value of walks and on-base percentage and not batting average or outs as the primary criteria for evaluating the true value of a player's performance.

Despite my 40 years in professional baseball spent mostly in player personnel and player evaluation, I fully recognize and accept that modern technology represents a change creating new and progressive methods and techniques and that there is nothing wrong in thinking outside the box. In fact, more often than not it's essential to do so in light of ever-changing challenges in today's environment. Yet despite the modern-day approach to player analysis, I still believe the intrinsic value of an experienced professional scout with a proven record of success must still play the more prominent role in evaluating a player's potential and future success. This is not to say that statistical analysis should not play a prominent role in the final and overall evaluation, but I just don't feel it should become the dominating factor. I am not intending to discredit statistical analyses because it does have value but just as long as we recognize its limitations.

In my opinion, the current *Moneyball* approach that some general managers have adopted overlooks certain important aspects of the game. On-base percentage is obviously a factor in winning ball games, but for me a major factor in winning ball games is not giving up outs needlessly. Your most precious possession on offense is your 27 outs, and you should give them up only to advance runners into scoring position or to win a ball game, not to mention that it is equally important to drive in runs once they are in scoring position. Getting runners on base is necessary, but the ability to drive them in once they are in scoring position is the most essential criteria for success.

I am also convinced that mental makeup and intelligence cannot be measured on a computer or defined by a statistic and that these qualities are essential in the overall and final analysis of a player's talent and potential. No matter the physical skills a player may possess, it is his drive, intensity, guts, and total commitment that will ultimately determine his true level of success as a ballplayer. No computer can ever measure those qualities in a player or a prospect, and too often in my career I have seen players with excellent physical skills but questionable makeups never perform at the full level of their God-given talents.

The value of statistics can be a great asset to any ball club, but the question, in my mind, is to what degree and of what nature. No one would discount the advancement in modern technology and its application to professional baseball, but, in my opinion, it should never discredit the basic intrinsic value of quality scouting intelligence. No organization will ever succeed without that intelligence, no matter how many methods of statistical analysis it has.

On the Red Sox at the time, we had some age on our scouting staff, but overall it was a quality staff. Our scouting director, Eddie Kasko, did an outstanding job. He was organized, capable, and hard working. I was fortunate to have Kasko and another veteran and extremely capable executive Eddie Kenney Sr., along with his son Eddie Jr., who ran our player development system. If I had any additional desire as the general manager of the Red Sox, I would like to have added one or two of the scouts who I had previously worked with and whose judgment I was very familiar with to give me a couple extra trusted advisers when it came to trading and acquiring talent.

We began to discuss the prospects within our organization who might be able to contribute at the major league level during the coming season. The majority of our staff felt a young outfielder named Phil Plantier just might help our offensive production with home runs from the left side of the plate. There were some questions about his defensive skills, but they felt he could be helped defensively if he was willing to work hard in extra sessions.

Some of our people felt that John Marzano, a young catcher we had been watching for a few seasons and who filled in for Rich Gedman in 1987, might also be only a season away from the big league ball club. They felt he could serve as an excellent backup to Tony Peña and in time become our number-one starting catcher.

We also had a young catching prospect in our farm system named Eric Wedge, who was probably a few years away but who just might develop into a front-line major league catcher. He was an All-American out of a fine baseball school, Wichita State University. He had tremendous makeup and a great work ethic and was a decent receiver with some bat potential, although there was some concern about his arm strength. Little did any of us realize at that early stage in his professional baseball career that, Wedge would one day become a major league manager and that he would go on to become the manager of the Cleveland Indians in 2003, and I'm certain that with his makeup and intelligence, he'll become an excellent major league manager.

There was also a strong indication that Carlos Quintana, one of the few Latin players we had signed and developed in our farm system, could prove to be a solid major league outfielder. He had average defensive skills with good bat contact and line drive power.

The one player, however, who was a consensus prospect by our staff was a young first baseman named Maurice "Mo" Vaughn. Our reports indicated that he could become a legitimate power hitter with All-Star potential. We had signed Vaughn, along with another young infield prospect named John Valentin, out of Seton Hall University after drafting him in the second round of the 1989 high school/college draft. Vaughn had been a three-time All-American and had set a Seton Hall school record for 57 home runs and 218 RBIs. He had also been named the Big East Player of the Decade. In 1990 at Pawtucket in only 108 games, he had hit 22 home runs and driven in 72 runs. It was our combined judgment that Vaughn would become our regular first baseman eventually and give us a potential 30 to 40 home runs from the left side of the plate. His defensive skills were average, but he was improving defensively with each passing season and we had every indication that in time he could develop into a good first baseman. We all felt he could be an impact player. I projected that Vaughn might have to open the 1991 season at Pawtucket, but at some point during the season I was hoping he could step in at the major league level.

We were also confident based on our judgment that Valentin was also not that far away from coming to our big league ball club and contributing as a regular infielder. He was playing in our minor league system as a shortstop, but I always felt that his physical skills were better suited for him to play third base and I projected him to play there in the future.

Tim Naehring was the young man we had projected to become our starting shortstop and replace Luis Rivera, although a number of our baseball people, as did I, felt his best position in time would be at third base. All of us in the organization felt that Naehring had the potential to become a major league All-Star. He had exceptional makeup, solid physical skills, a great work ethic, and the qualities of a team leader. He was the final piece of our projected infield with Wade Boggs at third, Naehring at shortstop, Jody Reed at second base, and Vaughn at first base—all products of our minor league system. We would have one of the better infields in the American League.

All of the other defensive positions were fairly well covered. Our outfield of Mike Greenfield, Ellis Burks, and Tom Brunansky starting and Randy Kutcher and Kevin Romine as backups was solid. Peña behind the plate gave us an outstanding starting defensive catcher.

Where we were really struggling was pitching. Even with Roger Clemens as our ace and the anchor of our staff; Greg Harris, a decent starter; and Jeff Reardon, an outstanding closer in the bullpen, we still desperately needed a number-two starter. We had veteran right-hander Dennis Lamp and rookie Jeff Gray to work out of the bullpen, but it was also in need of help. There was no question the loss of Mike Boddicker (17-8) to a free agency and Larry Andersen to an arbitrator's decision, which made Andersen a free agent, had opened up gaping holes in our overall pitching depth. I had my work cut out for me the upcoming winter to attempt to fill them. It would be no easy task.

I had acquired Joe Hesketh, a left-handed starting pitcher with five or six years of major league experience, last July as a free agent. I was hopeful that he might give us some depth either as a spot starter or middle reliever. During the 1990 season he had been a disappointment, but I still had confidence that based upon our scouting reports and his record of decent success that he might help us in the future.

Dana Kiecker, a right-hander out of our farm system, had pitched fairly well in his rookie season, winning eight ball games in a limited spot-starting role and earning a 3.67 ERA. It was our hope that Kiecker could continue to improve and end up as a fourth or fifth starter, or at worst, a spot starter or middle reliever. If he and Hesketh could meet our expectations, it would be a tremendous shot in the arm for our pitching staff.

One sleeper in our farm system who we thought just might become an effective right-handed reliever in our bullpen was Paul Quantrill. He was 12-8 combined between Double-A and Triple-A Pawtucket and had proved to be very effective against both left- and right-handed batters.

When I went off to the winter meetings that December, I was determined to find a way to trade for or acquire pitching through free agency if at all possible. A left-handed starting pitcher who could become a number-two or three starter would be ideal. There were one or two quality free-agent pitchers available, but they were signed by other ball clubs quickly and expensively. I spent a tremendous amount of time going from meeting to meeting with other major league general managers in the hope of finding some way to trade for pitching, but I came up empty handed. I did not want to trade away some of our best young prospects because I would have to rebuild with them. As a result I had little to bargain with, but it did not curtail my efforts to attempt to make something happen. I just struck out.

I now found myself really scurrying to find some pitching help somewhere, somehow. We could not gamble going into the next season maintaining status quo with our present pitching staff. As I scoured through our scouting reports and talked to our staff, right-hander Danny Darwin came to my attention. He was 35 years old and a 12-year major league veteran, but our reports indicated he was a tough competitor and he could still pitch effectively in a starting role. During the past two seasons he had won 22 ball games while losing only eight with around a 2.3 ERA. He appeared to be very durable despite his age, having appeared in 48 games in 1990 and 68 games the previous season. There was every indication he could still help us. Kasko and Wayne Britton, one of our top scouts, indicated that Darwin was an intense competitor and felt he just might help our pitching staff. I contacted his agent and worked out a contract for three years. I recognized it was a gamble to sign a veteran pitcher to a three-year contract, but he had averaged pitching close to 170 innings the past three or four seasons, and there was little reason to question his durability despite his age. I was certain that I would be questioned or criticized by the local media for giving this 35-year-old a three-year contract, but if he could give us 170 or 180 effective innings the next few seasons, he could be an asset to our overall pitching depth. Besides, I had very few options available, period.

A couple of our baseball staff brought up a left-hander named Matt Young. Young was a free agent, and his agent contacted me during the meetings to say that Young was interested in coming to Boston. Young had been a number-two draft choice by the Seattle Mariners out of UCLA in 1980 and was a highly touted high school and college player. He had pitched for the Dodgers, the A's, and the Mariners. In 1990 for Seattle he went 8-18, pitching in 225 innings and striking out 178, but walking 107 batters. As I read through our scouting reports on Young, they indicated that he had an above-average fastball and curveball, but his control was very inconsistent. I pondered whether Bill Fischer, our major league pitching coach and who was known during his pitching career for his control, could help Young. He was, however, left-handed, and we desperately needed a lefty in our rotation. I decided to take a gamble and sign Young to a three-year contract for $6 million, averaging $2 million a season—at that time about the average salary for a starting pitcher.

It turned out to be a bad gamble, probably my worst signing as the Red Sox general manager, because what our scouting reports failed to point out was that Young had a serious psychological block in throwing to a base, particularly first base. It would dramatically impact his effectiveness. He would struggle greatly, and his constant dilemma with his control and inability to throw to a base became a disaster. I may have read too much into our reports and gambled too much on Fischer's ability to help Young, but the fact that our reports did not point out his psychological block was an anomaly for the Red Sox scouting reports. They generally were always complete and in depth. It was an obvious flaw that we had failed to pick up on it. It was costly—not only financially but production-wise; he did little to help our pitching depth and our overall performance, and I heard a lot about it from our media. I deserved the criticism. I had let our desperate need for a left-handed starting pitcher overrule my judgment, and we got burned.

After I had signed Darwin and Young, I was hopeful that I had added some depth and strength to our pitching staff and I turned my attention to finding a bat with power to help our offense. During the course of this search, I, along with John Donovan, attended a special memorial service at the Carnegie Hall to pay homage to former commissioner of baseball A. Bartlett Giamatti, a huge Red Sox fan. Prior to his stint as commissioner, he was the president of the National League and he would, on occasion, visit Fenway Park. Whenever he was there, we would sequester him up in our private box and I'd get to spend some time with him. His knowledge and love of baseball and the Red Sox were impressive. He would banter back and forth with me over my trades or suggest moves I should consider that might improve our ball club. It was almost an oxymoron that Giamatti was the National League president and not the American League president. I have always felt that his untimely death was a tragic loss to baseball. Being the commissioner of baseball was not just a job to him, it was the fulfillment of a lifetime dream.

When the moving tribute to Giamatti was concluded, Tom Reich, a veteran-player-turned-agent who had also attended the ceremony, happened to be eating at the same restaurant that Donovan and I had selected, and so we invited him to sit with us. Reich happened to mention that Jack Clark, one of his clients who was now a free agent, had an interest in playing in Fenway Park. Clark was 34, a right-handed power hitter, having hit 35, 27, 26, and 25 home runs during the past five seasons, and a four-time National League All-Star. When I got back to Boston, I read through our scouting reports on Clark and also talked to our West Coast scouts who had covered the Padres to ask them for their judgment on Clark and whether he might be able to help our offense. The overall consensus was that Clark could be a definite power factor in Fenway. He could serve as a designated hitter, handle first base, or fill in as an outfielder. His average of 26 home runs and 90 RBIs over the past three or four seasons would be a welcome addition to our offensive production; I was hoping that the friendly confines of Fenway might produce at least a 30-home run, 100-RBI season out of Clark. I ended up negotiating a three-year contract for Clark with Reich. It was approximately $2.6 million average per season, with some incentives. Clark, with 14 years of major league service, nearly 280 career home runs, and nearly 1,000 RBIs, became a Red Sox player.

Just prior to the opening of the American League season and right before we broke camp, I made a trade to acquire another right-handed starting pitcher, Mike Gardiner from the Seattle Mariners, for Rob Murphy. Murphy had given us an excellent season in 1989 when he appeared in 74 games and posted a 2.74 ERA. I had acquired him in a trade from Cincinnati that same season. The past season Murphy had really struggled going 0-6 in 68 appearances while giving up 85 hits in 57 innings. Our reports on Gardiner were decent. He had been 12-8 with a league-leading 1.9 ERA in Double-A Williamsport in the Eastern League. In 179 innings he had struck out 149 batters. Our scouting reports indicated that Gardiner had some potential to pitch at the big league level as a starter, quite possibly in 1991. If he could make the jump to Boston and pitch effectively at the big league level, it would really add a great deal of depth to our pitching staff.

I made two other moves. I signed to a one-year contract a free-agent outfielder named John Moses, a switch hitter who had spent six years in the major leagues and who could help us as a hitter off the bench or as a backup outfielder. I also signed a left-handed relief pitcher, Tony Fossas, to a Pawtucket contract, but I invited him to spring training. Fossas was a short relief man, and although he had limited major league experience, our reports from Denver in the Triple-A Pacific Coast League indicated he was extremely effective in getting left-handed hitters out. As a short setup man he just might prove very effective in key situations.

I realized that I had added some age to the ball club in signing Darwin, Clark, and Young, but if they were capable of performing effectively, we just might, barring injuries, overcome the loss of Mike Boddicker's 17 victories and end up challenging once again for the league championship. We would also need another super season from Roger Clemens, but he was always capable of doing just that. I knew the media would be skeptical of the older players we had acquired. If they failed to live up to expectations, I would hear about it loud and clear. It would be nothing new, however, for you had to learn to live with the praise and the criticism if you were involved in sports or politics in Boston.

Our pitching rotation had the potential to be Clemens, Harris, Darwin, Young, and Dopson (if he was able to bounce back from elbow surgery), and the bullpen looked to have enough depth with Bolton, Lamp, Hesketh, Gray, Kiecker, Fossas, and Reardon. Only Gardiner would be a dark horse. The addition of Clark's bat along with Greenwell, Burks, Brunansky, Boggs, and Reed indicated an improvement in our offense. Our bench strength appeared to be very adequate. What we couldn't afford, however, were any major injuries, particularly to our pitching. On paper our ball club was improved, but we'd have to prove it on the playing field. Toronto, with their talented ball club and strong front-line pitching, was still the club to beat.

We had won the division title in 1990 by just two games over the Blue Jays. Toronto was a much improved ball club and on the verge of becoming a very strong ball club. With Joe Carter, Roberto Alomar, Devon White, John Olerud, pitcher Jimmy Key, Dave Stieb, Juan Guzman, and Tom Henke in the bullpen, they were a legitimate challenge to anyone and very capable of winning it all.

In late April I picked up one more utility player, Steve Lyons, to give us depth at a number of positions. Lyons could play a number of positions: first base, second base, shortstop, center field, right field, and catcher in an emergency. I had always considered his versatility a valuable asset to any ball club. It was the first of three different times that I would acquire Lyons during the next five seasons. He was a bit eccentric, but I personally liked him a great deal and honestly felt that he could really help our ball club. For whatever reason, I was never able to fathom that every time I acquired him, the sentiment in the clubhouse was always that he never seemed to fit in. To me he was personable, outgoing, and intensely competitive. It was a dilemma that I never understood.

On April 8 we opened the season in Toronto and Clemens bested Stieb to give us a 6-2 win over the Blue Jays. Clark also hit a grand slam in his debut in a Red Sox uniform. The Blue Jays, however, bounded back to beat us the next three straight in the SkyDome. By May 1 we were 11-8, but surprisingly in first place, clinging to a half-game lead. We proceeded to win seven out of the next nine games in Chicago and Minnesota. By May 12 we were now in first place at 18-9 with a two-game lead. At the start of June we continued to lead the division with a 26-20 record but were tied for first place. Reardon continued to pitch effectively, and despite our overall pitching problems, in a two-week period he would save six ball games.

Despite our strong overall start as a team, some individuals struggled at the plate. Although Clark's bat showed up in the season opener, he drove in only seven runs in the next 30 ball games. On June 6 Clark was hitting only .198, and the "boo birds" were out in force as the fans really got on him: They let him know in no uncertain terms what they thought of his performance. Ellis Burks also got off to a very slow start, hitting only .234 in April and a paltry .191 in June.

Injuries began to take their toll on our overall team performance. Dopson, who we had hoped might be able to become one of our starters, went down early in the first week of the season. It was ironic that Darwin had averaged nearly 166 innings of pitching the past four seasons, both as a starter and reliever. Just one month into our season he had to be put on the disabled list. We now had Dopson and Darwin, two starters I had banked on to bolster our starting rotation, who were recovering from injuries. On June 11, the starting rotation took another hit when Young had to be disabled with an incomplete tear in his left shoulder. He would remain disabled until August 1 while undergoing treatment for his injury. Adding to our now critical pitching situation, Kiecker, another pitcher who I had hoped would contribute to our pitching depth, was disabled on May 26 with a sore right shoulder. He would remain disabled until just about the end of July.

As our disabled list got longer, I continued to search for new talent. During the annual June draft, our number-one selection was a right-handed pitcher out of Washington State named Aaron Sele. He would later turn out to be an excellent front-line major league pitcher. We also drafted and signed his battery mate, Scott Hatteberg, who would also become a major league catcher and a decent major league hitter. It was encouraging, but unfortunately these two prospects would not be able to help us stop the rash of injuries that plagued our team.

I was convinced that Morgan, who was holding the pitching staff together with bailing wire, deserved an immense aount of credit for keeping our ball club competitive despite the serious injuries that were impacting our ball club's performance. In essence, he had now lost three of his projected starting pitchers. It would be extremely difficult for us to stay in contention or remain competitive without a miracle. Our pitching staff resembled the infirmary at the University of Massachusetts Hospital, and we were in deep trouble. As great as Clemens was, without a solid second, third, and fourth starter, it would be impossible to stay in contention with Toronto. By the end of June we had fallen into second place behind the Blue Jays, three and a half games out of the division lead.

It also wasn't limited to the pitching staff. Naehring, after an impressive spring, was limited to only 20 games because of injuries, and on May 20 I placed him on the disabled list. His season was over when he underwent back surgery on July 3 with a bone spur in his lower back.

Luis Rivera stepped in and became our regular shortstop for the rest of the season, hitting just under .260 with eight home runs. He also played well defensively. To give us some additional protection in the middle infield, I purchased the contract of veteran utility infielder Mike Brumley, who I had signed to a Pawtucket contract. Brumley had played in brief stints at the major league level as a backup middle infielder for the Cubs, the Tigers, and the Mariners. I had signed him to a Triple-A contract for just such an emergency, and I felt that with Brumley and Lyons, we had adequate backups.

One dramatic and stunning event occurred on July 30 when we were scheduled for a Sunday afternoon game at Fenway Park against the Texas Rangers. With our pitching rotation in disarray I had recalled a young 22-year-old left-handed pitcher named Kevin Morton from Pawtucket where he was 7-3. It was a desperate move to fill a gap in our depleted starting rotation. He would start the game for us against the Texas Rangers and Dennis "Oil Can" Boyd, a former Red Sox hurler who had been released after a series of injuries.

I arrived at the ballpark at 8:45 a.m. and drove into the players and staff parking lot. Al Forrester, a legendary Red Sox employee, was the first to greet me as I got out of my car. He told me one of our players had collapsed in our clubhouse, and Charlie Moss, our trainer, was out in front of Fenway waiting for an ambulance. I raced into our clubhouse, and the first thing I saw was pitcher Jeff Gray lying still on the floor in front of his locker. It was a sight I would not soon forget. Our other trainer, Rich Zawacki, was leaning over Gray and attending to him. I asked Zawacki if Dr. Pappas had arrived. He told me no, but he was due shortly. I asked him if he had any indication of what was wrong with Gray. Zawacki replied that he thought Gray had suffered a stroke and they had immediately called for an ambulance after Gray fell from his chair as he was starting to get dressed for the ball game. The clubhouse was like a morgue; the players were sitting in stunned disbelief at this tragic turn of events. As Zawacki continued to minister to Gray, Moss arrived with the ambulance crew. As they lifted him onto a gurney to carry him to the ambulance and the hospital, Dr. Pappas arrived and rode in the ambulance with Gray to the hospital.

Gray was a 28-year-old, well-conditioned athlete. It was all but inconceivable that he could have suffered a stroke. It was a tremendously emotional scene with a young man whose life was hanging in the balance who just hours ago was vibrant and full of life. The ball game we were about to play seemed totally insignificant. With a teammate's life at such a critical juncture, nothing else mattered.

The rest of the day unwound before me as though the ball game was being enacted on a stage outside my psyche. All I could think about was that a young man was battling for his life in the hospital a few blocks away. That we won the game 11-6 over Boyd and that Morton won his first major league game seemed totally insignificant. All I wanted to hear from Dr. Pappas was that Gray was alive and recovering. My thoughts, and the thoughts of the entire team, were with him in Beth Israel Hospital that Sunday afternoon. It was an unreal experience and an unforgettable day.

We finally received word from Dr. Pappas and the hospital indicating that Gray had suffered an irregularity in one of his arteries that supplied the brain with blood and that he was paralyzed on the right side of his body. He was obviously finished for the rest of the season and could well be finished for the rest of his professional baseball career. It seemed to put a pall over the rest of the season.

(Gray would eventually undergo months and years of therapy in the hope of recovering total mobility in the right side of his body and in his pitching arm. His attempt at total recovery is a classic story of courage and commitment. After two years he would nearly succeed. Unfortunately Gray would never regain the complete use of his right hand and fingers—he couldn't consistently hold the ball in his hands—and his playing career was over. He would go on to serve as a minor league pitching coach in the Red Sox organization for a period of time.)

Gray's collapse was the low point of a month that signaled a turnaround in the 1991 Red Sox's fortunes, thanks in a large part to Clark's bat. Although a serious groin and left calf injuries had severely handicapped Clark—his first 40 or 50 games he had driven in only 15 RBIs—he began to heal and his performance improved. On July 5 against the Tigers he drove in seven RBIs. On July 31 he would hit three home runs against the A's, including the game-winning home run in the 14th inning. From July on, Clark proceeded to drive in 75 runs. In August he hit .340 and drove in 16 runs in a 14-game stretch. In his last 20 games Clark hit .393. His bat would literally carry our ball club, despite a makeshift pitching staff, taking us from 11½ games out and in fourth place back to just a half game out on September 21.

On September 22 and after a remarkable 21-10 run, we were, miraculously, right back in contention. We faced the New York Yankees at Fenway Park. We took a 3-2 lead into the ninth inning, and with Reardon in relief—who had been brilliant all season long with 40 saves in 57 appearances, which established a new Red Sox save record, (he would end the season with 300 saves and second all time in major league history)—he faced Roberto Kelly. With two outs and two strikes on Kelly, Kelly swung and hit a solo home run to tie the ball game, rekindling some very painful memories from the past. Young, now activated, came on in relief and gave up a run in the 10th. We lost to the Yankees 4-3. The loss would send us into a downhill spiral, one from which we would never recover. We proceeded to lose 11 of the next 14 games and finish in second place seven games behind the Blue Jays, who finished 91-71; we finished at 84-78.

There were many factors that kept us from repeating as division champions and not the least of which was our injury hex that seemed to haunt us all season long. We had utilized the disabled list 13 times during the season and lost well over 1,000 days of playing time from numerous disabled players. Darwin won only three games and appeared in only 12 games; Young went 3-7. Dopson and Gray were lost for the entire season. Offensively we struggled also. Brunansky would hit only .229. Burks would hit .251 with only 14 home runs and drove in 56 RBIs. Greenwell would hit nine home runs, his lowest home run output in six seasons. We would finish seventh in the league in total home runs and seventh in pitching with a combined and ineffective team pitching ERA of 4.01.

Joe Morgan had kept the ship afloat as long as humanly possible despite crippling injuries to our pitching staff. The media, however, kept creating the perception that the club had gotten away from him and that there was dissension on the ball club. So often, unfortunately, the perception created by the media always becomes real in the eyes and ears of the fans. A good part of the blame for the last season's collapse was attributed to Morgan, and it was totally unjustified.

Despite the disappointment of our disastrous finish there were some highlights during the season. Clemens tied for the major league lead in strikeouts with 241, led in innings pitched with 271, and held hitting to only a combined .221 batting average against him. He would go on to win his third Cy Young award with an 18-10 won-lost record and a league-leading 2.62 ERA. Harris finished 11-12 but had 127 strikeouts, a career high, and he became only the second pitcher in Red Sox history to have 20 starts and relief appearances in one season. Hesketh, whom I had signed as a free agent, led the major leagues in winning percentage with .750 percentage. In his final 16 appearances, all after the All-Star break, he finished 10-3 with a 3.00 ERA, and he finished the season 12-4 with a 3.29 ERA. He was a lifesaver to a depleted pitching staff. Reardon had another outstanding season as our closer with 40 saves made and his 62nd save as a Red Sox closer since joining our ball club. Clark, after a horrendous early start, hit 28 home runs and drove in 87 to lead our ball club in both categories. Boggs finished second in the American League batting title race with a .332 batting average and 42 doubles (his seventh straight year with 40 or more doubles), and he was on base 270 times (only the third time in his career he didn't reach base 300 times in a season). Reed hit .283 played in 153 games with 60 RBIs and 175 hits, all career highs. He also handled second base extremely well, finishing with the fourth best defensive percentage in the American League. Peña, despite a disappointing season offensively, was brilliant behind the plate and finished the season as one of the best defensive catchers in the American League. His unique skills behind the plate salvaged an injury-ravaged pitching staff and kept the ball club in contention until the final two weeks of the season. He did so despite handling eight or 10 different starters throughout the season.

Some of the hopefuls we had been watching at the beginning of the season were able to make some progress as part of our major league club.

Plantier was called up from Pawtucket twice during the season and hit .331 with 11 home runs and 35 RBIs in 53 games. His offensive skills gave us a positive and hopeful outlook that he had the ability to make major contributions in the future as a starter. Quintana hit .295 with 11 home runs and 71 RBIs. He handled first base like he had played that position his entire career. He also played in both left field and right field. I recalled Vaughn from Pawtucket in late June, and in some 74 games he hit .260 with four home runs and 32 RBIs. His combined major league and Triple-A averages were 18 home runs and 82 RBIs. These were encouraging performances, and it boded well for the future. It was obvious that we had the foundation of some young talent to build upon. There were still, however, some big holes to fill in order for us to become a serious contender to win the division title and the American League championship.

When I sat down with owners Haywood Sullivan and John Harrington to discuss the overall status of the ball club and what we could do to turn things around for next season, the question about whether a change in managers should be made was brought up. Haywood broached the subject, and there seemed to be some dissatisfaction with the way Morgan had handled the ball club. In light of the problems we had encountered, it was difficult for me to point the finger at Morgan for our disappointing season. I recognized that despite the fact we had another great season attendance-wise as we drew 2,562,000 paid admissions (it was the sixth straight season of drawing more than two million fans, and it was a Red Sox record), the operating costs, primarily the continued escalation of players' salaries, and general costs continued to increase. In a ballpark like Fenway, which seats just over 35,000, we faced some limitations budget-wise because we had no parking income, minimal luxury boxes, and middle-level radio/television income that was well below the overall radio/television income of the Yankees. I fully understood ownership's concern with the bottom line and our need to rejuvenate fan interest after a losing season. On the other hand, however, I was strongly convinced that Morgan had done a great job in handling our ball club under very difficult circumstances, and I made known my feelings about Morgan to Haywood and John. After a bit more discussion, I assumed the issue of firing Morgan was shelved.

We then began discussing our coaching staff and if there was need to make some changes there. A few days before the season ended, Morgan and I had discussed the possibility of a change in our hitting coach. I told him that we would meet with ownership a day or two after the season was over and we would discuss the coaching staff in depth. I told him before the meeting that it was my understanding that all we would be discussing was the coaching staff.

After some very brief general comments, ownership proceeded to tell Morgan that they had decided to make a change and replace him. Morgan was stunned. He looked at me as if to say, "This isn't what you told me the meeting would be about," but I was as much taken aback by the decision as he was.

Morgan got to his feet stunned and angry and said, "I thought I did a good job with this ball club."

Before anyone in the room could reply, Morgan continued, "I don't understand this, but it's your ball club and I'm leaving."

He stormed out of the room and slammed the door.

The Joe Morgan era had ended abruptly. I felt a deep sense of sadness and remorse over his departure. I liked him a great deal personally and professionally, and I felt he had done an excellent job under difficult circumstances. I felt strongly that he should have been retained.

After Morgan left, I indicated that we had better prepare a press announcement on Morgan's dismissal immediately because word would spread quickly once the media got an inkling of the firing. When any press announcement has to be made concerning managerial changes, coaching changes, or player personnel moves, it is always handled by the general manager, whether you agree or disagree with the final decision by ownership. The general manager speaks for the entire organization, and he must support the decision totally.

A week or so after we had made the decision not to renew Morgan's contract, John suggested that I call Morgan and offer him a position in the organization. I decided to offer Morgan a position as a special assignment scout who reported directly to me. He was still smarting from the firing and told me he had no interest in the position. Still in all I was hopeful that he would mellow in time, change his mind, and return to the organization. Morgan was born to be in baseball, and he had been a dedicated, loyal, and successful Red Sox minor league manager, scout, and big league manager for a number of years. He belonged with the Red Sox.

The search for a new manager would now become my major priority along with a makeover of our coaching staff. I still had a great deal of work to do to fill the many holes on our ball club, but until we had a new manager on board, that challenge would have to be on the back burner.

I had always held Joe Torre in high regard since our days together in the Mets organization. I felt he had a very special approach in managing his players. He had tremendous patience, his players had a great deal of respect for him, and they seemed to love playing for him. He never seemed to put any additional pressure on them whenever they were struggling. He was a constant source of support and confidence that seemed to infect every player. He wasn't a holler guy who would rant and rave, but his message always seemed to come across loud and clear. I also felt that he had really matured as a manager since we last worked together. Torre had been out of managing for nearly five seasons while serving as a play-by-play announcer for the Angels. When Torre came to Boston, I mentioned to him how much I thought of him and indicated that if we ever had a managerial job open, I'd be calling him. But before the possibility ever developed he was hired by the St. Louis Cardinals and eventually he would go on to manage the New York Yankees to three world championships.

I had been associated with Lou Piniella at both the Baltimore Orioles and the Kansas City Royals. I always had the greatest respect for his intensely competitive nature. Piniella, however, had just taken over the managerial reins of the Cincinnati Reds the previous season, and despite my strong interest in Piniella, he was not available.

I began to draw up a list of other possible managerial candidates. One candidate that our organizational staff kept insisting for consideration was Cecil "Butch" Hobson, our Pawtucket manager. Hobson had played for six of nine seasons with the Red Sox. In 1977 he had hit 30 home runs and driven in 112 runs. In 1979 he hit 28 home runs and had 93 RBIs. Hobson also had managed in the minor leagues for five seasons, with the last two seasons in the Red Sox organization at New Britain, our Double-A club, and at Pawtucket, our Triple-A ball club. While managing the Pawsox, he took the previous season's last-place ball club and managed them to a first-place finish in 1991. It was a dramatic 18½-game turnaround from the past season. His accomplishments earned him the International League Manager of the Year honors. He was also selected as the Minor League Manager of the Year by *Baseball America*, a very prestigious honor. Hobson was as hardnosed, aggressive, tough, and intensely competitive.

As I began to draw up my list of possible future managers, I decided that Hobson should be given consideration. His track record the past two seasons managing in our farm system was excellent, and as I talked with our development staff, they had extremely positive things to say about him. I suggested that John and Haywood sit in with me when I brought Hobson in for an interview.

John, Haywood, and I decided to hold the interview away from Fenway Park at the J.R.Y. Foundation offices in Dedham. We spent the better part of two hours questioning him at length about his overall managerial philosophy and his methods for motivating players and dealing with them and the media. He made a very positive impression on all of us because he was so positive, polished, prepared, and hungry to win. He had to be our man.

By the end of the interview, we all agreed that Butch Hobson would become the 38th manager in Red Sox history.

On October 8 we held a press conference in the Diamond Room at Fenway Park to introduce Hobson as the new Red Sox manager. The Diamond Room was jammed with media, and a number of them were still critical of our decision not to retain Morgan. Hobson handled the press conference well, and his initial rapport with the media was positive. Over the course of the questioning by the media, I was asked if there was interest in Hobson by other major league teams and whether that influenced my decision to hire him. My exact response to that question was simply that two or three scouts from other organizations had made inquiries about Hobson's future with the Red Sox. That was my verbatim answer to the question. I never stated or implied that I had received direct inquiries asking for permission to talk to Hobson about a managerial position from other general managers.

As is not uncommon in Boston, my statement was taken out of context. Dan Shaughnessy of *The Boston Globe*, would continue to proclaim that I had stated that other organizations had a strong interest in hiring Hobson. The implication was that the interest had greatly influenced the Red Sox to hire Hobson as the big league manager. Nothing was further from the truth. Hobson was hired to manage the Red Sox based on his spirit, his success in managing within our organization, and the recommendation of many of our baseball operations staff. It was my opinion, and that of our ownership also, that Hobson had earned the privilege of managing the Red Sox.

After meeting with Hobson to select and hire his coaching staff, I then spent the better part of two days discussing and analyzing our present ball club—its strengths, weaknesses, and needs with Hobson so he was prepared for the annual winter meetings, which were to be held in early December, and the upcoming annual organizational meetings in Florida in late October.

At our internal offseason meetings, we spent five days critiquing our entire minor league system with emphasis on players who might be able to help our big league club next season. We also discussed what players, if any, who might be available for acquisition and might contribute to our ball club. One of the players we discussed was Frank Viola, a left-hander and a former Cy Young award recipient, who had played out his free agency with the New York Mets. In 1990 he was 20-12 with a 2.67 ERA, and in 1991 he was 13-15 with a 3.97 ERA, having suffered an infected fingernail on his pitching hand for the second half of the season. It turned out to be a glomus tumor that required surgery.

But from what I had witnessed from Viola and what our scouting reports indicated, the hurler was a gutsy, hard-nosed competitor every time he was handed the baseball and wouldn't allow this injury to impair his talent. That observation was in every scouting report and evident in all the times I had observed Viola pitch. I had seen him pitch for St. John's University against Yale University and Ron Darling in the NCAA Regional playoffs in probably the greatest collegiate baseball game ever played. It was scoreless through 11 innings. Darling and Viola carried a no-hitter into the 12th inning. Viola was matching Darling pitch for pitch until St. John's finally won 1-0. Our scouts had also seen Viola pitch often for both the Twins and the Mets. There was no question in my mind that Viola would give the Red Sox that same commitment and toughness on the mound. I was excited about obtaining Viola and his potential impact on our starting pitching.

I made contact with Viola's agent and immediately indicated our strong interest in signing him. I told him once we were able to agree to terms and to the length of the contract, we'd also have to have his left hand and finger examined by our team doctor. The final execution of the contract would be contingent upon a clean bill of health from Dr. Pappas. The agent and Viola agreed, and I proceeded to negotiate a three-year contract through the 1994 season. Viola was 31 at the time of our negotiations, and I was confident that a physically sound Viola as the number-two starter behind Clemens would give us one of the best one-two starters in the league.

Darwin could now also overcome his physical problems and take over as a productive third starter; it would dramatically impact our entire ball club. Our bullpen should be decent. With Reardon once again as our closer, I had high hopes that we could bounce back from our disappointing 1991 season.

In late January I signed an eight-year major league veteran outfielder named Herm Winningham to a one-year contract. I felt he could contribute to our ball club off the bench in various roles and he would be a solid addition to our ball club. Winningham was 30 years old and had been a number-one draft pick, who I had personally scouted when I was with the Mets. With the Cincinnati Reds in 1991, Winningham had been the second best pinch hitter in the National League, hitting .394 off the bench. I was also aware that Winningham was an above-average defensive outfielder with good speed. In his second season in professional baseball at Lynchburg, Virginia, in the Carolina League, Winningham had stolen 50 bases in 120 games. He had also been a very effective base stealer at the major league level while playing mostly in a limited role off the bench.

In our farm system we had some young players who gave indications that they just might be on the verge of contributing to the major league club during the upcoming season. Scott Cooper, a young third baseman, had been the International League All-Star third baseman, hitting .277 with 15 home runs and 72 RBIs in 135 ball games. He had been voted the Best Defensive Third Baseman in the International League for the second straight season. Another young player out of the farm system, who had a brief stint with our major league club in 1991, was an excellent defensive outfielder with a strong throwing arm named Bob Zupcic. At Pawtucket in 1991 he hit 18 home runs and 70 RBIs while making only two errors the entire season. Our staff felt that both Cooper and Zupcic might contribute to the big league club in the upcoming season.

There was also the strong possibility that Vaughn just might be ready to step up to the major league ball club and take over at first base. He had appeared in 74 games at the major league level the season before. After the better part of two seasons at Pawtucket, our reports and staff felt this might be the season for Vaughn to establish himself as our regular first baseman.

Just prior to the start of spring training as we continued to be optimistic about the young guns in our farm system, we received the very disheartening news from Caracas, Venezuela. Carlos Quintana was seriously injured when his car was broadsided on February 23, 1992, while he was rushing his brother who had been shot, to the hospital. He suffered multiple injuries, including a broken right foot and broken left arm, and he underwent five hours of surgery. He also required a lengthy stay in the hospital. When he was able to travel, we flew him into Boston to be re-examined by Dr. Pappas. Upon examination it was discovered that Quintana had infected tissue in his right pelvis, and Dr. Pappas had to perform a 40-minute operation to remove it.

The prognosis for recovery was not good, and as originally expected Quintana would miss the entire season. I had hoped that the loss of Quintana was not a bad omen for the season ahead.

But our current lineup was still very strong. I felt good about our outfield strength with Mike Greenwell in left—although his power output in 1991 was disappointing—Ellis Burks in center, and Tom Brunansky in right, and our bench strength now included Winningham, Zupcic, and Plantier. Our catching strength was strong also with Peña as our number-one receiver. Peña had caught over 140 games the previous season and was one of the top defensive receivers in the league. We had Marzano and Wedge, both out of our farm system, as backups. Marzano's defensive skills were more than adequate, and Wedge, although a bit short defensively, could fill in and serve as a pinch hitter off the bench.

There were a couple of question marks for the future of some Red Sox greats. Wade Boggs's and Ellis Burks's contracts would be up at the end of the upcoming season, and I wanted to secure both players' futures with our organization. I pursued Boggs first, and his agent was interested in negotiating. But there was some concern about Boggs's back. It had become an off-and-on problem for him. Dr. Pappas had some serious concerns that his flaring back problems could affect Boggs's longevity and his ability to perform at 100 percent. Nonetheless, we were still willing to discuss a contract extension with him because Boggs was still one of the best hitters in the game; not to mention our younger prospects for that position were not ready to start regularly. I discussed the Boggs contract situation with John and Haywood. They told me that they would be willing to sit in with me during spring training and help finalize a deal with Boggs.

Boggs had been very happy with the Red Sox after his previous round of contract negotiations. We had agreed to a three-year deal covering from 1990 through 1992 seasons for a total of around $7.3 million, exclusive of incentives he had earned. At the time he had signed that contract, it was considered to be an excellent contract for the marketplace and he told Mrs. Yawkey that he was elated with the contract and he was thrilled that the team had such faith in him.

Prior to our arrival at spring training, I put together a proposal. The contract was for three years with an option for a fourth year; after discussing his physical problems with Dr. Pappas and with ownership, it was decided that we should not tender Boggs a multiyear contract for more than three years. I had also included attainable incentives, which would potentially enable

Boggs to earn an additional $250,000 each season. The overall contract would pay Boggs $11.5 million for three years, and if the fourth year of the contract kicked in, he could earn a total of $15.5 million. The fourth-year option could automatically apply if Boggs was healthy and played "X" number of games during the 1995 season. If the Red Sox decided not to pick up the option for the fourth season, they would pay Boggs a $350,000 buyout.

Boggs was entering his 11th season in a Red Sox uniform. He would be 34 during the 1992 season, and the proposed contract would be guaranteed to Boggs through his 37th year or 38th if the fourth year kicked in. Even so, we were taking a risk because the guarantee would pay Boggs the total contract amount even if he were unable to perform. But I felt the risk was worth taking for a .340 career hitter. Hitters like Boggs just didn't come around very often, and he was a definite candidate for baseball's Hall of Fame.

When we finally met with his agent Alan Nero at our new family home in Winter Haven, Florida, I asked Nero for his proposal. He told me that he did not have a proposal. I was taken aback by his response.

"Alan, you have been calling me since last June to meet with me to work out a contract extension for Wade and you now have no proposal whatever to offer us?" I replied. "I am frankly stunned by your answer."

"The only thing I can tell you now is that Wade has to have a five-year guaranteed contract or we can't even begin to crunch numbers," he responded.

I told Nero a five-year guaranteed contract was out of the question. He responded that he would like to have Boggs join us at the end of the workout that afternoon. I told him that if he and Boggs were to insist on a five-year guaranteed contract then we were at an impasse and ownership would not sit in on any negotiations to finalize an agreement. When the meeting ended, Nero told me that Boggs was adamant about a five-year contract. I tried to convince him that our contract offer would only be for three years, period.

Around 3 p.m. Nero called me and told me he and Boggs were available to meet with us to continue the discussion of Boggs's contract. John Donovan, Elaine Weddington Steward, and I came in to meet with Nero and Boggs, and Nero asked me if John Harrington and Haywood were going to sit in on the negotiations. I told him that because he had insisted upon a five-year guaranteed contract, ownership would not sit in on this negotiation. Boggs told me he was extremely upset at their position.

Nero then handed me a contract proposal, which he had scribbled on the backside of one of our daily training camp press releases. He had casually jotted down a five-year guaranteed contract proposal, totaling around $23 million with some additional incentives that would add approximately $2 million more over the tenure of the contract. As we looked over it, Nero admitted his disappointment that John and Haywood were not present. I reiterated our position, regarding the three-year proposal and said that unless it was feasible, ownership would not attend the negotiations. Boggs got very upset and began criticizing the Red Sox and me for refusing to consider their demand for a five-year proposal. He continued to point out that he felt the Red Sox did not appreciate what he had done for the ball club, and I told him the Red Sox had compensated him very well for his past contributions. At that point he and Nero abruptly left the room.

The next Sunday I was in my office around 9 a.m. when I received a phone call from Nero indicating he'd like to visit with me to discuss some new thoughts on Boggs's contract proposal. I set up a 10:30 a.m. meeting in my office. When he arrived, he told me that Boggs really wanted to remain with the Red Sox, but the five-year guaranteed contract was extremely important to him. They were willing to adjust their financial requests, but the duration had to be for five years.

"Alan, I cannot be any more sincere with you—we are not going to give Wade a five-year contract. Absolutely not," I replied.

Nero presented me with a new contract proposal that was around $20 million with incentives, but for five years. I turned to face him after reading his proposal.

"Alan, we are just spinning our wheels until you and Wade are willing to talk about a three-year guaranteed contract," I responded. "I am willing to include a fourth-year option, but as a club option and/or it could kick in automatically if Wade plays in 'X' number of games in the third year of the contract, but that is it."

Nero asked me if he could bring Boggs back to meet with us once again at the end of the day's workout. I told him we would be willing to talk some more in the hope of closing the gap, but that ownership would not be present if he kept insisting on a five-year guaranteed contract. At the end of the day's workout, Boggs and Nero returned to our office complex and Steward, Donovan, and I met with them once again.

"I'm very upset that Harrington and Sullivan weren't willing to be present for these discussions," Boggs began. "I've done a great dealt for this ball club, and they won't show me that courtesy."

"Wade, we made it eminently clear to you and Alan that they are more than willing to sit in and finalize a contract with you, but only if we're talking about a three-year guaranteed contract," I interrupted him before he could continue.

Boggs then proceeded to angrily vent about our indifference and lack of appreciation of what he meant to the franchise. He went on to extol his accomplishments and to point out what he considered his value in the marketplace. He then turned to face me directly.

"If you aren't willing to consider giving me a five-year guaranteed contract offer, I have nothing further to say to you or the ball club," he stated. "As far as I am concerned, I will not discuss a contract with you for the rest of spring or during the season."

He and Nero rose to leave.

"Wade, I'm sorry we can't work something out right now, but if you don't care to discuss a contract during the season, that's fine with me," I said. "I hope you'll change your mind this spring or at any time, my door is always open to you."

Boggs and Nero left, and neither ever made any attempt to contact me again that spring or at any time during the season. Boggs continued to play for the Red Sox, but I knew it could be his last season with us although I sincerely hoped it would not be.

In addition to the disappointing impasse with Boggs's contract negotiations, spring training produced a few surprises—including Clemens who did not report on the first day. We heard nothing from the MIA hurler, and the media noticed his absence and waited to see how Hobson, a rookie manager, would handle his star pitcher's tardiness.

A few days later, I got a call from Randy Hendricks, Clemens's agent, telling me that Clemens would be at camp the next day. I went down to Hobson to let him know and see what he wanted to do about it. Hobson said he would handle it.

The next day Clemens showed up at the field in his sweatpants ready to work out, and Hobson took him aside to talk. After the short exchange, they began to run laps as though nothing had happened.

After the workout, I approached Hobson and asked him what Clemens had said.

"He apologized and said he was wrong," Hobson told me. "That's what I was looking for. So we shook hands and left it at that."

I was satisfied that the fiasco had blown over, but the media took Hobson's lack of sternness as a sign that he was going to let his veteran players walk all over him—an accusation that never proved to be true.

We were in the late stages of spring training in Winter Haven, Florida, when Haywood called us all together in our main conference room at the ballpark to break some bad news. He told us that Mrs. Yawkey had died; she had suffered a stroke two days earlier, and although it had appeared that she had made a recovery, it was short lived. As I walked away from the meeting and back to the solace of my office, I began to recall my memories of Jean Yawkey.

I had heard about her reputation for being very aloof, cold, and difficult to get close to. But when I first joined the Red Sox organization after leaving the New York Mets in 1984, Mrs. Yawkey had gone out of her way to make my wife, Mary Lou, and me extremely welcome. Once she accepted you, she could be caring and compassionate. She had a tender heart and a very kind nature. I came to know her kindness on more than one occasion.

My most poignant memory of her, however, came vividly to mind as I sat in my office and looked out at the playing field. I began to recall that agonizingly painful look that came over her face when we finally lost Game 6 of the World Series in October 1986. We had been a single pitch away from the ultimate glory of a world championship, the very first ever under the Yawkey's ownership of the Red Sox, a ball club they had owned for more than 40 years. We had let it slip away. Hesitatingly, as we had prepared to leave Shea Stadium, I glanced in her direction and the agony of that heartbreaking defeat was so visibly etched in the pain on her face, I could only begin to surmise her emotions and thoughts were at that moment. It hurt me to look at her, and I felt then that she was more emotionally distraught over that loss than any other defeat since she and her husband had bought the team. That memory would stay with me forever.

I also remembered how she would sit up in the owner's box at every single home game, tabulating every pitch and every play in the scorebook she kept religiously. Often she would invite me there to discuss a particular player whom I had acquired, an individual play that occurred during the ball game, or a specific strategy that the manager or opposing manager had employed. I was often surprised by her comprehension of some of the intricacies of the game and how emotionally she involved herself in the game-by-game fortunes of the ball club. She had a deep attachment not only to the team on the field, but also to the entire organization and staff.

She was a very private person who was not big on extravagant social functions or a lot of media attention; however, she always enjoyed small social gatherings with those she was close to. My wife and I always enjoyed her company. She was extremely loyal to those she was close to and expected the same loyalty in return. I came to understand her more during my tenure as general manager and came to develop an emotional attachment to her as a person and as my boss.

My last memory of her came at a difficult time in my position as general manager because she and Haywood, for reasons I was never privy to, had reached an impasse in their relationship and had parted company. Mrs. Yawkey would not acknowledge Haywood, talk to him, or remain in the same room with him. It was very painful to observe the dissolution of a friendship that had been established when Haywood joined the Red Sox organization. Most of all, it placed me in a very tenuous and all but impossible position to function as general manager without complication. I had two managing partners at odds with each other and on some occasions my ability to make decisions and take action in regard to baseball operations was impacted by their ongoing disagreement. I liked them both a great deal and that made the entire situation even more difficult.

Over the course of the last three years, I had sensed that Mrs. Yawkey was beginning to fade physically, and I desperately wanted to win it all for her. My greatest disappointment was my failure to do just that.

As I continued to gaze out my window, I began to regret that I hadn't had an opportunity to say goodbye to her, but I hoped she knew I cared for her and she would be in my prayers.

Unfortunately baseball and life continued on down in Florida as we mourned Mrs. Yawkey's death and began looking toward the season ahead. A lot of our prospects showed very encouraging signs of improvement. Cooper had a fine spring, and he gave every indication he was ready to step in and become the Red Sox third baseman of the future. Tim Naehring, who was disabled nearly the entire 1991 season with a back injury that eventually required surgery, came into camp after a winter of rehabilitation and appeared ready to meet our expectations. Zupcic also had a fine spring. Hobson felt, as did our coaching staff, that Zupcic could play a definite role on our ball club in the upcoming season. He would add additional defensive depth in the outfield. If he improved offensively, he could take over as

a starter in any one of the outfield positions. It was also the consensus judgment of our baseball people that Vaughn and Valentin were ready to step up
and to contribute at the big league level. Valentin had improved defensively and showed a great deal of promise with the bat. We knew that he might
have to start the season at Pawtucket, but Valentin and Cooper gave us great
depth at third base for the future.

At the beginning of spring training Valentin had had an error-plagued
start, and his performance set off a media blitz of criticism. Valentin, who
was not one to offer excuses, claimed that the new infield surface at City of
the Palms Park was still rough and the ball had taken some funny
bounces—it is not unusual for new infield dirt to take some time to settle
and smooth out.

After a few rough days in the field the Boston media began to joke open-
ly about his defensive skills. I happened to wander into the press box during a ballgame to talk to vice president of public relations Dick Bresciani
when I overheard the jabs at Valentin. Totally out of character, I became
incensed at the criticism and I turned to the assembled media.

"If it were possible for me to make a friendly bet for dinner, I would predict that John Valentin will one day be an All-Star, become a solid defensive
player, and have the potential 20 plus home runs on a regular basis," I blurted out. "That's of course if I were permitted to bet."

I made the claim tongue in cheek realizing I could never make a bet
under any conditions. At first the media was taken aback by my reaction,
but they all began to smile or laugh at my retort.

Naturally Dan Shaughnessy scoffed at my comments, and then Nick
Carfardo of *The Boston Globe* and Joe Guiliotti of the *Boston Herald* joined
in.

"You've got to be kidding," they said. "With that guy at shortstop you're
in trouble."

From that moment on I began to become the butt of some humor for
my defense of Valentin, and it carried over into the season.

As the season got underway Valentin began to settle down, but some of
the talk show criticism and second-guessing continued.

In mid-April I received an invitation to speak at the downtown Boston
Public Library for an appearance in late May. It was part of an annual seminar dealing with culture, literature, and sports. I assumed that I was to be
the principal and only speaker at the seminar. I unfortunately assumed
incorrectly. When I arrived at the lecture hall of the library, I was dismayed

to find that Shaughnessy and Peter Gammons, the featured columnist for *The Boston Globe*, would be members of the panel, and *The Boston Globe*'s sports editor would serve as the moderator of the seminar.

Our ball club was struggling at that time so I knew with Shaughnessy and Gammons involved, I was in for an unpleasant evening. I would have to say in fairness, however, that Gammons was more objective and on a number of occasions very complimentary of me, for which I was grateful.

When the lecture got underway the lecture hall was full. As the evening progressed, I found myself under siege and in a defensive posture nearly the entire evening. The criticism about Valentin, Vaughn, and just about the entire ball club, particularly from Shaughnessy, continued throughout the seminar. I was constantly defending our ball club, player by player and point by point. The questions from the audience, spurred on by the critical assessment of our ball club from the stage, kept coming at me throughout the evening. I began to wonder why I had ever volunteered to endure such an evening on an off night when I could have been home enjoying the company of my wife.

After enduring the beating of negative question after question, a gentleman sitting in about a fifth or sixth row raised his hand. He was a heavy-set gentleman with a baseball cap on and because he had the visor raised, I was unable to determine which team's logo was on the hat. He looked to me like a taxi driver. I was leery of his question as the moderator acknowledged him.

"I never read *The Globe* because it's too negative," he began. "Every time I read about the Red Sox or the other sports teams, it puts me in a bad mood. That gentleman sitting up there on the stage," and he pointed directly at Shaughnessy, "is the most negative of all."

Shaughnessy was obviously greatly agitated at the accusation. I could have jumped off the stage and hugged the gentleman. I was absolutely elated, and it made my day and my appearance at the event well worthwhile. Gammons and the sports editor began to defend Shaughnessy, citing the numerous awards for sports reporting that Shaughnessy had received in his career, but it did little to appease his detractor, nor dim my elation.

The media fuss that stemmed from spring training eventually died down, the team turned to focusing on the coming season. Hobson was extremely anxious for opening day. For the first time in his major league career he was in the Red Sox dugout as the team manager and not as a player. It was an exciting challenge for him and he was chomping at the bit. I was also confident that Don Zimmer, whom Hobson had personally requested we hire as his bench coach, would prove to be a tremendous asset to the rookie manager. Zimmer had a wealth of experience, and I felt his knowledge and counsel could prove to be a huge advantage for Hobson.

Right before the season opened, I attempted to sit down with Burks to negotiate a contract extension. I really wanted to convince Burks that this organization valued him and his contributions on the field. He had excellent overall physical skills and he was exactly what we needed to play center field for us. He had great quickness, speed, and a good range in the outfield along with solid offensive skills to hit with some power and for average. But during the meeting Burks told me how unhappy he was playing in Boston, and he said if I could make a trade for him, I should seriously consider doing so. I was convinced that Burks's potential was still a long way from being fulfilled. I desperately wanted to find a way to convince him to stay in Boston because he was an outstanding young man with great talent. I did everything possible to dissuade him from thinking about leaving. After our discussion, I thought I had him leaning toward staying with us.

Unfortunately, I couldn't convince him to sign the extension, and the season began with another player's future status unknown. I began to finally realize that I just might, regretfully, be forced to trade him at some point in the season if we were not in a pennant race. To let him go would be a huge loss; my only hope was to get value in return.

Clemens opened the season at Yankee Stadium and lost 4-3. After the game I went down from the press box to our clubhouse, and as I walked into Hobson's office, I saw he was inundated with 30 or 35 media with microphones, cameras, and notebooks stuck in his face. He sat at his desk in almost a state of bewilderment, dazed by the entourage of media bombarding him with questions. It was a far cry from the two or three media personnel who would interview him after a game in Pawtucket. He wasn't quite ready for this spectacle.

When the media cleared his office, I asked him, "What do you think about the media coverage now?"

"Do I go through this same thing every day?" he asked back.

I laughed and said, "Butch, not quite this bad, but you'll be on stage to a helluva lot of media in Boston every day, so you may as well get used to it."

I had gotten used to the rabid nature of the local media after dealing with them for so long. The Boston sports media are probably the most passionate, aggressive, critical, opinionated, oftentimes negative, and on occasion mean spirited of any sports media in America. (I'm certain that there are sports fans and listeners in New York or in Philadelphia who would take issue with that statement and lay claim to the title instead.) I do, however, also admit that there are some members of the local media who are definite exceptions to my denunciation, but they are too often in the minority. It is not unusual in the Boston media market for a media "authority" to rant and rave on any given topic or personality, analyzing, reanalyzing, second-guessing, always after the fact on whatever the current issue might be. Too often they seem to wallow in a sea of negativity and appear elated with the opportunity to do so.

One example was during a previous season when Clemens had been experiencing some tightness in his pitching shoulder and went to see Dr. Pappas. Recognizing that we were dealing with an exceptional talent and the mainstay of our pitching staff, Dr. Pappas told me he'd like to meet with Clemens and me. As I came into the clubhouse, there were still a number of media milling around, and when they noticed that Dr. Pappas, Clemens, and I were heading into the doctor's office, they speculated that something must be up.

When I met with them, Dr. Pappas said he felt that Clemens's problem was not serious, but as a precaution he would like him to come to the UMass Hospital for an MRI. Clemens agreed but asked us not to publicize anything about his hospital visit. I gave Clemens my word I would not mention it.

While we were meeting, some of the reporters approached manager Joe Morgan for a comment. Morgan played down the situation.

"Probably nothing serious just some tightness in his shoulder, and the Doc may take a look at him at the hospital tomorrow," he responded.

That evening before the game, our talented vice president of public relations Dick Bresciani told me the media wanted to meet with me before the game. I sensed it was about the Clemens situation.

I went up to our pressroom and was confronted by a host of reporters. My friendly nemesis, Dan Shaughnessy, was right up front, pencil and notepad poised for my answers. They immediately began shouting questions about Clemens.

"Is his shoulder all right?"

"Is he going to be examined at the hospital tomorrow?"

I kept my word to Clemens.

"No, he is not going to be examined at the UMass Hospital in Worcester tomorrow."

I could tell from their expressions they were perplexed by my response. They came back at me once again.

"Clemens will not be examined at the hospital by Dr. Pappas tomorrow?" Shaughnessy asked.

"No, he will not."

With no further questions and one or two local TV stations asking for personal one-on-one interviews, the formal press conference was terminated. Eventually I left the pressroom to go to my box to watch the ball game.

The next day Clemens went to the UMass Hospital per Dr. Pappas's request, and an MRI was conducted. Clemens had a severe case of tendonitis and he was given a shot of cortisone. It was also our decision to have Clemens miss his next regular turn in the starting rotation to give him at least eight or nine days before his next start.

As a result of his treatment and the fact he would also miss a start, we had to prepare a press release to notify the media. I knew as the press release was being prepared for distribution before that night's home game that I would be on the hot seat that evening.

Later that day, Bresciani brought a copy of the press release for me to look over.

"Lou, I know the media will be insisting on talking to you tonight before the game about the Clemens situation. I don't envy you the task."

I thanked him and told him I'd be in the pressroom at 6:45 p.m.

"Good luck," he said as he left.

As I entered the pressroom, I somehow had the feeling that the huge media assemblage were waiting for the kill and that I was to be the victim. Most of the media were holding our press release in their hands.

The first question to me came from Shaughnessy.

"You lied to us last night about Roger Clemens, didn't you?"

I cleared my throat to respond.

"Yes, I told you all a white lie. Clemens asked me not to inform the media or anyone about his visit to the hospital for an examination by Dr. Pappas and to keep it totally confidential. I made a promise to him I would keep it confidential and I honored my promise to him. I consider that a white lie. My responsibility is to our players first and foremost, and my credibility with our players is essential and sacrosanct with me." The media said nothing and just kept staring at me. I continued, "Have any of you ever told a white lie?"

No one said a word. I looked around the room into the faces of the assembled media entourage and they just kept staring at me. Shaughnessy was standing directly in front of me his pencil poised above his notepad, and I anticipated a critical question from him, but he said nothing either.

After a pause I began to speak again, "I'll tell you all what I consider a white lie to be. If my wife had to go the hospital with a very serious ailment and she asked me not to tell her family the seriousness of the ailment, I would tell a white lie to her family when they asked me about her condition to honor her request. Would any of you do anything different?"

Again, no one said a word in answer to my query. I looked around and then walked out of the pressroom without a further word.

The next morning Shaughnessy writing in *The Boston Globe* wrote a column entitled, "Gorman the Moralist," and he went on to write about "white lies," "blue lies," "red lies," green lies," etc., mimicking my defense of my statement about Clemens and the white lie. Shaughnessy would always find a way to damn me with faint praise or be critical of some of my decisions.

The Clemens scenario was a common incident where many times certain writers, such as Mike Shalin, a beat writer for the *Boston Herald*, would go to a source to get a story or the background for a story—obviously the more controversial the better—and then come to me with questions after already having background facts or opinions about a particular issue. I would never be aware as he questioned me that he had already spoken with others. It was the perfect situation to create a controversy if my facts differed from what he had already been privy to.

I always understood that the media have to be diligent in researching their stories, but I also believe that the reporter should at least say to the interviewee, "I've heard this story or that story on this issue, what is your response?" It seemed that the questions were searching for controversy, not facts.

I personally always appreciated a media reporter who was upfront with me and did not attempt to trap me in a controversy. Joe Guilliotti was always upfront in his dealings with me. I sincerely felt that he was honestly seeking the facts on both sides of an issue, and I went out of my way to be more open and more accessible to him because of the fairness in his approach and his objectivity. Bob Ryan of *The Boston Globe* and Steve

Buckley of the *Boston Herald* were always also fair, honest, and objective in their dealings with me, and I was more open to them because of their methods and frankness. There were other media personnel that dealt with me in a similar fashion, writers such as Nick Carfardo and Larry Whiteside of *The Boston Globe*, Dave O'Hara of the Associated Press, Sean McAdams of the *Providence Journal/Bulletin* and a very knowledgeable baseball writer, and Seth Livingston of the *Patriot Ledger* were also writers I found looking for both sides of a story and not seeking to entrap me.

If I had made a bad trade, signed an inept free agent, or participated in a general screw-up, I expected to be criticized and/or castigated by the media in all its forms. The aforementioned writers, when I deserved it, would take me to task, and I fully understood that it went with the territory. What was unnecessary, however, was the unceasing, unrelenting criticism that would seemingly go on forever on any issue. They just seemed to beat it to death. Many times I would read, hear, listen to, or see on television a story that I would recognize was not completely accurate or completely factual and I often wondered whether it was intentional or just bad reporting. It reminded me of a story by Mark Twain in which he describes when he is hired as a news reporter for a newspaper in San Francisco. The day he was hired his editor called him into his office to give him some advice. According to Twain, his man said to him, "I want you to go out and find a great story, dig up all the facts, and then distort them anyway you can."

Hobson eventually learned how to work the Boston media as the season continued. In the second game of the season Viola lost to the Yankees 3-2. We finally went on to Cleveland and won two of three games against the Indians. We came home on April 13 to face the Orioles. By the end of April we were playing .500 ball at 9-9 and we were tied for fourth place, five games out of first place. By the end of May we were still in fourth place at 24-21. Reardon had already saved 12 games in relief. Clemens had won eight games and Viola four. We were able to move within two and a half games of the division lead on May 26, the high mark for the season. We never came any closer to contending as we slowly kept falling further behind toward the basement of the Eastern Division.

During this dark time on June 15, Reardon recorded his 342nd save against the New York Yankees, breaking former A's reliever Rollie Fingers's record to become the all-time save leader in Major League Baseball. Even that highlight was not enough to shock us into a turnaround. On June 18 we proceeded to lose seven straight games to fall eight and a half games behind and out of contention for good.

As our team continued to flounder, I made a series of moves that I hoped would stave off the losing. After playing only 39 games at Pawtucket, I recalled Vaughn from Pawtucket to attempt to jump-start our offense. He would end up playing in 113 games at the major league level, hitting only .234 with 13 home runs and 57 RBIs. It was an inauspicious start for a player who would eventually go on to become an American League MVP, All-Star performer, and one of the top home run hitters in the league. I also called up Valentin, the shortstop who showed so much promise, to replace a struggling Luis Rivera. Rivera was in a slump, hitting .215 after registering a .260 batting average in 1991. In 56 big league games Valentin would hit .276 and establish himself as a major league player. Cooper and Zupcic also made debuts at the major league level, hitting .278 and .276 respectively. Zupcic would hit three home runs, two of which were grand slams, which tied a rookie record.

On July 9 I traded a longtime minor league left-handed pitcher Tom Bolton to the Cincinnati Reds for outfielder Billy Hatcher. Hatcher had 196 career stolen bases and was an above-average defensive outfielder. The loss of Bolton was not going to impact of pitching staff, but Hatcher could provide us with some badly needed speed, serve also as a right-handed hitter off the bench, and give us more depth in the outfield with the loss of Greenwell and Burks to injuries.

I also reacquired utility player Steve Lyons by purchasing his contract for just about the waiver price. I was convinced that he could play a role on our ball club and protect us at any number of positions as a capable backup. Lyons ended up filling in as a backup at first base, second base, and center field, doing an adequate job at all these positions. He played in 21 games, hitting .250 but filled the role for which we had gotten him. Once again, however, the managers and coaches were not too happy about having Lyons on the ball club, and he, for whatever reason, was not too popular in the clubhouse. When the season concluded, Lyons again became a free agent.

In late August I traded Reardon to the Atlanta Braves for a future prospect because I noticed that he was starting to slow down and show signs of his age. (Reardon would save a total of 10 games after the trade, and in 1994 he would be signed by the New York Yankees, pitching only nine and two thirds innings and ending up with two saves and 8.38 ERA. His great career was over. He would finish with a total of 367 saves and in my opinion will be a definite candidate for baseball's Hall of Fame.)

Despite the adjustments I made during the season, we struggled badly the rest of the way because of injuries and poor performances. Our ball club played poorly on the road—29-52—throughout the season. Our entire ball club would hit only 84 home runs for the season. It was one of the lowest overall Red Sox home run totals in modern times. Brunansky would finish at .266 with 15 home runs and 74 RBIs to lead our ball club in both categories. This very modest offensive production was abundant evidence just how badly we had struggled the entire season. Our opponents scored nearly 70 more runs, and we left nearly 100 more men on base than our opposition, a direct result of our struggling offense.

Going into September we were still struggling, but we totally buried ourselves starting on September 6. We proceeded to lose 13 the of next 17 games, seven of them by one run. We finished the last three games of the season by taking two of three from the hated Yankees, and we won seven of our last 10 ball games. We ended the season with a disastrous 73-89 won-lost record, an embarrassing 23 games out of first place.

Greenwell appeared in only 49 games, none after mid-June. He underwent surgery on his right elbow and his right knee and was lost for the rest of the season. He ended up hitting only .233, with two home runs and 18 RBIs, far below his career average.

After a slow start, Burks was picking up his offensive production when he hurt a disc in his back in June. Burks appeared in only 66 games, and he finished with only 30 RBIs and a .255 batting average. Although his small offensive contribution led to our struggles on the field, I was more concerned with the questions surrounding his ending contract. There was some concern that his back injury could hamper his overall performance for the rest of his career, and although it was my very best intention to keep him in a Red Sox uniform, I was unsure about offering a one-year guaranteed contract extension (assuming he would agree to one) with the questions surrounding his physical well being. I also was having trouble finding a club that would be willing to trade for his full value as a player. I was backed into a corner with few options.

Clark also struggled through one of his worst seasons ever because he was consistently hampered by rib cage and right shoulder injuries. After hitting 28 home runs and driving in 87 RBIs in 1991, he dropped off to .210 with five home runs and 33 RBIs.

Besides the physical problems that Clark incurred during the season, he was also in serious financial trouble. He was deeply in debt and facing bankruptcy. Clark was an extremely likeable and highly competitive individual, and he was generous to a fault. I really liked him, and I tried to see if there was any way we could help him with his problems, but they were so diverse and extensive that there was little we could do.

The combined physical problems and his critical financial problems were a constant nightmare to Clark, and I am convinced the emotional pressure he was experiencing dramatically impacted his performance on the field. Whether he was at home or on the field, he was being verbally abused and insulted on a daily basis and it really was beginning to get to him. At our home games, I was extremely concerned about some unruly fans who were close to our dugout and were riding Clark incessantly. I asked our longtime vice president of stadium operations and security Joe McDermott to station a security guard nearby just in case Clark reacted to the abuse. It got so bad that at one point during the season, Clark went into Hobson's office and told the manager that with his injuries and personal problems, he was in such an emotional state that he didn't know if he could help the ball club.

The pressure and the injuries eventually got to Clark, and he decided to end his major league career after the 1992 season.

Another disappointment was Phil Plantier, who after showing promise and power balked at working with the staff to improve his defensive skills. He came to the big leagues in 1991 and hit .331 with 11 home runs and 35 RBIs in 53 games, but he still needed to work on his fielding. After returning from offseason elbow surgery, Hobson noticed that Plantier didn't seem committed to improving his outfield performance so he sat Plantier down and told him he was going to have to work harder if the young outfielder wanted to remain in the big leagues. Hobson wanted him to attend special workouts, which Plantier was not interested in. As the season progressed, Plantier and Hobson had a couple of shouting matches focusing around Plantier's lack of commitment. To make matters worse, Plantier was having a disappointing season at the plate. Finally on August 12, Hobson decided that the best thing would be to send Plantier back to Pawtucket to get untracked.

Once Plantier found out about the move, he was furious and went into Hobson's office to confront him. A nasty shouting match occurred. As Plantier left Hobson's office, he screamed that he would never play for

Hobson again and then took his complaints to an all-too-eager press, who ate up the controversy and relished the negativity.

With the loss of Greenwell, Burks, and Clark and the demotion of Plantier, our offensive production was critically impacted and it would have taken miraculous pitching to carry us if we had any hope at all of competing. Clemens, despite our lack of an offensive punch, won 18 ball games, posted a 2.41 ERA (which led the American League), and struck out more than 200 hitters for the seventh consecutive season. He would finish third in the Cy Young award balloting but was named Pitcher of the Year by the writers association and Man of the Year by the BoSox Club, a longtime Red Sox booster club. Other than Clemens's 18-11 season, Viola's 13-12 season, and Darwin's 9-9 season, our pitching struggled badly also.

The Boston media continued to place a great deal of blame on Hobson for the ball club's poor performance. The prevailing criticism was that Hobson did not have the total respect of his players and that his managerial and leadership skills were questionable. They kept pointing out that Hobson would discipline only the younger or rookie players while the veterans on the club had the run of the clubhouse and could do no wrong. He was still "Daddy Butch" as far as the media was concerned.

It was, for the most part, an unfair criticism. Hobson, to his credit, never disciplined a player, rookie or veteran, in public. He dealt with all players, including some veteran players, in the privacy of his office and tongue-lashed them for various disciplinary reasons or violations of club rules, but these issues never left his office or reached media's eyes and ears.

If Hobson had any faults, he would tend to err on the side of leniency before he decided to take action against a player, and some of the players would take advantage of that. However, when he did address a problem, he treated veterans and rookies alike in meting out his discipline. Most of the rookie players on the ball club Hobson had managed at Double-A or Triple-A on their way to the big leagues and he had already developed a rapport with them. Tactically, Hobson had room for improvement and had he leaned more on the advice and experience that Zimmer could impart to him, it could have helped him immeasurably and well could have made him a better manager. He made his share of mistakes, but he also was dealt a difficult hand. And that was my responsibility.

Unfortunately, my hopes of Zimmer, with his wealth of baseball knowledge, mentoring Hobson through the next season would remain unfulfilled. Before we began our offseason planning, Zimmer told me that he did not want to return for the next season, because he was thinking about retiring. I responded with obvious disappointment, but in retrospect I should have made more of an effort to convince him to stay, because I could sense that he wasn't serious about retiring and I thought he felt underutilized by Hobson. If I had tried to bring Zimmer and Hobson together for a casual meeting, we might have been able to resolve the problems and get them working together as a team. I regret not having done so.

At the end of the 1992 season, we also lost Boggs and Burks to free agency. Ironically, Boggs had had the worst season of his career. He had come into the 1992 season with 10 consecutive seasons of hitting more than .300, seven seasons as an American League All-Star, six league batting titles, and a .345 career batting average. For the first time in his major league career he hit under .300 finishing at only .259 with 50 RBIs, his lowest RBI total ever. In the early stages, it appeared that he had only a three-year offer from the Dodgers for around $7 million dollars. When it looked like the Dodgers' offer might be the only one, the Yankees came to the table to fill the void left by the Rockies selecting third baseman Charlie Hayes in the expansion draft. The Yankees then proceeded to offer Boggs a three-year contract, totaling around $11 million, with a $3 million signing bonus and $8 million in salary and averaging around $2.7 million per season. Boggs accepted the Yankees' offer and turned in his Red Sox uniform after 12 seasons for Yankees pinstripes.

Burks signed a contract with the Chicago White Sox. He struggled for a while but eventually went on to have some extremely productive seasons for the Rockies and Indians.

After all of the offseason reshuffling, we turned to planning strategies for improvement for 1993. We had now suffered through two losing seasons. The media, besides targeting Hobson as a primary culprit for our losing season, began to turn their attention to me, placing a good degree of the blame on me for our ball club's failures—Clark's problem, Matt Young's struggles, the Jeff Bagwell trade, and our failure to win. I was well aware, however, that the buck stopped with me as the general manager, and I'd made my share of mistakes. Without question, though, injuries dramatically impacted our performance in the field, and our offensive production was severely impaired. Hobson, the staff, and I knew we needed to bolster our offense if we wanted to turn things around.

In late November, an opportunity to do just that presented itself. Ron Shapiro, an agent, called me. Shapiro was one of the most respected agents in the game. I had dealt with him in the past on a number of players, and I found him to be knowledgeable, reasonable, fair, and a man of his word. He was a dealmaker, not a deal breaker, and his preparation before negotiations was always thorough and complete. He always understood what the market for any player was, and his goal was always to negotiate within that to finalize a deal. I had great respect for his negotiating skills and for his character.

Shapiro wanted to pass along that Kirby Puckett, one of his clients, might be willing to leave the Twins after nine brilliant seasons. Puckett was an exceptional talent and a tremendous competitor. He had speed, power, and excellent defensive skills in center field or right field, and he played with total abandonment. He was all but a legend in Minnesota. From what I was able to determine, Andy MacPhail, the Twins' general manager and a quality baseball executive as well as a longtime friend, had made an offer to Shapiro for Puckett, which was a multiyear deal totaling $26 million. Puckett decided to accept the offer, because his whole career had been with the Twins and both he and his wife, Tonya, were very happy in Minnesota. Everything seemed to be settled. But when MacPhail went to his owner, Carl Pohlard, to get his final approval for the contract, Pohlard rejected it, figuring they could get Puckett for less. When word got back to Puckett via Shapiro that the deal was off, Puckett was visibly upset and now convinced that the Twins organization did not appreciate his contributions to the ball club and decided that maybe it was time to move on. Shapiro was also very upset at Pohlard's decision, because he had assumed he had a deal. After a great deal of discussion with Puckett regarding the owner's refusal to agree to the contract proposal, Kirby convinced Shapiro he was ready to listen to other offers from other ball clubs.

I had been in contact with Shapiro regarding other players, and he mentioned that Puckett was now serious about talking to other ball clubs and would definitely consider leaving the Twins. I immediately told Shapiro that the Red Sox had a strong interest in him, and we were prepared to meet with him to negotiate a contract. I knew he would be a brilliant addition to our ball club offensively and defensively, and he would become a fan favorite overnight. Shapiro told me he would be back in touch with me soon.

Puckett wrote in *I Love This Game*, "I've already said the reason I signed with Ron Shapiro was because he had a reputation as a straight shooter and I knew I didn't want to jeopardize that by playing teams off, one against the other in the 'Kirby Derby,' as some of the media called this business. Time, energy, and credibility were at stake, so Ron wanted me to decide once and for all and for real: 'Was I prepared to leave the Twins?' My answer was, 'Yes, I was prepared to leave the Twins.'

"Within days Boston and Philadelphia got serious, too. They were definitely interested in me and I was interested in them, and both of these teams could handle a contract in the $35 million range."

As we set out to sell them on our ball club, our organization, and our city as a place to live and play, the question of Boston's reputation, justified or unjustified, for black athletes was definitely on their minds.

"The exchange concerning Boston's reputation for racial trouble was pretty frank...," Puckett wrote. "Several players had told me during the season, long before I really got serious about free agency, that I shouldn't even consider Boston. It was a bad place for black athletes."

We were all well aware that unfortunately and certainly in recent times, unfairly, the reputation of Boston was not a positive one with minority players. I have always felt that our fans and the region, having grown up in New England myself, have been very accepting of minority players and have treated them and judged them based not on their race but solely on their performance on the playing field. Hopefully, we hoped to convince the Pucketts that they would be welcome with open arms in Boston.

I had some players—Mike Easler, Frank Viola, and Roger Clemens—call Puckett to tell him about the ball club and the city. Viola had been a fellow teammate in Minnesota and a close friend of Puckett's. I also asked Al Bumbry, a former outstanding outfielder for the Baltimore Orioles and now one of our coaches, to convince him that the racial issue regarding Boston was overstated and that many minority athletes who had played in Boston had enjoyed playing here.

I kept at Shapiro and finally got him to agree to bring Puckett and his wife into Boston for a face-to-face meeting. I was sincerely excited about the prospect of signing Puckett and somewhat confident that we could get it done.

When the Pucketts agreed to come to Boston, I had them listed on their flight to Boston and also registered them at the Four Seasons under the names Mr. and Mrs. Johns. I had also spoken to the hotel manager about our desire to keep the visit a secret as much as possible and to provide them with some hotel security to ensure their privacy.

But somehow the Boston media discovered I had been talking to Shapiro and we were interested in Puckett. They kept watch, and when the Pucketts arrived at Logan Airport, a local television station had a cameraman and TV sportscaster waiting. Our attempts at privacy were abruptly forgotten. Every media outlet in the area was now aware that Puckett was in town.

When they arrived at Logan, we immediately got them into the Lifestyle Limousine and hustled them off to the Four Seasons. Once we had them in their suite and Shapiro in his room, I arranged for a private dinner early that first evening.

The Pucketts, Shapiro, and his assistant, Michael Maas, joined John Harrington, Elaine Weddington Steward, and me for a social, informal meeting. I wanted all of us to get to know each other in a very casual, personal environment. I am a strong believer in the philosophy that before you sell anything, you sell yourself.

As we sat around for dinner, we made a very low-key but concerted pitch to sell our organization, the lifestyle and culture of our great city of Boston, and our enormous and passionate fan base. We told Tonya that Steward would take her around the entire city during the visit to look at housing, schools, and our great hospitals.

It was very important that we made the most of this visit because we were in competition with the Phillies, whom I assumed the Pucketts would visit after their trip to Boston. I wanted to sell them completely on Boston and the Red Sox so that any other proposal would be insignificant. We set out to make every moment of the days of our visit with the Pucketts so positive, so memorable, and so convincing that we just might be able to get him under contract before he ever left Boston.

"I was really impressed with Boston," Puckett wrote. "I believed their presentation was sincere. I had visions of tattooing the Green Monster with about 50 line drive doubles and slamming the occasional curve into the net above the wall. That night it finally sank into me that for the first time in my career I was seriously talking about playing baseball for someone other than the Minnesota Twins. ...The idea of a change had taken a hold of me and especially with Tonya."

The next evening we ate dinner with the Pucketts again. At this point I was absolutely convinced that neither Shapiro nor Puckett was using us and that they were serious about signing with us.

As the dinner was concluding, I pulled Shapiro aside.

"What are we talking about to get Kirby signed?" I asked.

"In the range of $30 million plus."

"We are prepared to negotiate a contract in that range right now," I told him.

"Lou, your people have done a great job in selling the Pucketts on coming to Boston. I honestly believe they are finally ready to make the change. I assure you I'll be back in touch with you soon after we caucus and I'll tell you what it will take to sign Kirby."

A day passed after the Pucketts and Shapiro left Boston, still unsigned despite my desperate attempts to get him under contract before they left. I got back on the phone to Shapiro to let him know that we were ready to sign Puckett right them. Shapiro mentioned that the owner of the Twins had asked to meet with Puckett and his wife personally.

"Lou, we are not going to play one offer against another, you know I don't deal that way," he assured me.

"Ron, we are prepared to offer a contract for $33 million now."

Shapiro indicated that it might take a package of $35 million to close the deal. I told him we stood ready to talk and get Kirby signed.

After the phone call, I became concerned that Puckett was wavering and that the Twins were about to jump into negotiations. I knew the Phillies had made a strong pitch to sign him, yet I felt that everything considered, he would rather come to Boston unless the Twins now came back into the picture. I knew Pohlard was not one to change his mind very often, but the pressure from media and fans in Minnesota had all but reached a crescendo of protest, and Pohlard began to realize that Puckett was loved by the fans and he was the "heart and soul" of the Twins. He was beginning to realize that his loss would be a disaster for the organization and one that would critically impact their attendance.

I must have called Shapiro five or six times during the next week to put some pressure on him and to let Puckett know how much we really wanted him in a Red Sox uniform. But MacPhail implored Pohlard to re-evaluate and re-offer a better contract to Puckett to keep him in Minnesota. Pohlard reluctantly agreed, and Puckett accepted the proposed five-year $30 million offer from the Twins that Friday. Shapiro called me to let me know of Kirby's decision.

"Lou, Kirby has decided to accept an offer from the Twins and remain in Minnesota," he told me. "I want you to know, however, that you came so very, very close to getting Kirby in a Red Sox uniform. He anguished over his decision until 2 a.m. between coming to Boston or staying in Minnesota. He was sincerely emotionally torn apart in making his decision.

You folks did one helluva job in selling Tonya and him on coming to Boston."

"Did the Twins increase their original offer?" I asked.

He indicated they had.

We had been so close, and I remained convinced that if Pohlard had not changed his mind and increased their offer, Puckett would have been in center field for the Red Sox in 1993, despite the murmurings of the local media who said we had merely been used again.

With the distraction of trying to sign Puckett behind me, I had to find a way to turn things around and put a competitive ball club on the field in the upcoming season. Internally there were a few changes that I thought would help us get back on the winning track. I hired Mike Port as our assistant general manager. Port was a longtime veteran baseball executive and former general manager for the California Angels, who I believe never fully appreciated him and his managerial skills. I had known him for more than 30 years during his years with the San Diego Padres and the Angels. He was highly respected throughout all of professional baseball as a bright, dedicated, extremely hard-working and knowledgeable individual. He was a solid baseball executive with a quiet sense of humor and a thorough knowledge of baseball rules and regulations. I was thrilled to have him on board, because his administrative skills, experience and judgment would be a huge asset to me personally.

Another major change was the elevation of Eddie Kasko, our director of scouting, to vice president and director of player development. In his new position he would oversee our entire minor league system and be an invaluable assistant to me. I had great respect for his judgment and his baseball savvy. Kasko's career had been an exceptional one. He had done it all—and done it well. He had been a major league player, major league coach, a minor league manager, a special assignment scout, and a scouting director. He had drafted some outstanding young talent for the Red Sox organization. We had developed a close personal relationship over the past nine years, and I had great respect for his talents.

At the end of the 1994 season Kasko would decide to step down from his position as the vice president of player development and return to his home in Richmond, Virginia. He had contributed a great deal to the past success of the Red Sox organization.

To replace Kasko as the director of scouting, we had an 18-year talented veteran of our scouting staff with outstanding judgment named Wayne

Britton. Britton had done it all. He was a dedicated, hard-working, organized, and talented individual, who was highly respected throughout all of professional baseball. He had played briefly in the minor leagues, and then after retiring as a player he was signed by the New York Mets as a territory scout in 1974. Some five or six years later he joined the Red Sox scouting staff. When I came to the Red Sox, I was well aware of his reputation and his ability in judging talent and so were other clubs.

At one point in my tenure as the general manager of the Red Sox, Britton indicated that the Pirates were interested in him for their scouting director position. The position would have paid him considerably more, and he asked me whether he had any future for advancement within the Red Sox organization. I promised Britton that one day when the position of scouting director was available with the Red Sox, he would be my man for the job. I convinced him, despite passing up a big increase in his salary, to remain a member of the Red Sox organization. A few years later the Expos, when Dan Duquette was their general manager, expressed an interest in hiring Britton as their scouting director. Once again and despite the potential of a sizeable increase in his salary, I convinced him to stay.

In his first year as our scouting director he selected Trot Nixon and Jeff Suppan. That year, as I did in every draft session, I sat in with the scouting director and our top scouts in the drafting room and read the scouting reports on each player being considered for selection. As I read through every report of the players we were considering, I ran across a strong follow report on a young player from Georgia Tech named Nomar Garciaparra and the report was highlighted. I asked Britton about the young shortstop.

"Lou, this guy might be something special, and we're going to have to really take a hard look at him for next year's draft," he said. "He just might be a top draft choice."

Our advance scouting report on Garciaparra was amazingly prophetic. In Britton's second year as director, he selected Nomar Garciaparra as our first-round selection.

Along with changes made to the front office staff, we decided to reanalyze our coaching staff as well. I, along with Mike Port, also met with Hobson and his coaching staff to get their input on the pros and cons of the past season and their judgment as to what they felt we needed to do to improve our ball club. It was an interesting and productive meeting. When we finished the meeting, I held a one- or two-hour meeting in my office with Hobson and Port to talk about our coaching staff because I was keenly aware that Hobson was not completely satisfied with all of the members of his staff.

From my conversation with Hobson I determined he was perturbed with third base coach Rick Burleson, who he felt was, on occasion, second-guessing him on some of his game decisions. Burleson was a fiery and intensely competitive athlete. He took every loss as a personal affront. Over the course of a season when we lost some tough ball games, Burleson in frustration would pop off about a call or decision that Hobson had made to no one in particular. He was in essence venting over the loss, but Hobson felt it was undermining and derogatory.

A day later Hobson, Port, and I met with John Harrington and Haywood Sullivan to discuss our ball club and our coaching staff. As we talked in detail about each member, a decision was made to replace Burleson and Al Bumbry, our first base coach. (I personally liked Bumbry a great deal, and it had been my recommendation to hire him. Burleson was also a good worker and instructor in working with our infielders, but I understood Hobson's feelings in the matter.) We also talked about Rich Gale, our pitching coach, and replacing him with a veteran pitching coach, but that decision was never made at that meeting.

When we left the meeting with ownership, Hobson, Port, and I met briefly, and we agreed to each make up a list of potential candidates to replace Burleson and Bumbry. I scheduled a conference call for after the organizational and general manager meetings in Florida to go over the individual lists and finalize two replacement coaches.

The art of selecting coaches is always thorough and exhaustive, because to find a talented, hard-working, knowledgeable person, who is also a good instructor and communicator, is essential to the success of any field manager or ball club. Before I left for Florida, I drew up a list of potential candidates to later discuss with Hobson and Port.

As I prepared to head down to Florida, I realized that my challenge as I faced the 1993 season would in all probability be the greatest challenge I would face since I became the Red Sox general manager.

Jack Clark would be gone, and Ellis Burks and Wade Boggs would also not be back. Mike Greenwell would be coming off surgery in the offseason, and his status would be in question. Our pitching staff was in desperate need of depth, both in the starting rotation in the bullpen. I was also well aware that our failure to make it back to the playoffs these past two seasons had not set well with ownership. I had my work cut out for me, and I would have to do whatever it took to turn our fortunes around today, as in this coming season. It could not be a rebuilding process, because Red Sox fans had suffered through enough anguish for the past 74 seasons. Rebuilding teams don't survive in Boston, particularly when you've waited nearly a century for a world championship.

I had an enormous challenge, but it was my responsibility to turn things around. I was well aware of the pressure that the media and ownership would bring to bear, but I had to expect it and accept it. Progress would always involve risk and pressure, but only someone who fears failure will always limit his chances to succeed.

CHAPTER 7

1993
The Change of Command

I went off to Florida at the end of the 1993 season for our annual organizational meetings to get a look at our young talent in our instructional league team for three straight days and nights. Mike Port and I would oversee long comprehensive and detailed evaluations of our entire farm system and exhaustive discussions with our scouting staff and minor league field managers about possible acquisitions from other organizations who might turn around the fortunes of the major league club for the upcoming season. The meetings were intensive and tiring, but critical to our future.

I once again concentrated on pointing out our basic need to dramatically improve our concentration on scouting coverage of the Latin countries. I made a point to spend a good deal of time with Wayne Britton, our scouting director, and to emphasize our need to dramatically increase our scouting coverage in the Latin countries. I told him we'd find a way to fund the hiring of more fulltime scouts and a number of part-time scouts to increase our exposure and production in these countries and to make a concerted effort to become a major player in these areas.

I also spent a great deal of time with our major league scouts, getting their input on the possibility of players on other ball clubs who might be available to us either for trade or through free agency. Our organizational managers and the scouts who covered minor league clubs in other organizations, at the Triple-A and Double-A levels in particular, spent time with me as we analyzed their prospects.

Finally, after an exhausting examination of our own organization, I concluded our meetings with a reception and dinner at which time we honored Eddie Kasko for his many years of dedicated and productive service to the Red Sox.

I went on to Naples, Florida, where I was to serve as the co-chairman of the annual major league general manager meetings with my friend Bob Quinn, the general manager of the San Francisco Giants.

It was coincidental that Quinn had worked for me many years before— I had hired him as the general manager of our Triple-A ball club, the Omaha Royals, when I was then the vice president and director of player development and procurement with the Kansas City Royals. Quinn served as the general manager of our Omaha club for three or four years before becoming the director of player development for the Milwaukee Brewers. He would eventually rise rapidly through the administrative ranks of Major League Baseball to become the general manager of the San Francisco Giants.

Once I arrived at the Registry Hotel, I made contact with Quinn. When Quinn and I got together in my suite, we discussed the agenda for the meeting and some of the ongoing administrative details. In keeping with the long-standing tradition of these meetings, the night before the actual meeting session and the seminars got underway, a reception and dinner were held to bring all the general managers and their spouses together to socialize and on occasion honor a former colleague or a former retired general manager. It was also a great opportunity to mingle and talk business, man to man with the other general managers at the meetings. The entire three- or four-day period, in addition to the formal sessions, became a great opportunity to explore trade possibilities with every organization present. Throughout the days of the meeting it was commonplace to see two general managers huddled together between coffee breaks, at lunch, or in the evenings in deep conversations about trade possibilities. Port and I, together or individually, did likewise as we attempted to find out what trade possibilities might develop to help our ball club.

Recognizing I had to do something dramatic to revitalize our team after two mediocre seasons, I made the very difficult decision to trade Roger Clemens. During my more than 40 years in professional baseball, I have seen, scouted, been associated with, or had signed some of the great pitchers in the league. In my judgment Clemens ranks among the very best major league pitchers ever. Certainly he is one of, if not the greatest, pitcher in current Red Sox history and may well have been the most misunderstood and underappreciated ever.

I had enormous respect for Clemens because he had been the heart and soul of our ball club. He was the most dedicated and hardest-working athlete I had ever been associated with. For me to consider trading him was a desperate and excruciating move for me to make.

I was convinced that if I were able to trade Clemens, he would relish going home to Houston so I made contact with Bob Watson, the general manager of the Houston Astros, in strict confidence. I mentioned that I would consider trading Clemens, but it would have to be a trade that would benefit the Red Sox greatly. We agreed upon a nine-player trade—five coming to us and four, including Clemens, going to the Astros. The Astros had been discussing sending us Steve Finley, Pete Harnisch, and Craig Biggio, but when Houston's ownership refused to include Biggio in the trade, the deal fell apart.

I had mixed emotions about failing to make the trade happen because I felt it would have improved our ball club a great deal. On the other hand, Clemens, our ace and the most dominant pitcher in the major leagues, was still in a Red Sox uniform.

On the second or third day of the meetings when I went back to my suite at the hotel prior to heading out for a meeting with another general manager, my wife told me that John and Haywood had called and wanted to talk to me at 6 p.m. I proceeded to reschedule my meeting with the other general manager and waited around for the conference call.

In the course of our conference call, Haywood and John asked how our search for our coaching replacements was going, because a couple of weeks earlier Haywood, John, Hobson, Port, and I had met and decided to replace our first and third base coaches. In the meantime, the media had gotten wind of the changes and there were a number of names being bantered around by local media. Haywood and John inquired on how the media were getting the names of some of the coaches we had under consideration.

"Nothing that our media finds out surprises me," I replied. "How they find out the things they do and speculate, sometimes accurately, sometimes inaccurately, is frustrating, but they have their sources."

"Have you compiled some names for the pitching coach position?" John asked.

I was taken aback by his question. At the meeting, we had discussed the pitching coach position but had never determined that a change needed to be made.

"John, Rich Gale is our pitching coach." I replied.

"I thought from our discussions about our coaching staff back in Boston in my office, it was understood that we were going to make a change in the pitching coaches position also."

"John, that was not my understanding."

"I thought you understood that we were to replace our pitching coach with a veteran coach for next season," he retorted.

I was confused by that statement, but it was now eminently clear that they wanted me to replace Gale as well as the other two coaches and restructure our entire coaching staff. When we finished the conference call, I realized I was going to have to call Hobson and tell him that we would have to replace Gale.

I called Hobson, who was home in Alabama, and after some casual conversation began to talk about some candidates for our coaching staff. I then proceeded to tell Hobson that we would also have to replace Gale as our pitching coach. Hobson couldn't believe it.

I told him of my conversation with Haywood and John an hour before and told Hobson that it was their understanding we were to replace Gale too.

"But that wasn't my understanding, was it yours?" Hobson responded.

"No, Butch, it wasn't, but they feel we should replace him with a veteran pitching coach." Hobson was silent, but I continued, "Butch, you're going to have to call Gale and tell him we are not going to re-hire him for next season."

Hobson was beside himself.

"But, Lou, I just talked to him earlier today and per our discussions told him he was re-hired for next season, and we spent an hour or more going over our pitching staff and our spring training workout schedule," he blurted out. "How am I going to call him back now on the same day and tell him he's fired?"

It was a helluva question, and there was no easy answer.

"Butch, let me call you back in the next half hour. I'll give it some thought."

I sat back, decided to have a drink, and discuss my dilemma with my wife. Finally I realized there was going to be no easy way to do this, and we were going to have egg on our face no matter how we handled it. I picked up the phone and called Hobson.

"Butch," I said, "you'll have to call Gale and tell him that we're replacing him, and it was my decision not to re-hire him."

"He's going to think we've lost it. It will be an embarrassing phone call."

"Butch, I understand, but it has to be our decision and not ownership's, and it has to be done," I stated directly.

Hobson hung up obviously upset, confused, and in a quandary as to how to tell Gale he would not be returning to the club.

When word reached the Boston media that Gale had been hired and then fired on the same day, they had a field day in ripping both ownership and me in grand fashion. It was an embarrassing predicament that made us all look like we didn't have a clue what was going on. The media loved it. We became the village idiots in print and on the local talk shows all week long and deservedly so. Gale was also totally flabbergasted, confused, angered, and vocal about the entire situation. John was particularly incensed at the media criticism, but he had always been ultra-sensitive to any public criticism, either personal or in general.

The media also made contact with me in Naples and began to literally interrogate me regarding the Gale situation. They were heartless and relentless as to how and why we could hire and fire Gale on the same day. It was all but impossible to defend our actions. I knew it and the media knew it, and there was no way to skirt the issue. I had to face the music, too.

Whether it was related or not, a week after I returned from Florida, John called me into his office, still rankled by the media criticism, and told me that he wanted to make a change in the general manager position, but he'd like me to remain with the Red Sox. I would now have the title of senior vice president of baseball operations. He also told me he would like me to help him hire the new general manager. He asked me to draw up a list of baseball executives who I felt we should interview for the job.

I was extremely upset at John's decision to replace me. I recognized that we had suffered through back-to-back losing seasons, but I was still confident that with the young talent in our system and with another capable starting pitcher, we could become very competitive quickly. We had drawn nearly 2.5 million paid admissions once again and the franchise was making money, but in the end it always comes down to winning ball games on the field. We had a pitching rotation of Clemens, Sele, Viola, and Darwin on which to build, but nonetheless, it would have to translate into wins on the field, and that was always the bottom line.

I was able, a few days after John told me he wanted to replace me, to visit Haywood. I wanted to find out if Haywood was in agreement. He had initially recommended me to John and Mrs. Yawkey. I liked Haywood personally, however, and we developed a mutually respectful friendship. I enjoyed working with him because he was a baseball man per se, even though on occasion we didn't see eye to eye on every issue. He was always upfront, and there was no pretension or deception. I always knew where I stood with him, but even with Haywood serving as the general partner, he had been much more involved in the baseball operations of the ball club than I would have desired or anticipated. I never had autonomous control, which did create some problems for me in the long run.

When I met with Haywood, he told me that he had just agreed to a buyout with John and the lawyers for the Yawkey Foundation and that he was no longer making ownership decisions. It was rumored after the buyout was announced that received in the neighborhood of $30 million. I felt some sense of betrayal that Haywood may not have spoken up to argue against my dismissal as general manager because it was on his recommendation that the Red Sox hire me away from the New York Mets. On the other hand I fully understood that the transaction he was involved in was obviously more significant than John's decision to replace me as the general manager.

When I left Haywood's office, I went back to my office and began to slowly gather together my personal files and memorabilia, realizing that one day in the very near future this office would no longer be mine. I sat back in my chair and began to look back on the pluses and minuses of my tenure as the club's general manager for the past 10 years.

We had won three American League Eastern Division titles and one American League championship, and we came within one pitch of winning a world championship. No other Red Sox ball club since 1918 had ever been that close to winning a World Series. During those 10 years of my watch, we set an all-time attendance record in 1991, drawing 2,562,435 fans into Fenway Park, and for eight straight seasons we averaged more than 2.3 million paid attendance, including five straight years of averaging 2.5 million. It had never been done before in Red Sox history.

We also had developed some 40 major league players in our minor league system who went on to play in the big leagues. Those players included Roger Clemens, Mo Vaughn, John Valentin, Aaron Sele, Ellis Burks, Mike Greenwell, Jody Reed, Dennis "Oil Can" Boyd, Tim Naehring, Curt Schilling, Jeff Bagwell, Phil Plantier, Rich Gedman, Ken Ryan, Carlos Quintana, John Marzano, Todd Benzinger, Sam Horn, Paul Quantrill, John Flaherty, Scott Hatteberg, Jeff Suppan, Lou Merloni, Trot Nixon, Scott Cooper, Danny Scheaffer, Kevin Romine, Tom Bolton, Al Nipper, Bob Zupcic, Rob Woodward, Marty Barrett, Mike Smithson, and others.

I had also pulled off some solid trades to give us a chance at returning to the World Series. Curt Schilling and Brady Anderson to the Orioles to acquire veteran right-hander Mike Boddicker. I had been hopeful that a starting staff of Clemens, Hurst, and Boddicker would provide a dominant front-line rotation, and with Lee Smith as our closer in the bullpen we had the nucleus of a highly competitive pitching staff. That fall, however, Hurst had left us to sign a multiyear contract with the Padres. It was a big loss and a move that Hurst would later tell me, "It was one of the biggest mistakes I've ever made in my entire career in leaving the Red Sox." At the time I traded Schilling, it was our consensus judgment that he was probably five seasons away from pitching successfully in the major leagues and Boddicker could help us now. Schilling would spend two seasons with the Orioles, but mostly at Triple-A Rochester. After two seasons, the Orioles traded him to the Astros where he would spend most of his time there pitching at the Triple-A level before he was finally traded away to the Phillies, where he eventually evolved into a major league pitcher.

I had traded for first baseman Nick Esasky from the Cincinnati Reds along with reliever Rob Murphy, giving up Todd Benzinger as the principal in the trade to the Reds. Esasky came to us and hit 304 home runs and drove in more than 100 RBIs, and Murphy appeared in some 74 games in relief. They were both major contributors to our ball club during the 1989 season, but we lost Esasky to free agency and the Atlanta Braves at the end of the season. Benzinger never became a major contributor for the Reds.

The acquisition of Smith for Al Nipper and Calvin Schiraldi was also a major coup for us. It gave us a dominant closer in our bullpen who already had 180 major league saves at the time we acquired him.

The trade for Dave Henderson and shortstop Spike Owen also became a major factor in our American League championship team that battled the New York Mets for the world championship in 1986.

In the first six seasons of my term as the Red Sox general manager, our ball club posted a 514-457 won-lost record with a winning percentage of .560. Overall, our ball club's record for my entire tenure was 837-781 games with a winning percentage of .517. The disastrous season of 1992 in which we finished 16 games under .500 was a huge disappointment and had a major negative impact on the overall winning percentage of my tenure.

During my time as Red Sox general manager, I faced several of the toughest decisions I had to make as a baseball executive. Some of them were obvious and had to be done; others have been criticized and debated, but I faced these challenges head on and tried to do what was best for the ball club. The hardest decision, and one that ultimately did not come to fruition, was when I decided to trade Clemens in 1993. This choice was made behind closed doors and I struggled with my admiration of Clemens as our star pitcher and with the need to shake things up in our lineup. The other challenges were the release of future Red Sox Hall of Famer Jim Rice, the firing of Joe Morgan, the release of future Red Sox Hall of Famer Dwight Evans, my inability to re-sign Wade Boggs and Ellis Burks in 1992, the release of Bill Buckner, my inability to re-sign Bruce Hurst, and, finally, the Jeff Bagwell trade, the most debated and vilified move of my career.

The greatest disappointment to me, however, was my failure to bring home a world championship to New England. It would have been the fulfillment of a lifetime dream for someone who grew up in Rhode Island idolizing Ted Williams and devoted to the Red Sox from age 10.

The last three years of my reign were probably the most difficult and the most challenging because of the unfortunate disagreement between Mrs. Yawkey and Haywood, which became very unpleasant and greatly affected my opportunity to function without certain difficulties or constraints.

As I looked back on the entire scenario, I have become convinced that the column that Dan Shaughnessy wrote in *The Boston Globe* during the closing weeks of the 1992 season, indicating that the Red Sox should fire me as the general manager, and the embarrassment to the organization over the Gale incident were the factors that prompted John's decision to replace me. The Gale situation was a totally unjustified charge, because I was never told we should replace our pitching coach when we discussed coaching staff changes in the meeting with ownership. Nonetheless, John made the decision to replace me, and as chief operating officer of the Red Sox, he was the boss.

I began to draw up a list of six or seven potential candidates to replace me as the general manager. I placed Port at the very head of my list, convinced that he would be the ideal man for the job. He was eminently qualified in every regard—experienced, talented, and with a solid track record.

As John and I began to set up interviews for the prospective candidates for the general manager position, Peter Gammons in *The Boston Globe* began to beat the drums for Dan Duquette, then the general manager of the Montreal Expos. Gammons extolled Duquette's baseball skills and expertise, and after one or two interviews were conducted, John told me he felt he had his man for the job and not to set up any other interviews. On January 27, 1994, John introduced Duquette as the new general manager of the Boston Red Sox. Duquette wisely retained Port as assistant general manager.

When John hired Duquette, he gave Duquette absolute and autonomous control of baseball operations to hire, fire, and restructure the organization according to his operational philosophy and judgment. It was a sound and sensible business decision. When an organization or industry hires an expert or chief executive officer, it is a basic axiom of good business to give that executive the total control and responsibility to operate, make decisions, and control his own destiny. If he doesn't do the job, you replace him—but give him control of his own destiny and give him the means to get the job done.

I found it coincidental that Duquette and I had both grown up in New England—he in western New England and I in Rhode Island—and graduated from the region's outstanding liberal arts colleges—he from Amherst College as a literature major and I from Stonehill College as a literature major. We also had both been hired for our first major league jobs by Harry Dalton, the former Orioles', Brewers', and Angels' general manager. We were, however, totally different personalities with different operating philosophies, for better or worse.

As I walked away from the press conference announcing Duquette as the new Red Sox general manager, I now held the title of executive vice president of baseball operations, but I knew it was a hollow title with Duquette in total charge of all baseball decisions.

My days of making player personnel decisions were over. Duquette would run his own ship his way, and my input would be minimal at least; every captain should command his own ship in his own way and sail his own course. My Navy days had taught me that.

After some 36 years of living and breathing baseball operations on a daily basis, often 12 to 13 hours a day for 365 days of the year, my days of dealing with players and player personnel had finally come to an end. I would miss it greatly, and I was certain to experience some withdrawal. If, however, there was any consolation whatever, I was at least still a member of the Red Sox organization.

The former talented and extremely gifted commissioner of baseball, A. Bartlett Giamatti, once wrote, "The game begins in the spring, when everything else begins again, and it blossoms in the summer, filling the afternoons and evenings, and then as soon as the chill rains come, it stops and leaves you to face the fall alone."

Somehow those words came to mind as I stood in the cold, dreary, and empty Fenway Park after the press conference. I began to reminisce about past seasons, both the good and the bad. I sensed I was leaving behind something that had been a big part of my life, but it would not be a part of me ever again. I recalled a verse from an A.E. Housman poem my classmates at college had chosen to inscribe on the campus in our memory at our most recent reunion. I suddenly realized how poignantly and painfully appropriate it was to my present status:

This is the land of lost content,
I see it shining plain,
The happy highways where I went
And cannot come again.

I had traveled down that highway for 36 years, but I cannot and would not go there again. I felt sad and woebegone. Still I knew however, that the sun would set. The sun would also rise again tomorrow. I'd have lunch; life would go on as always. I'd still contribute to the Red Sox organization whenever and wherever ownership or management asked me to, because my love of the game and of the Red Sox ran ever so deep.

The Curse Has Finally Ended

"You know the ending, but you just don't know the hour. They are the Red Sox. Just as Hamlet dies every night, the Red Sox die every time they take the stage."
—Anonymous

Some 35,000 plus fans of Red Sox Nation jammed Fenway Park, and everywhere you looked you saw signs in the stands stating, "We believe," "We kept the faith," "Why not us?" or "We always believed." Even the Prudential Building, standing tall over the right-field bleachers and clearly visible to the entire ballpark and city of Boston, spelled out in lights to the entire viewing audience, "Go Sox."

It was October 23, 2004, and the Red Sox had made it to the World Series. Game 1 was moments away from beginning.

It had been 18 years since their previous visit, and I can recall every pitch, every inning, and every ball game, because they are ever so painfully engraved in my memory. I was the general manager of that Red Sox ball club.

As the 2004 World Series pregame ceremonies began to unfold in the field at Fenway Park, I felt the memories from that 1986 team flood back into my mind. I thought of Bruce Hurst, Jim Rice, Wade Boggs, Roger Clemens, Dwight Evans, Dave Henderson, and Bill Buckner, and a New York Mets team I had known so well after having spent nearly five years working for the Mets as the director of baseball operations where I was intimately involved in the procurement and development of many of the Mets players. I recalled a certain sense of absolute joy and elation as we prepared to head into our clubhouse to accept the World Series trophy as Game 6 wound down. We were one strike away, with two outs and a two-run lead.

There just wasn't any way we could lose that ball game and not take home the world championship to Boston and New England.

But tragically we did.

That defeat was so painful that, even as I watched the St. Louis Cardinal players and then our Red Sox players being introduced, I could not get out of my mind the disappointment and heartache of that loss.

This organization had endured so many losses and so much heartbreak in the 86 years since the franchise's last world championship. We always seemed to fall short of success and be one out, one hit, or one pitch from achieving our dream—to bring a championship to Boston. It happened to me in 1986 and it had happened more recently to other Red Sox teams.

In 2003, the Red Sox had been on the brink of eliminating the New York Yankees from postseason play. We had our ace, Pedro Martinez, on the mound in the eighth inning with a 5-2 lead in Game 7 of the American League Championship Series. Martinez retired the first batter and the Red Sox were five outs away from the World Series. But then suddenly Martinez gave up a single and then a double, and manager Grady Little came up to the mound to confer with his star hurler. The conference led to Martinez's staying in the game—and the Yankees tying the score 5-5. It was a big mistake and one that ultimately might have cost Little his job.

The game continued until Yankee Aaron Boone killed the Red Sox's World Series dream with the game-winning home run in the 11th inning off reliever Tim Wakefield's first pitch.

"Red Sox seasons die the deaths of spaghetti western cowboys: never graceful, but rather writhing, painful, and melodramatic," *Sports Illustrated* wrote about the game. "The ending at the hands of Aaron Boone and the Yankees was true to form. Five outs from the World Series, with a three-run lead, no one on base, and their best starting pitcher on the mound, the Red Sox lost without ever using their bullpen. Nobody but the Red Sox could lose a game so spectacularly."

And so in 2004 when the Red Sox and Yankees faced off again, the stage was set for more drama. In the first three games the Yankees crushed the hearts of Boston's fans as they stormed on to victory at home and then in Fenway. The Red Sox were down three games to one, and no team in the history of baseball had beaten that deficit.

With the Red Sox on the verge of another disastrous and tragic loss to the Yankees, the critics and doomsayers were out en masse. They were ready to blame manager Terry Francona, or the players, or the organization, or anybody in sight, and "The Curse of the Bambino" would once again raise its ugly head.

The mythic "Curse" was more of a created phenomenon that Boston fans clung to in times of tight competition. Over the past two decades when balls took inexplicable bounces at crucial points of important games, the Red Sox Nation muttered something about "The Curse" under their breath. It was the explanation for the impossible—when a team steps up to the almost assured threshold of glory and then tragically trips and falls short yet again. As Game 4 approached, the so-called "Curse" and all of the heart-break fans had endured was in the forefront of their minds.

With the champagne on ice, the Yankees had prepared for a huge cele-bration that night. In the home team's clubhouse, the Red Sox players found a message attached to the door: "We can change history. ... Believe!" And they may have been the only people in the park to whom those words did-n't sound like hollow braggadocio, because every die-hard fan felt it would take a miracle for the Red Sox to survive.

Through the fifth inning, the Yankees held a 2-0 lead, and the fans of Fenway had been silenced, awaiting the inevitable.

But then David Ortiz hit a two-run double, and suddenly the score was tied. By the end of the fifth, another run had scored, and the Red Sox were leading 3-2.

The lead was short lived. The next inning the Yankees took it back, scor-ing two runs. In the eighth, it was 4-3 when the Yankees brought in their brilliant reliever Mariano Rivera, who would hold the Red Sox scoreless. Then came the bottom of the ninth—three outs away from a Yankee sweep. Red Sox fans held their breath, praying for a miracle and that the team could live for at least one more game.

And then the miraculous happened. Kevin Millar drew a walk, and Dave Roberts, with his exceptional speed, was sent in to pinch run. Roberts stole second—probably the most dramatic stolen base in Red Sox history. Rivera threw a fastball to third baseman Bill Mueller, who lined it right back at Rivera. The ball bounced and made its way to center field. Roberts scored; he tied the game 4-4. There was hope.

But that glimmer of hope almost faded in the ninth. With Gary Sheffield on first and only one out, the Yankees sent up Tony Clark to pinch-hit. He hit a line drive into the right-field corner that just barely—by inches—cleared the low right-field fence. It was a ground-rule double, holding Sheffield at third and Clark at second. Closer Keith Foulke retired the next two batters to end the threat and keep the Red Sox alive. Ironically had the ball ricocheted off the wall, Sheffield could have scored, and with Boston held scoreless in the ninth, the Yankees would have swept the series—all by the bounce of another ball and just a couple of inches.

For two and a half more innings the score remained tied. The Red Sox faced Yankee reliever Paul Quantrill, and he quickly struck out the first two batters. Then Manny Ramirez singled to left field. Ortiz walked up to the plate, Quantrill unloaded, and Ortiz blasted a shot out of the park. The Red Sox were going to live to play another game. There would be no sweep by the "Evil Empire."

In Game 5 both teams kept fans teetering on the edge of insanity and delight. The Red Sox struck first with two runs. They held on to the lead until the sixth when the Yankees struck back with three runs, taking a 4-2 lead. The Sox were held scoreless in the sixth and in the seventh. And then in the eighth inning Ortiz stepped up to the plate, faced pitcher Tom Gordon, and blasted a two-run home run over the Green Monster, tying the game 4-4. The marathon match continued until the 14th inning when Ortiz battled Esteban Loaiza for nine pitches before lobbing the 10th pitch to center field for an RBI single that scored Johnny Damon. As Damon hit home, it set off a wild celebration throughout Fenway and the Red Sox Nation in the early hours of October 19.

Suddenly and for the very first time, the fans began to wonder, "Could they really begin to 'believe' that something, quite possibly even a miracle or maybe the fulfillment of an impossible dream, was about to happen?" The younger generation was ready, but the older fans still had their enthusiasm tempered by memories of past failures. But whatever the outcome, the series was now three games to two, and the Red Sox were, without question, alive and well.

The series went back to Yankee Stadium for Game 6, and Curt Schilling, with his dislocated tendon stitched to his skin and wearing his bloody sock, valiantly pitched the Red Sox out of trouble. In the fourth inning, Mark Bellhorn smacked a three-run homer to left, and by the end of the inning the Red Sox took a 4-0 lead that they never relinquished because Schilling, Foulke, and Bronson Arroyo held the Yankees bats to two runs. They had tied the series; the Red Sox were on the verge of rewriting history.

But so often in the past the Red Sox would reach the pinnacle of victory, only to stumble and fall. Now, once again, the Red Sox were ready to score a spectacular victory, but even the most passionate Red Sox fan could not conceive what was about to happen.

Game 7 began with bang—a grand slam from Damon, and the team never looked back. They continued their offensive, crushing the Yankees 10-3, making Major League Baseball history, and assuring themselves a shot at the world championship. It was amazing. Four days before they had been down three games to none, and now the team that was "cursed" had come back from the dead to score a glorious victory.

Here I was again at the World Series, watching my beloved Red Sox play for it all. As the dark memories of the past revisited my mind, I could feel the excitement in the stands on this very chilly October night. The fans had still not recovered from the frenzy of the comeback victory over the Yankees, and it was hard not to get caught up in the energy as Game 1 began.

But after the drama of the ALCS, the World Series against the Cardinals seemed anticlimactic. The first game kept Red Sox fans on the edge of their seats, with the Cardinals rallying in the sixth to pull even with the Red Sox. The next inning the Red Sox added two more runs and were only six outs away from a World Series win. But then Ramirez made two errors on consecutive plays, allowing the Cardinals to tie the game 9-9, and the park grew silent, wondering if the baseball gods had decided to rescind the team's newfound favor.

The Red Sox came up to bat. With one out Jason Varitek reached first on the Cardinals' single error of the game. Bellhorn came up to bat. Bellhorn knocked a shot down the right-field line that smashed off the Pesky Pole—barely fair with the strong wind blowing toward right. The baseball gods were smiling on the Red Sox, and the fans went into a state of euphoria. The Sox won 11-9.

That was as tight as the Series got. The Red Sox went on to sweep the Cardinals and bring home their first world championship in 86 years. After winning Game 4 a wild celebration took place in the middle of the infield in Busch Stadium, under a blood red moon, as the Red Sox players began a long-awaited jubilee. The merriment would reverberate throughout New England and, in fact, in many parts of the world, as Red Sox fans everywhere joined in.

The Red Sox ownership had generously offered to fly the entire organization, including front office personnel, to St. Louis for the World Series; I had decided, however, to remain behind and watch the games on television in the comfort of my own home with my wife. In my 41 years in baseball I had been to 38 World Series, including the 1966 World Series when I was the director of player development for the Baltimore Orioles and when we swept the Los Angeles Dodgers to capture the world championship. In the process we defeated two future Hall of Fame pitchers, the great Sandy Koufax and Don Drysdale. There are so many pregame and postgame social events, celebrations, and galas that are a part of any monumental event, such as a World Series, that I decided to just stay at home and enjoy the games without the pomp and circumstance.

I had beside me a bottle of my favorite chardonnay (because I can't stand champagne) and as the final out was made with the ball clutched securely in Doug Mientkiewicz's glove, the Red Sox were for finally the first time in 86 years world champions. The very first thought that came to my mind was Jean Yawkey. How I wished she had been here to witness and share this monumental victory. Somehow as I raised my glass to celebrate, I had to believe that she, Tom Yawkey, and Haywood Sullivan would be enjoying this great moment and I toasted their memories.

I turned to my wife, and as we both toasted the victory, I said, "Mary Louise, we came close to witnessing history 18 years ago, but tonight we finally did."

As I sat back to watch the jubilation taking place on the playing field and in the visitors' clubhouse, I regretted that during my years as the Red Sox's general manager, I had failed to win a world championship and I felt some pangs of remorse. It would have been such a glorious accomplishment personally,

I thought of former general manager Dan Duquette and what he must be thinking at this moment because he had helped acquire a great deal of the talent on this ball club. I drank a toast to him.

As I watched our current ownership, chief executive officer Larry Lucchino, and general manager Theo Epstein participating in the joyous celebration in the clubhouse, I drank my last toast to them. Ownership and Lucchino had done an outstanding job in every aspect of marketing and promotions, Epstein had skillfully and brilliantly orchestrated the acquiring of the remaining talent needed to create a world championship team. They deserved all of the accolades that would come their way. It was a glorious victory.

I sat back and said to myself, "It didn't happen on my watch unfortunately, but it's still one helluva an accomplishment and I'm thrilled to be a small part of it."

My phone began to ring and it would ring into the wee hours of the morning. Our friends, former scouts, former managers, and front office personnel I had worked with or for called to offer congratulations.

Finally late in the morning I fell asleep on the couch with the television still on. It had been a special night, certainly one for the ages.

Mayor Tom Menino of Boston, a great Red Sox fan, scheduled a parade to honor the world champions on October 30, three days after the Sox had won it all. It was a rainy, misty day, but that did little to dampen the spirits or enthusiasm of the 3.5 million fans who would turn out to pay tribute to their heroes.

For me, it brought back some very poignant memories of our parade through downtown Boston after we lost to the Mets in the 1986 World Series. At that time, the reigning mayor was Raymond Flynn, and he had insisted that the fans of Boston and New England wanted to honor our Red Sox ball club for a great season, despite the fact we had come within one strike of capturing the world championship. I had fought against us participating in the parade, because I felt we had not won it all, but the mayor was unrelenting and the parade went on. An estimated crowd of a little over a million fans turned out to honor our ball club, and in the end it was a memorable moment for every member of the organization. Our parade route took us to City Hall Plaza, where Governor Michael Dukakis, Mayor Flynn, and 2,000 or 3,000 fans were jammed into the plaza to pay tribute to our ball club. It is a memory that still remains to this day for all the members of the 1986 ball club.

But that parade was nothing compared to the revelry of 2004. That celebration dwarfed any celebration for any Boston sports team ever in the history of the city and the commonwealth. Three and a half million passionate and adoring fans, some who arrived at 3 or 4 a.m. to get a good view, jammed every nook and cranny of the parade route to catch a glimpse of their favorite player.

Jack MacMullan (one of my favorite people and writers) wrote about the crowds, "You wonder why someone would do such a thing. You wonder why millions of people woke up so early and stood in the rain, just for a glimpse of a baseball player that was here and then gone before they knew it. The answer is simple. The Red Sox are the World Series champions and this is their day. Whether it's five, 20 or 50 years from now, fans from New England all want to say the same thing: I was there.'"

This 2004 incredible season, culminating with a world championship for the Boston Red Sox in a history-making playoff, was over, but its memory will live on forever. It was so very sweet and so very special. But most of all, it ends forever "The Curse" that had haunted Red Sox teams for decades, literally since the Warren G. Harding administration. It has also rewarded the faith of many of the most passionate fans in Red Sox Nation, who always "believed" that someday in their lifetime the Red Sox would win a World Series.

There will be some critics or skeptics who will wonder what might have been had the Minnesota Twins retained David Ortiz or the Houston Astros not let Johan Santana get away. For me, however, I am totally convinced that this gutsy, talented Red Sox ball club was destined or ordained to win it all, and nothing, or no man, was going to prevent them from fulfilling their destiny. They were on a mission that had to be successful; it was just that simple.

After the parade, there were the Trophy Tours, as management and, generally one or two players, would take the World Series trophy to all the capital cities and towns throughout New England and to various special events. Fans by the thousands flocked to the events and to the presentations to see, to touch, and to take pictures with the trophy for posterity, for their grandchildren, but primarily for themselves to fully believe that the Red Sox were finally champions and that the anguish and the suffering was truly now finally over.

Like all Red Sox fans who grew up in New England and who lived and died with our beloved Red Sox, we recognize that being a Red Sox fan is part of the culture of our region and that, once a Red Sox fan, you are a Red Sox fan forever. We now know that "The Curse" is finally over, and we are all "free at last, thank God Almighty, we are free at last."

My Basic Principles of Leadership

Throughout a 41-year career in Major League Baseball I have always believed in certain basic qualities that define the kind of leadership I believe inspires and engenders successful results. These principles are not all inclusive, but they are, in my opinion, essential for a leader to create a productive environment for those you work with and for within your organization. They are the principles I followed throughout my career, including during my tenure with the Red Sox, and they influenced all of the decisions I was asked to make as a general manager.

Lead—Don't Manage.

For me a leader's responsibility is to lead—to establish the goals, the vision, and the mission of an organization and not to become entrapped in the daily functions of the organization. The manager oversees the how of an organization while the leader addresses the why.

The commanding officer, or C.O., of a commissioned Navy ship is a perfect example of a leader at work. The C.O. is in charge of the mission of his ship and setting the course his ship must sail to fulfill it. The officers serving under the C.O. manage the daily tasks of the ship, which will allow the ship to complete its mission.

Should the leader become a manager, he has lost his ability to be a good leader. The success of any organization is ultimately the product of effective direction.

Also, a true leader is not the one with the most followers but the one who creates the most leaders.

Hire the Very Best People.

For any organization to succeed you need to hire the very best people available. It is a basic precept of good business that the higher quality of people you have in one's company, the greater the opportunity of success. This principle should also be taken one step further: Not only should you hire the best, but always recognize your staff comprises people, not just employees. An organization is not a machine with precision parts, but a body of people and their relationships.

The overall success of a group is the result of good people implementing good policies.

Foster Loyalty.

Loyalty is a two-way street; it goes up as well as down. It is vitally important for the people working for you in any organization to expect and receive a sense of total commitment from the company's leadership—an impression of dedication to their needs and those of their families. Your interest and concern for your employees, however, must be sincere—not superficial.

If it is anything less, you have lost you ability to lead.

Always be consistent, fair, and objective in dealing with your employees. Praise in public, but criticize in private. Always give commendations for a job well done because that recognition is a powerful motivational tool.

It is also vital for your employees to respond in kind with total commitment and loyalty to an organization and to its leadership.

The heart and soul of any company is its people at all levels and their commitment to the company—that makes the bonding within an organization happen. If you are always fair and consistent in dealing with those you work for and with, loyalty is greatly enhanced and nurtured.

Communicate.

No organization can, or will, succeed without effective communication. It is important for every member of an organization to feel that they have a voice that will be heard by management and leadership alike. That ability to listen is an important quality of effective and productive management.

The door to my office was always open and was closed only out of necessity during a confidential call or a player contract discussion. I was always willing to listen to the opinions, suggestions, and evaluations—both positive and negative—of everyone within the organization. I welcomed and encouraged other views and recommendations from others within the organization. I also wanted everyone to be apprised of what was going on and to make everyone, regardless of their position, feel that he or she was a vitally significant member of the group who was key to our overall success.

Also, remember there are no foolish questions and man becomes a fool only if he stops asking them. Someone once said, "You can tell whether a man is clever by his answers, but you can tell whether a man is wise by his questions. He who is ashamed of asking is ashamed of learning."

Generate and Sustain Enthusiasm.

In my opinion, nothing of value can ever be accomplished without enthusiasm. Bill Gates said, "What I give to my organization is my enthusiasm." I can't stand negativity because it drags you down and it inhibits your chance for success. Enthusiasm is uplifting and inspiring. When we approach any task or job challenge with positive energy, our possibility of success is greatly enhanced. I love enthusiastic people; for me they are the kind of people I want to be working for and with.

Don't Micro-Manage.

I could never accept leadership or management that would micro-manage the people working with them or for them. Delegate responsibility and the authority required to get a job done and don't constantly look over their shoulders. If you micro-manage the people working for you, you inhibit their talents, their imagination, and their vision. Yes, sometimes, they will fail, but more often than not, they'll succeed above and beyond your greatest expectations.

Create a "We" Organization, not an "I" Organization.

For me the success of any organization is the result of an entire organization's contributions and not just the efforts of one individual. No organization will ever find success unless it's a total team effort.

A leader may receive the credit for an organization's achievements, but it won't happen unless everyone within the organization has contributed. No single employee should ever be led to believe that he or she is not important to the company's success. To put this concept in perspective, professional tennis player Althea Gibson said, "No matter what accomplishments you attain, somebody helped you along the way."

Be Willing to Deal with Failure and the Criticism That Will Follow.

As the leader of an organization, always remember that the buck stops with you. When a group encounters failure, you as the leader must be willing to accept the criticism that will follow. If you make a mistake, admit it and move on. Never let failure or criticism drag you or your company down. Learn from the situation and move on. Someone once said, "Don't waste time hating failure. Failure is a greater teacher than success."

Be Willing to Take a Risk If You Are Convinced It Is in the Best Interest of Your Organization.

Someone once said, "Only those who are willing to take risks will ever know how far they might go." Any leader must be willing on occasion to take risks or face failure. Conservatism, in my judgment, breeds mediocrity.

When the judgment of a leader, based on all of the intelligence that he has at hand, is that taking the risk is in the best interest of his organization in order to bring success, I am convinced it has to be taken. He has to be willing to do so or regret forever what might have been. Andre Gillson, the writer, once wrote, "Man cannot discover new oceans unless he has the courage to lose sight of the shore."

Risks are often the greatest challenges that a leader must face, and if he is not willing to face them, he shouldn't be leading an organization. A journalist named Richard Reeves wrote, "All leaders must face some crisis where their own strength of character is the enemy."

In the final analysis it is a leader's ability to motivate and to inspire his employees that determines an organization's success. No matter how brilliant or visionary the organization's policies may be, it is the employees—the people—who make it effective. Leadership is the ability to deal with and motivate people, period. Leaders give confidence to those around them. They set the tone, the feeling, and the culture of the entire organization.

Index